HOLLYWOOD VAMPIRE
The Unofficial Guide to *Angel*

Keith Topping

Virgin

This edition first published in 2000 by
Virgin Publishing Ltd
Thames Wharf Studios
Rainville Road
London
W6 9HA

Reprinted 2001 (twice)

A catalogue record for this book is available from the British
Library.

ISBN 0 7535 0531 2

Typeset by TW Typesetting, Plymouth, Devon
Printed and bound in Great Britain by
Mackays of Chatham PLC

For Rob Francis
Who didn't just 'go for doughnuts' this time . . .

And Paul Simpson
An inspiration and a friend.

And Susannah Tiller
Who saved my life more than once.

Acknowledgements

Round up the usual suspects. My thanks for encouragement and contributions to this book go to: Ian and Janet Abrahams, Jessica Allen, Ian Atkins, Daniel Ben-Zvi, Stephen Booth, Kini Brooks-Smith, Will Cameron, Suze Campagna, Paul Comeau, Paul Cornell, Tony Dryer, Irene Finn, Simona Fischer, Robert Franks, Paul Gibson and Colleen Laffey, Cath Grey, Lea Hays, Theresa Lambert, Andy and Helen Lane, Gary Leigh, Shaun Lyon, John McLaughlin, John Mosby, Ian Reid, Jill Sherwin, Trina Short, Dave Stone, Jim Swallow, Deb Walsh, everyone at *Gallifrey One* and *CONvergence* (especially Anna Bliss, Stephanie Lindorff and Jody Wurl for the '*Giles, Get a Job!*' panel) and the *wholly inspirational* Vincent Tang.

Steve Purcell and Chris Cornwell provided several (much needed) 'business lunches' during the writing of this book and Jackie Cox, Dave Arkley and Carol Watson also deserve a mention for covering for me.

The Watcher's Web (www.watchers.web.com) is an invaluable source of analysis and information on both *Buffy* and *Angel* from a largely British perspective. I'd also like to thank the numerous website custodians who spared the time to answer my, no doubt annoying, emails. Details of these sites can be found in the chapter 'Angel and the Internet'.

A special tribute to my *Slayerettes*: Jo Brooks (my editor at Virgin), Wendy Comeau, Martin Day ('PC-Fixer-By-Phone to The Stars'), Mike Lee, Ruth Thomas, Graeme Topping and Mark Wyman, all of whom (once again) loaned me their enthusiasm and talent for the duration. Plus Kathy Sullivan without whom there would, simply, have been *no* book.

And my family who have supported my writing for the past decade.

Preface

'You're vampire detective now? What next? Vampire cowboy? Vampire fireman? Vampire ballerina?'

– 'In the Dark'

It's one of the fallacies of the TV age that there's no such thing as a genuinely great spin-off from an already successful show. There haven't been very many, it's true, but there *are* a few.

Angel is one of the best.

Crawling from the apocalyptic emotional wreckage of *Buffy the Vampire Slayer*'s third season, *Angel* was a chance for its creators Joss Whedon and David Greenwalt to escape the teenage-and-growing world that Whedon had fashioned in Sunnydale and step into the adult morass of Los Angeles. If one element defines the fundamental differences between the two series, then it's *Angel*'s ability to get down into the gutter of The Big City while *Buffy* is stuck in the confines of small-town America. 'Because *Angel* is set in Los Angeles,' notes *Science Fiction World*, 'a certain degree of reality creeps in. We're talking about an existing city and the speculation of its seamy underside.' Producer Marti Noxon adds: 'Los Angeles was the place that Joss picked for very specific reasons. It's a town with so many different characters [and] flavours. There's a lot of preconceptions about what the city is, but there's also a lot of truths. It's a pretty competitive, intense town where a lot of lonely, isolated and desperate people end up. It's a good place for monsters.' For this reason *Angel*'s shape was drawn in many people's minds (and in the American Gothic tradition of *The Legend of Sleepy Hollow* and its followers) before the show even began. It would be 'darker' than *Buffy*, most fans decided. More graphic. More visceral.

It hasn't quite happened that way. '*Buffy* is definitely aimed at a younger audience,' Marti Noxon insists. *Angel*, on the other hand, has an audience including: 'People who are potentially out of college and making their way in the big city. We noticed in our premiere episode we had a much stronger male audience.' In reality, *Angel* treads a contextually similar path to its predecessor featuring a near-identical mixture of soundbite-friendly dialogue and eye-bulging set-pieces. When Associated Press's Ted Anthony called *Buffy*: 'a vivid piece of hip TV splatterpunk, a hybrid of *Fast Times at Ridgemont High*, Gothic romance and one of the video games you might think was favoured by Columbine's "Trench Coat Mafia", while peppered with cartoonish violence,' he could equally have been describing *Angel*. Essentially, the two series began as halves of a single whole. But *Angel* did, quickly, establish an identity of its own, together with themes that it intended to explore. And, like those in *Buffy*, these were both universal and timeless. Another quality that the two series share is an ability to avoid being constrained by aesthetics. *Angel* might look like *The Matrix*, but the story is pure *King Lear*.

Hollywood Vampire, then, is a book about where *Angel* came from, how it reached the screen and what it looked like when it got there. It's about the creation and development of a major TV series as it became hugely successful across the world. Strap yourselves in for a few surprises along the way.

Headings

Dreaming (as *Buffy* Often Proves) is Free: Lots of TV series do *cool* dream sequences. Joss Whedon's shows differ from their contemporaries in that *they* do *magnificent*, surreal, scary, funny ones. You'll find them listed here.

Dudes and Babes: A meditation on all of the pretty girls and boys that catch our attention on *Angel*. Even more than Sunnydale, Los Angeles is full of beautiful people and most have an interesting story to tell.

It's a Designer Label!: In *Buffy the Vampire Slayer* Cordelia Chase is envious of Buffy Summers' L.A. past. 'I'd kill to be *that* close to that many shoes,' she notes. Now she is. Here the quality is checked *and* the width felt.

References: Joss Whedon's shows delight in slipping pop-culture references into both their dialogue and visuals. Whether it's the recurring *Batman* motif that runs throughout *Angel*, or Cordelia's name-dropping of movie-stars, this category tries to catch all of them.

'West Hollywood'?: The debate in *Buffy* fandom about Angel's sexuality is a fierce one. After some fans misheard Doyle's question 'Are you game?' as 'Are you gay?' many writers have used subsequent scripts to indulge a few slash-fiction fantasies.

The Charisma Show: For many, even before the cameras started rolling, the main centre of attention wasn't Angel himself, David Boreanaz, but rather his female co-star. Charisma Carpenter, who plays Cordelia, is often the best reason for watching *Angel*. 'There aren't many people who are that funny *and* that beautiful,' David Greenwalt told *TV Guide*. 'She can do every colour of the rainbow.'

Sex and Drugs and Rock'n'Roll: In Los Angeles *all* are rife, even in TV shows. The city may have, as Raymond Chandler noted, 'the personality of a paper cup', but it's a place where literally *anything* goes.

There's a Ghost in My House: An occasional category that lists the activities and (lack of) appearances of Cordelia's less-than-substantial housemate, Dennis.

Logic, Let Me Introduce You to This Window: An acknowledgement that even in the best shows there are sometimes logic flaws, bits of bad continuity or just plain foul-ups. Part of the job of being a fan is looking for these, laughing at them when they occur and then aggressively defending them to your non-fan friends.

Quote/Unquote: The dialogue that's worth stopping the video for.
Other categories will appear occasionally, including some old friends.

'That ain't a Mexican name, is it? Angel?'

– 'The Prodigal'

Keith Topping.
His Gaff.
Merrie Albion.
July 2000 (Common Era).

Previously on *Buffy the Vampire Slayer . . .*

'A vampire in love with a Slayer. It's rather poetic. In a maudlin sort of way.'

– 'Out of Sight, Out of Mind'

Born in Galway, Ireland in the eighteenth century, Angel was, according to Margaret (one of his victims): 'A drunken, whoring layabout and a terrible disappointment to your parents'. Though, as he told his vampire sire Darla, 'With the exception of an honest day's work, there's no challenge I'm not prepared to face.' Asking her to 'show me your world', Angel became a vampire in 1753. Angel is the nickname of his possessing demon, *Angelus* ('the one with the angelic face'). He created sheer havoc and terror across Europe for decades and was, according to the elite vampire The Master: 'The most vicious creature I ever met'. His *modus operandi* involved sending his victims insane firstly by killing their family and friends before finally murdering them without mercy or pity.

However, all bad things come to and end and in 1898, after he murdered a Romanian gypsy from the Kalderash Clan, Angelus was cursed by her people to regain his soul and have knowledge of the dreadful crimes he had committed against humanity.

'You don't remember? . . . In a moment, you will. The face of everyone you killed . . . They will haunt you, and you will know what true suffering is.'

– 'Becoming' Part 1

Damned to walk the Earth, Angel – the vampire with a soul – spent most of the following century in misery over his past deeds, shunning other vampires, coming to America and living in the gutter. Rescued by a friendly demon, Whistler, in New York in 1996 and shown a path of hope in the shape of the Vampire Slayer, Buffy Summers, Angel accepted that he had a destiny after all and travelled to the Hellmouth, the California town of Sunnydale.

> *'Things used to be pretty simple. A hundred years, just hanging out, feeling guilty . . . I really honed my brooding skills. Then she comes along.'*

– 'Lie to Me'

Once there, he spent almost two years helping the Slayer and her friends Willow Rosenberg, Xander Harris, Cordelia Chase, Daniel Osborne and Rupert Giles fight vampires, demons and the forces of darkness. He finally killed his sire and nemesis, Darla, and helped Buffy defeat the powerful Master and prevent the opening of the Hellmouth and the end of the world.

Briefly, he lost his soul again after enjoying a single moment of true happiness with Buffy, and returned to his evil ways, killing Giles's girlfriend Jenny Calendar and stalking Buffy with the help of his 'offspring', the English vampire couple Spike and Drusilla.

He was eventually cured by a reversal spell performed by Willow just before being sent to Hell by Buffy to save the world from the coming of the demon Acathla.

On his return, Angel slowly regained his humanity and resumed his relationship with Buffy. But he spent much time questioning the reason why he was allowed to escape from Hell by The Powers That Be.

> *'I'm trying to think with my head instead of my heart.'*

– 'The Prom'

Realising that there could be no future in a lasting relationship with Buffy, and after helping her to defeat the apocalyptic schemes of Mayor Wilkins and the rogue Slayer, Faith, he left Sunnydale for Los Angeles. Here, he continues to fight demons and monsters while searching for the reason why he was returned to this dimension and trying to forget the girl he left behind.

'Angel, you have the power to do real good, to make amends. But if you die now, then all that you ever were was a monster.'

       – 'Amends'

'If you hang with me and mine, you'll be accepted in no time. Of course, we do have to test your coolness factor. You're from L.A., so you can skip the written . . .'

       – 'Welcome to the Hellmouth'

Cordelia Chase was born into a wealthy Sunnydale family and spent most of her formative years developing a willfully narcissistic view of herself at the centre of the universe (simultaneously inspiring the existence of the 'We Hate Cordelia' club: Founder member *and* treasurer, Alexander Harris).

In high school, she was at the centre of a group of similarly minded schoolgirls known as 'The Cordettes', who spent their time avoiding learning anything remotely educational, wearing the latest fashionable clothes and dating rock musicians and football jocks.

However, beneath Cordelia's bitchy, selfish exterior was a very different person, someone who realised that she had become a magnet for people who just wanted to be 'in the popular zone', and had little interest in the *real* Cordelia (albeit she preferred being alone in a crowd to 'being lonely all by yourself').

'Thank you for making the right choice and for showing me how much you all love me. Being this popular is not just my right, but my responsibility.'

       – 'Out of Sight, Out of Mind'

Once Cordelia's life had been saved by Buffy Summers when attacked by the demented invisible girl, Marcie Ross, she became a reluctant, if occasionally vital, member of the Scooby Gang and even dated Xander before discovering his attraction to Willow. After surviving a near fatal injury shortly after this trauma, Cordelia was further horrified to discover that her family had lost all of their money (her father failing to declare any taxes . . . for twelve years) and that she actually had to work for the first time in her life.

> *'Excuse me? Who gave you permission to exist?'*
>
> – 'The Harvest'

Consumed by bitterness over her break-up with Xander, she briefly wished Sunnydale into an alternative-reality but now Cordelia, her dreams of going to college shattered by financial considerations, has come to Los Angeles to begin an aspiring acting career and forget all about Sunnydale.

> *'I should leave you in there, but I'm a great humanitarian. You'll just have to think of a way to pay me back sometime.'*
>
> – 'Doppelgängland'

Into the City of Angel

'A lot of people who worked on Buffy including David and Charisma, obviously, are on it [Angel] ... We check the ratings to see if they came out a little ahead or a little behind but it's really one big family.'

– Joss Whedon

Creators of cult shows often fail to strike lucky with their second projects (*Crusade* and *Millennium* are recent examples). In a revealing interview with Rob Francis for *DreamWatch*, Joss Whedon was asked the secret of getting a spin-off up and running while simultaneously maintaining the standards on the parent-show: 'We were very careful to learn while we were doing *Angel* not to set a formula until we had seen the results. What they meant, how people responded to them. I was determined not to have a second show that brought down the quality of the first.' It was during the *Buffy* episode 'I Only Have Eyes For You' that Whedon began thinking about a spin-off: 'Seeing David open himself up to playing this really emotional female role and doing it excellently – without overdoing it or being silly, without shying away from it as a lot of male action stars might have – was extraordinary. That was the moment when I thought "this guy could carry his own show."'

As *Angel* entered production David Boreanaz explained to *TV Guide* that his character 'goes to L.A. and fights for humanity ... A lot of people from *Buffy* will come visit me and I'll come back and visit them.' Though Sarah Michelle Gellar told *Sci-Fi TV Magazine*, 'I probably won't be making crossovers. I may do one at the beginning of *Angel*, but that will be it,' in the event, links between the two shows *did* become a major part of the schedules on *Buffy* and *Angel*, with three crossover events strategically placed throughout the year.

Angel initially co-starred Glenn Quinn as Doyle, Angel's half-demon spiritual mentor. Joss Whedon told *Entertainment Weekly*: 'The higher powers have called Doyle to be Angel's guide. He's the last person in the world who wants to – or should – be doing this. He just wants to play the ponies and drink a lot. But he has unexpected wisdom in the midst of his extreme foibles.'

Whedon, having succeeded in getting *Buffy* and *Angel* scheduled back-to-back on the WB was keen, at first, to stress the differences between the series, noting that *Angel* 'is more of an anthology show than *Buffy*. There's not a soap opera at the centre of it.' We also saw a more humorous side to Angel, but good old Cordelia was still reliably 'self-involved and in her Cordelia-bubble, which is her charm', according to Whedon. Boreanaz also revealed that the plan was to 'explore Angel's past [and the] period when he [was] wandering the streets in abject misery, cursed by the gypsies'. This element took a while to manifest itself, and it's not until **11**, 'Somnambulist' that Angel's history is delved into in any significant way.

In the event, *Angel* quickly became a hit, achieving respectable ratings on the back of *Buffy* (it was the top-rated new WB show of the year) and impressive critical backing. Fans immediately took to the central trio of characters and there was a huge outcry at the first change in the regular cast (see **9**, 'Hero'). Long before the end of the season, *Angel* (along with *Buffy*) had been renewed for the 2000–2001 schedules. In Britain, Sky quickly bought the series and opted to follow US scheduling, showing *Buffy* and *Angel* back-to-back on Friday in early 2000. These proved to be very popular, gaining the satellite company some of its highest ratings. Sadly, as with their purchase of *Buffy* two years previously, the BBC dithered over *Angel*, unsure whether they could find a suitable timeslot for a series with such adult content. This allowed another terrestrial company, Channel 4, to buy *Angel*. Channel 4's current plan is to show *Angel* in the autumn of 2000 and episodes should be on air by the time this book is published. Rumours abound, however, of yet another early time-slot and more potential cuts with a blunt hacksaw for the UK audience. Time will tell.

The Angel Demo Reel: 'I figured life didn't have any more surprises . . . I thought I'd seen everything. Then I came to L.A.' In May 1999, as an advertising tool for the forthcoming series, Whedon and Greenwalt prepared a six-minute promotional video of specially shot sequences (and clips from *Buffy*). It begins with Angel on a rooftop doing the *Who I Am And How I Came To Be* bit. 'I was born 244 years ago in Ireland,' he notes. 'Life as a vampire was a constant thrill. The power. The danger. The outfits. *Good* outfits. Never getting old was also a plus.' The flashbacks include clips from 'Becoming' Part 2, 'Amends', 'Anne', 'Passion', 'Graduation Day' Part 2, 'I Only Have Eyes For You', 'Reptile Boy', 'Doppelgängland', 'Beauty and the Beasts' and the memorable bit from 'The Wish' of Cordelia getting out of her car wearing *that* leather skirt. Over a pounding rock soundtrack (Vast's 'Here'), Angel and Doyle share a scene that almost mirrors the street sequences in 1, 'City Of' ('one hell of a city,' notes Doyle. 'Buckets of fun if you're a nasty creature'), while Cordelia tells Angel (uniquely wearing a white T-shirt) that they should 'charge the helpless'. There's also some great dialogue exchanges like when Doyle tells Angel that there are dangerous people in this town. Angel: 'They're not gonna like me stirring up the water.' Doyle: 'You're *afraid* of that?' Angel: 'I'm *counting* on it.' Doyle: 'Quite the masculine fellah, aren't you?'

Extracts from the demo were put to good use in the subsequent *Angel* title sequence along with several of the travelogue scene-breaks of Los Angeles at night.

Did You Know?: Despite the disparity in their ages on the series, Charisma Carpenter is actually nine months *older* than David Boreanaz.

'The idea of a vampire in a white hat,
probably seems a little "gimme a break-y".'

– 'War Zone'

'After centuries of terror, redemption has a price . . .'

Angel – Season One
(1999–2000)

**Mutant Enemy Inc/Greenwolf Corp[1]/Kuzui
Enterprises/Sandollar Television/20th Century Fox**

Created by Joss Whedon and David Greenwalt
Consulting Producer: Marti Noxon, Howard Gordon
(1–16), Jim Kouf (18–22)
Producer: Tracey Stern (1–7), Tim Minear (1–13),
Kelly A. Manners, Gareth Davies (1)
Supervising Producer: Tim Minear (14–22)
Co-Producer: Skip Schoolnik, James A. Contner
(2–6, 10, 18)
Associate Producer: R.D. Price
Executive Producers: Sandy Gallin, Gail Berman, Fran
Rubel Kuzui, Kaz Kuzui, Joss Whedon, David Greenwalt

Regular Cast
David Boreanaz (Angel/Angelus)
Charisma Carpenter (Cordelia Chase)
Glenn Quinn (Allen Francis Doyle, 1–9[2], 14[3])
Sarah Michelle Gellar (Buffy Summers, 1[4], 7[5], 8, 19)

---

[1] Except **1**, 'City Of' which does not carry the 'Greenwolf Corp' logo.
[2] Although Glenn Quinn appears in the title sequence of **10**, 'Parting Gift'
(and in the 'previously on *Angel*' scene repeated from **9**, 'Hero'), he is
not present in the episode itself.
[3] Uncredited, voice only in **14**, 'I've Got You Under My Skin'.
[4] Uncredited, voice heard on the telephone and seen in flashbacks in **1**,
'City Of'.
[5] Uncredited, seen in flashback in **7**, 'The Bachelor Party'.

Michael Mantell (Oliver Simon, 1[6], 17)
Christian Kane (Lindsey McDonald, 1, 18–19, 21–22)
Elisabeth Rohm (Detective Kate Lockley, 2, 4, 6, 11,
14–15, 19, 22)
John Mahon (Trevor Lockley, 6, 15)
Thomas Barr (Lee Mercer, 6, 18–19, 21)
Carry Cannon (Female Oracle, 8, 10, 22)
Randall Slavin (Male Oracle, 8, 10, 22)
Alexis Denisof (Wesley Wyndham-Price, 10–22)
Julie Benz (Darla, 15, 18, 22)
Stephanie Romanov (Lilah Morgan, 16, 18–19, 21–22)
Eliza Dushku (Faith, 18–19)
J. August Richards (Gunn, 20[7], 21–22)
David Herman (David Nabbit, 20, 22)
Sam Anderson (Holland, 21–22)

1
City Of

US Transmission Date: 5 October 1999
UK Transmission Date: 7 January 2000 (Sky)

Writers: David Greenwalt, Joss Whedon
Director: Joss Whedon
Cast: Tracy Middendorf (Tina),
Vyto Ruginis (Russell Winters), Jon Ingrassia (Stacy),
Renee Ridgeley (Margo), Sam Pancake (Manager),
Josh Wolloway (Good-Looking Guy),
Gina McClain (Janice),

In a Los Angeles bar Angel tells a stranger the story of his
lost love. He watches some men and women playing pool
and follows when they leave. The men are vampires but
Angel interrupts their work and, in the ensuing fight, kills
two of them and incapacitates the third. When one of the

---

[6] Uncredited in **1**, 'City Of'.
[7] Uncredited in **20**, 'War Zone'.

women thanks him, Angel scares her with his vampire face. He stakes the last vampire and slips into the night.

Angel arrives home. He senses that he is not alone and finds Doyle, who describes himself as half-human (on his mother's side). Doyle has been sent by 'The Powers That Be' and implies that unless Angel gets involved with people he will prey on humans again. Doyle explains that he gets visions of people in trouble and that they both have things they must atone for. He tells Angel to meet 'Tina at the Coffee Spot' where she is a waitress. Angel strikes up an awkward conversation with the woman but she mistakenly thinks he's working for a man called Russell who is harassing her. Angel convinces her otherwise and offers her a lift to a party. While Tina is busy with the hostess, Margo, Angel is surprised to meet Cordelia, one of Buffy's old friends from Sunnydale, now a jobbing actress. She is worried that Angel may be evil again, but he assures her that, while he is still a vampire ('there isn't actually a cure for *that*') his soul remains intact. Angel spots Tina struggling with a man named Stacy. After a confrontation, Angel and Tina escape. In Cordelia's apartment she listens to a message from her agent which implies that no one wants to see her audition.

Tina asks if this is the part where Angel 'comforts' her, but he says that enough people have taken advantage of her. Tina tells him about her friend Denise, who has disappeared. As Tina sleeps Angel looks up information at the L.A. Public Library. His research leads him to believe that Denise was killed. Angel tells Tina about his suspicions, but she spots Doyle's note containing her name and thinks Angel was sent by Russell. Angel is unable to follow her into the sunlight and, seeing his true face, Tina returns to her apartment where Russell is waiting for her. Tina tells Russell about Angel's transformation. Russell reveals that he is also a vampire and kills Tina, leaving her to be found by Angel. Russell is briefed by his lawyer, Lindsey McDonald from the firm Wolfram & Hart. Viewing the party video, Russell sees Cordelia and says he wants something to eat. Angel, with Doyle's help, finds Stacy who reveals Russell's whereabouts.

Margo calls Cordelia and tells her that Russell wants to help her career. At Russell's mansion Cordelia notices some oddities and realises that he is a vampire. Then the power goes out and Angel arrives. Russell and Angel fight and, despite Angel being shot, he and Cordelia escape. Next day Russell is meeting Lindsey when Angel walks in on them. Russell offers to make peace saying that in L.A. they do things differently, but Angel kicks him out of the window before anyone can stop him. Lindsey calls his people to warn them about Angel. Doyle tells Angel that Cordelia will make a useful link to humanity. Cordelia thinks they need a business that helps people and volunteers to organise it. Angel says he's game.

What Might Have Been: The first-draft script (entitled 'Angel Pilot') follows the basic plot of 1, 'City Of' but includes some elements not taken forward. It confirms what many fans suspected: that the role of Angel's mentor was originally written with the character of Whistler (see *Buffy*: 'Becoming') in mind. 'You know what I don't need?' Angel asks when meeting his old friend. 'A wacky sidekick from Hell.'

The opening scene has Angel bitter over Buffy, commenting, 'Women, they're just . . . so round and comfy and then they say, "Oh, could you pass me that fork, honey? And your heart, too, come on." Then they [pounds pretend fork into a heart on the bar]. I'm not bitter.' After this, with the exception of the odd line of dialogue and Stacy being spelt 'Stacey' throughout, the script proceeds much as per 1, 'City Of'. However . . .

What a Shame They Dropped . . .: The following gem. Tina: 'You kinda remind of the cowboys back home. 'Cept you're not drunk.' Angel: [deadpan] 'I'm high on life.'

Dudes and Babes: Much cleavage is on display at Margo's party. The hostess, Tina and (especially) Cordelia's dresses giving a new meaning to 'low cut'. Plus a girl wearing a *very* tight black PVC skirt. Also worth mentioning are those scenes when Angel first meets Doyle and David Boreanaz gets to show off his rippling biceps.

It's a Designer Label!: Cordelia's red party dress is a Neiman-Marcus. Angel pulls the 'wearing a Hawaiian shirt to convince the villain that he's a tourist' trick for the first time (see **6**, 'Sense and Sensitivity').

References: Apart from the Gotham City look of twilight Los Angeles and Angel walking down the alley at the end of both the tag-sequence and the titles (it's the same shot), with his coat billowing behind him like a cape, there's the first of many *Batman* references; Doyle noting Angel's home 'has a nice *bat-cave* sort-of an air to it'.

Doyle's being half-human 'on my mother's side' is a characteristic he shares not only with Mr Spock in *Star Trek* and the Doctor in *Doctor Who*, but also with Jesus, the mythical Hercules of *Legendary Journeys* and many literary and comic-book characters. The plot is similar to an obscure animated movie *Vampire Hunter D*, in which a brooding half-vampire helps a woman stalked by an ancient vampire. 'I'm parched from all this yakkin', man. Let's go treat me to a Billy Dee,' refers to Colt .45 beer and actor Billy Dee Williams (*The Empire Strikes Back*, *Batman*) who did commercials for the brand. Also references to the notorious L.A. nightclub The Lido, Grandmaster Flash and the Furious Five's 'The Message' and the Minnesota Vikings football team.

The Charisma Show: Charisma steals the episode from her first appearance at the party asking Angel, 'Are you still . . . *GRRR*?' Plus the memorable exchange with Russell at his mansion. 'I finally get invited to a nice place with no mirrors and lots of curtains. Hey, you're a *vampire.*' Russell: 'What? No, I'm not.' Cordelia: '*Are too.*' Russell: 'I don't know what you're talking about.' Cordelia: 'I'm from Sunnydale. We had our own Hellmouth. I think I know a vampire when I'm alone with him in his fortress-like home.'

'West Hollywood'?: Readers without Internet access may be astonished at the number of fans who *totally* misheard Doyle and Angel's closing 'Are you game?', 'I'm game,' as

'Are you gay?', 'I'm gay.' Oliver tells Angel he is a 'beautiful man', but denies that he is coming on to him, noting that he (Oliver) is in a serious relationship with a landscape architect.

'You May Remember Me from Such Films and TV Series as . . .': Born in Buffalo where his father is a TV weatherman, David Boreanaz had done very little acting before landing the role of Angel on *Buffy*. Aside from a couple of low-budget movies, his only claim to fame was a brief guest slot on *Married: With Children*. A former cheerleader for the San Diego Chargers, Charisma Carpenter began her acting career in the *Baywatch* episode 'Air Buchanon', playing Hobie's girlfriend Wendie. Aaron Spelling personally auditioned her for the part of the deliciously saucy 'über-vixen-bitch' Ashley Green in NBC's *Malibu Shores*, a performance described by *TV Guide* as: 'The Shannen Doherty bad-girl role is taken by *sultry stunner*, Charisma Carpenter, who comes across as the most beguiling and fleshed-out character on-screen.' She also landed another role in a short-lived series, Beth Sullivan in the *Josh Kirby: Time Warrior* TV movies, plus a legendary advert for Spree sweets ('It's a kick in the mouth!'). Glenn Quinn spent seven years playing Mark Healy, Becky's husband, on *Roseanne* (where he worked with Joss Whedon). Among his movies is the delightfully named *Live Nude Girls*.

Tracy Middendorf played Risa Holmes in *Ally McBeal*, Laura Kingman in *Beverly Hills 90210* and Carrie Brady on the soap *Days of Our Lives*. Her guest appearances read like a list of most of the important US TV series of the 90s: *The X-Files, Millennium, Chicago Hope, Star Trek: Deep Space 9, Murder, She Wrote* and *The Practice*. 'It seems like I always get cast as very emotional women in crisis,' she complained to *TV Guide* in 1999. Still, it's a living, isn't it?

Vyto Ruginis has also been a guest-star on *Ally McBeal*, along with *Star Trek: The Next Generation* and *NYPD Blue*. His movies include a brilliant cameo in *The Devil's Advocate, Phenomenon, Descending Angel* and *Jumpin'*

Jack Flash. Christian Kane played Wick Lobo on *Rescue 77* and Flyboy Leggat on *Fame L.A.* Michael Mantell, who appears uncredited, has been in movies like *The Velocity of Gary*, *Dead Funny*, *Quiz Show*, *Passion Fish* and *The Brother from Another Planet* and in TV series as diverse as *Charmed*, *ER*, *Party of Five*, *The X-Files* and *Matlock*. Readers may recognise him as Howard Sewell in *Space: Above and Beyond*.

The Men Behind the Camera: When asked how much like *Buffy*'s Xander Harris Joss Whedon was as a teenager, the writer noted: 'Less-and-less as he gets laid more-and-more.' Whedon is a third-generation Hollywood script-writer (his grandfather wrote for *Leave It To Beaver*, his father worked on *The Golden Girls*). His education included a period at Winchester, a public school in England ('My mother was a teacher,' he told Rob Francis. 'She was on sabbatical in England so I had to go somewhere.'). After writing many speculative scripts in his teens, he landed a writing job on the enormously popular sitcom *Roseanne* (he also produced the TV version of *Parenthood*). 'My life was completely about film, night and day,' he told *teen movieline* magazine. '[I] learned about filmmaking by analysing two particular movies – the Western *Johnny Guitar* and the melodrama *The Naked Kiss*.' However, with an encyclopedic knowledge of horror movies and comics Whedon had always wanted to write for that market (his favourite film remains Kubrick's *The Shining*). 'I watched a lot of horror movies,' he admitted to *The Big Breakfast*. 'I saw all these blonde women going down alleys and getting killed and I felt bad for them. I wanted one of them to kill a monster for a change so I came up with *Buffy*.' His movie script for *Buffy the Vampire Slayer* suffered four years of rejection before being produced in 1992. Subsequently, Whedon became one of Hollywood's hottest properties, Oscar-nominated for his script for *Toy Story*, writing *Alien: Resurrection* and contributing (often un-credited) rewrites to *Twister*, *Speed* and *Waterworld*. At the time of writing it seems sadly unlikely that his *The X-Men* script will be the one that reaches the big screen in the summer of 2000. His next major movie project is a science-fiction thriller called *Afterlife*, due to enter production later in the year.

One of David Greenwalt's first industry jobs was as Jeff Bridges' body-double before he become a director on *The Wonder Years*, preceding a period as writer and producer on *The X-Files*, *Doogie Howser M.D.* and, in 1997, *Buffy the Vampire Slayer*. His film scripts include *Class*, *American Dreamer* and *Secret Admirer* (which he also directed) and one acting role as 'Uniformed Cop' in a 1981 horror-spoof called *Wacko* (see **18**, 'Five by Five'). Producer Skip Schoolnik was the regular editor on *Buffy the Vampire Slayer* along with over 30 films and TV movies.

An explanation of the role of the various producers is provided by Tim Minear: 'The title "producer" on a TV show can mean anything from writer to line-producer (the man or woman in the trenches running the day-to-day operations of the set) to someone billed as an "executive producer" who might have some stake in the property but wouldn't be let through the gate by the security guard for lack of recognition. On our show, most of those producers you see are the writers. David Greenwalt, Joss, Marti Noxon, Howard Gordon, Tracey Stern, Jim Kouf. Kelly Manners is our on-set producer. He has the thankless task of making sure the show gets made for a price and on a schedule. R.D. Price, our associate producer, is a catch-all producing entity. He baby-sits the set when one of us can't be there, shoots second unit material and directed **14**, "I've Got You Under My Skin". Skip Schoolnik runs our post-production department. So far as my involvement, I've had the chance to get my hands dirty in all aspects of the production. I'm in the early concept meetings with the other writers as we pitch story ideas. When one of my scripts is in prep, I work with the director and the production department heads – my bosses, David and Joss, of course – going over all the elements. This includes casting, wardrobe, sets, locations. I "tone" with directors, meaning going over the script scene-by-scene trying to get across what we want the tone of [the] episode to be. After it's shot and the director has had his cut, I sit with the editors and work through the cuts, sometimes redesigning sequences which don't work and deciding what additional material is needed. I work with post-sound on the sound design and talking to the composer about music. Then, when it's ready to put in the oven, we mix the sound and sometimes I'm on the dubbing stage for that.' Do these guys ever sleep?

'The full time *Angel* writing staff is small,' concluded Minear. 'David Greenwalt, Howard Gordon, Jeannine Renshaw and myself at the moment. There's plenty for me to do on *Angel*.'

L.A.-Speak: Tina: 'I'm sort-of having relationship issues.'

Cordelia: 'Wow, what a nice place. Love your curtains. Not afraid to emphasise the curtains.'

Cordelia, as Doyle extracts bullets from Angel's chest: 'Finally. I thought I was going to faint while *barfing*.'

Cordelia: 'You need somebody to organise things and you're not exactly rolling in it Mr I-was-alive-for-200-years-and-never-developed-an-investment-portfolio.'

Classic *Double Entendre*: Angel, on Cordelia: 'You think she's a Hottie?' Doyle: 'She's a stiffener all right, I can't lie about that. But, you know, she could use a hand.'

Sex and Drugs and Rock'n'Roll: There are wholly unsubtle hints from Tina and Cordelia that 'helping' someone in Los Angeles usually means that you get to have sex with them afterwards. Tina is astonished when she is ready to give herself to Angel only for him to turn down the offer. 'Boy, are you ever in the wrong town.' In addition to being a vampire, there are hints to a dark side to Russell's sexuality, Tina alleging that he 'likes pain'. Margo takes some pills while on the phone to Cordelia. She's also drinking what looks like tomato juice, but it could be blood. Is she a junkie, or a vampire, or both?

Logic, Let Me Introduce You to This Window: As with various *Buffy* episodes (for instance, 'What's My Line?')

Angel can be seen on videotape, despite video cameras using mirrors as part of their focusing mechanism. When Angel pretends to be drunk in the bar his sleeves don't have the retractable stakes that he wears one scene later. Doyle uses the fact that he walked uninvited into Angel's home as proof he (Doyle) isn't a vampire, but it's later established that vampire's homes are not protected from unwanted vampires entering, since the owner is dead. (This also, presumably, explains how Angel can get into both Tina's apartment after she's been killed and into Russell's house. Russell's ability to enter Tina's apartment is specifically explained by the fact that he owns the building.)

In the coffee shop, Angel's reflection is visible on a table top. The bomb Angel sets says '30' on the display when he triggers it. Although it ticks quickly, the numbers don't change. When Angel is handed Oliver's business card, he holds it between a finger and his thumb. Next shot, it's between two fingers. When Angel picks up Cordelia to escape Russell's guards she is wearing different shoes to those seen when they jump to the floor. The fight between Angel and Russell features a pair of stuntmen who look *nothing whatsoever* like David Boreanaz and Vyto Ruginis. As Russell falls and bursts into flames his reflection is visible in the building's windows. Angel dials seven numbers when calling Buffy. Sunnydale, although in the same state, should not be a local call from Los Angeles.

I Just *Love* Your Accent: Contrary to popular belief, Glenn Quinn *is* Irish and uses his natural accent in his appearances on *Angel*.

Asked about a perceived British influence in his writing and whether his time in England during the early 1980s and exposure to British Telefantasy had scarred him for life, Joss Whedon noted: 'I saw *Blake's 7*, *Sapphire and Steel* and *Doctor Who* but not a great deal. I was at boarding school and didn't have much opportunity. What we watched were our heroes like *Starsky and Hutch* but I watched a huge amount of British TV while I lived in America. That's one of the reasons I was so anxious to come. I was an entire PBS kid. *Masterpiece Theatre, Monty Python*, BBC Shakespeares.' Asked if he believed his time in Britain had helped to get characters like Giles and Wesley 'right', Joss confirmed: 'You want the contrast between Giles and Buffy but at the same time I hope he's been a little more human than just stuffy. Of course the great thing is there are dirty words that the American audience don't know.'

Motors: Angel drives a black 1968 Plymouth Belvedere GTX convertible. Stacy's car is a 'grey 87 Black Mercedes 300E, [which is] going to need some serious work on the bumper'.

Quote/Unquote: Doyle: 'I've been sent. By The Powers That Be.' Angel: 'The powers that be what?'

Doyle describes the plot for anyone who's never watched *Buffy the Vampire Slayer*: 'Once upon a time there was a vampire. And he was the meanest vampire in all the land. All the other vampires were afraid of him, he was such a bastard. Then one day he's cursed by gypsies. They restore his human soul. And all of a sudden he's mad with guilt . . . It's a fairly dull tale. It needs a little sex is my feeling. So, sure enough, enter the girl. Pretty little blonde thing, Vampire Slayer by trade, and our vampire fell madly in love with her. Eventually the two of them get fleshy with one another. The technical term is "perfect happiness". But when our boy gets there, he goes bad again . . . So when he gets his soul back for a second time, he figures he can't be anywhere near Miss-Young-Puppy-Eyes without endangering them both. So, what does he do? He takes off. Goes to L.A., to fight evil and atone for his crimes. He's a shadow. A faceless champion of the hapless human race.'

Doyle, when Angel asks why The Powers That Be are using Doyle as their instrument: 'We've all got *something* to atone for.'

Angel, on Cordelia: 'It's nice that she's grown as a person.'

Angel: 'I don't want to share my feelings, I don't want to open up. I want to find Russell and I want to look him in the eye.' Doyle: 'Then what?' Angel: '*Then* I'm going to share my feelings.'

Cordelia: 'A cockroach. In the corner. I think it's a bantamweight.'

Notes: 'Los Angeles. You see it at night and it shines. Like a beacon. People are drawn to it. People and other things. They come for all sorts of reasons. My reason? No surprise there. It started with a girl.' A cracking beginning, setting up all of the elements that *Angel* will focus on – guilt and redemption, the quest for happiness, the cheapness of life in Los Angeles and the hollowness of 'status', the cost of 'fighting the good fight' – and yet still having time to tell a story. Nicely paced and with a rather appealing sense of irony. The visuals are *tremendous*, particularly the recurring shots of the sun rising and setting in speed-motion above the L.A. skyline that crop up throughout the season (see *The Angel Demo Reel*; this trick had been used to great effect in the movie *Blade* which came out while *Angel* would have been in pre-production). Not as dark (in several senses) as was expected by many but, perhaps, more interesting for exactly that reason.

While Doyle tells the story of Angel's past, we see flashbacks from the *Buffy* episodes 'Amends', 'Innocence', 'Becoming' Part 1, 'Anne' and 'Graduation Day' Part 2. Cordelia summarises her own back-story from 'Lover's Walk' and 'The Prom': 'I grew up in a nice home. It wasn't like this, but we did have a room or two that we didn't even know what they were for. Until the IRS got all huffy about my folks not paying taxes for, well, ever. They took it all.' There's a subtle crossover to 'The Freshman' episode of *Buffy* which was shown immediately prior to 1, 'City Of' when Angel calls Buffy and then hangs up when she answers. Doyle indicates that Angel drinks exclusively pig's blood. Angel confirms that the last human blood he tasted was Buffy's (see *Buffy*: 'Graduation Day' Part 2). Angel has seen fourteen wars in his lifetime, not including Vietnam (which was never, officially, declared). He has tea in his apartment but not milk or sugar. He seems able to differentiate between humans and demons by smell. He has good reflexes and admits to Tina that he is lonely.

Cordelia says she lives in 'Malibu. A small condo on the beach. It's not a private beach, but I'm young so I forbear.' When we actually see her apartment, however, it's neither a beach condo *nor* in Malibu. Her agent is called Joe and she seems to have had plenty of auditions with the networks to such an extent that they've seen enough of her. She tells Russell that she's had 'a lot of opportunities. The hands in the liquid-gel commercial were almost mine, bar one or two girls'. She practises yoga and is reading a book called *Meditation for a Successful Life*. Doyle notes: 'I get visions. Which is to say great splitting migraines that come with pictures. A name, a face. I don't know who sends them. I just know whoever sends them is more powerful than me or you and they're just trying to make things right.' Tina comes from Missoula, Montana. Angel says he was there 'during the Depression'.

The episode was rated 'TV 14'. The subject matter probably would have justified it anyway, but including a 'piss off' and a 'bastard' in the opening scenes made certain. Some filming took place in the basement car park of the exclusive L.A. Restaurant, the Argyle.

Soundtrack: The theme is by Darling Violetta (accompanying the stunning title sequence designed by Regis Kimble). Also 'Right of Left Field' by Wellwater Conspiracy and 'Maybe I Belong' by Howie Beck. The two songs used during Margo's party are 'Ladyshave' and 'Teenage Sensation' both by Gus Gus.

Much of the music on Angel is performed by Robert J. Kral (whose previous work included soundtracks for *The Legend of Billy the Kid*, *Cyberkidz* and *Sliders*). He told Rob Francis: 'I owe my break into the TV industry to Chris Beck. He hired me as an assistant on a TV show called *TWO*. Chris would also hire me for assistance on several HBO and TV movies. He recommended me to Danny Lux, so I ended up writing for 41 episodes of *Sliders*. Chris was offered *Angel*, but knew he wanted to turn more energy toward feature films. He took up the offer, but had explained to the producers that I would be coming on board.'

Explaining in detail the equipment he uses, Robert noted: 'A G3 Macintosh computer running Digital Performer which is the command centre for the rest of the studio, comprised of Roland and Emu samplers and the Gigasampler. Gigasampler is totally revolutionary in that it isn't restricted to memory limitations like the other samplers. I spent an entire session recording the insides of a grand piano: scraping the strings etc. There are some truly terrifying sounds lurking under the hood of that instrument. I haven't managed to use the bulk of those sounds on *Angel* yet because I haven't had the time to program them in the sampler. The most unusual thing might be my three-year-old daughter's toy that when you press a button a trap door opens and it has this hilarious "boing" sound from a spring being released. Play it down about four octaves and it's scary. That's the fun thing about samplers: it's "open season" on anything that makes a sound.'

Did You Know?: The sequence in which Angel is approached by an agent at the party was, as Marti Noxon told *Science Fiction World*: 'Something very similar [to what] happened to David. His manager saw him walking his dog and went up and said, "I'm going to represent you." Although Boreanaz was already an actor, his discovery was very much like that.'

Critique: *TV Guide* trailed *Angel* as: 'One of the best new shows'. Noted *Buffy* fan and critic Matt Roush said *Angel* 'best preserves the virtues of the original – the wit and danger of *Buffy* are here – while giving us an entirely new experience . . . *Angel* is grimmer than *Buffy* which is why Cordelia is so welcome, still unflappably spouting such lines as, "I've known a lot of demons and, slime aside, not a lot goin' on there." Gotta love her!'

The Novelisation: Nancy Holder's novel of **1**, 'City Of' (Pocket Pulse Books, December 1999) is a classic TV tie-in (in the best traditions of this underrated literary sub-genre), taking the script and fleshing it out with pop culture references (*Beverly Hills Cop*, *Gone With the Wind*). Holder used the opportunity to tell Angel's back-story in interludes set in Galway 1753 (see *Buffy*: 'Becoming' Part 1, although much of Holder's Angelus-origin speculation is contradicted in **15**, 'The Prodigal'), Manhattan 1996 (see *Buffy*: 'Becoming' Part 1), the death of Jenny Calendar (see *Buffy*: 'Passion'), Dublin 1838 (see *Buffy*: 'Amends'), London 1860 (see *Buffy*: 'Becoming' Part 1), a marvellous Spike and Drusilla fragment set in Hungary during the 1956 Russian invasion, Rumania 1898 (see *Buffy*: 'Becoming' Part 1, **19**, 'Sanctuary') and the collapse of Buffy and Angel's relationship (see *Buffy*: 'The Prom').

What Might Have Been . . .: Writer David Fury, speaking in April 2000 at the Canadian Film Centre, responded to an audience question about whether any of his scripts had been spiked: 'The one script I've written that was never produced was the second episode of *Angel* . . . [It] was going to be a much darker show. Far more adult. An example is in the first episode, when he finds a girl he's protecting dead, he has her blood on his hands; he was going to start licking the blood off his fingers like he can't control himself. Then, being repulsed, he goes to the bathroom and scrubs his hands. It was about recovering alcoholics, that was the allegory. We were going to [have] him struggling to remain good. Along those lines the second episode which I'd written was called "Corrupt". It was about junkie prostitutes, not usually what you see on the WB. Kate was an undercover cop who was addicted to cocaine and was sleeping with men because she got a bit too far into her work. About two days before shooting, the network got a hold of the script and went, "WOAH. This is the WB." They said "Corrupt" was far too dark and disturbing, we'd like something nice and friendly and with pretty people in it. So I had to very quickly turn over a new script.'

Tim Minear revealed: 'It's true that the initial first episode after the pilot was scrubbed. The network wasn't really asking for anything Joss didn't agree with. It really wasn't a big drama, we were still in the formative stages. As for the "dark" episodes, before the network ever approached us with their concerns, each *Angel* writer was developing their first script. Mine happened to be **11**, "Somnambulist" [which was] conceived and first-draft written before we started shooting. We always understood that *Angel* had its dark side and never shrinked from that. I don't think you'll find the main character on any other WB show, or any other show for that matter, eating his family any time soon!'

2
Lonely Hearts

US Transmission Date: 12 October 1999
UK Transmission Date: 14 January 2000 (Sky)

Writer: David Fury
Director: James A. Contner
Cast: Lillian Birdsell (Sharon Richler),
Obi Ndefo (Bartender), Derek Hughs (Neil),
Johnny Messner (Kevin),
Jennifer Tung (Neil's Pick-up Girl),
Tracy Stone (Pretty Girl), David Nisic (Slick Guy),
Ken Rush (Guy), Connor Kelly (Regular)

During a discussion with Cordelia regarding the emblem on their new business cards, Doyle has a vision of a 'terminally-stuck-in-the-eighties' bar, D'Oblique. In the bar Kevin and Sharon are getting to know one another as Angel, Doyle and Cordelia arrive. Angel questions the bartender, while Cordelia works the tables, passing out their card. Doyle tactfully cautions her about her methods as they notice Kevin and Sharon leaving together. Angel meets an attractive blonde called Kate. When she asks his occupation, Angel says he's a veterinarian. A man asks Cordelia and Doyle about the 'services' they provide, insinuating that Cordelia is a hooker. Angel and Kate are getting on very well and she asks if he'd like to go somewhere quiet. He reluctantly refuses, claiming he has to remain at the bar. Doyle's situation quickly deteriorates and a fight begins. Angel joins in and the troublemakers are thrown out by the bartender. Kate leaves and Angel watches her go with regret.

Next morning Sharon is getting dressed and Kevin lies dead, his body eviscerated and decaying. Angel and friends search newspapers and the Internet for incidents near D'Oblique. They discover two attacks that are linked to the bar. Angel returns to it and meets Kate. He tries to warn her against going in but she takes offence and ignores him. Kate sits at the bar, next to Sharon who is flirting with a man she has just met and they leave together. A man asks the bartender if Kevin is around. As Angel listens, the bartender says he last saw Kevin with Sharon the night before. Sharon and her new friend are in bed, as Angel rushes in search of her apartment building. Sharon pulls her male companion close and a creature burrows from her chest into his back. Angel crashes through the door to find Sharon dead and her companion pulling on his shirt, as the tail of the parasitic demon disappears into his body. Angel confronts the demon and they fight but the demon is stronger than Angel and throws him across the room before making his escape. Angel gets to his feet to find Kate holding a gun on him and flashing her police badge.

Angel tries to convince Kate that he is not the killer. She doesn't believe him and starts to put him in handcuffs. He apologises and knocks her down then jumps out of the window. Angel arrives at Cordelia's apartment and gives his friends a description of the parasitic demon they're dealing with. While Doyle and Cordelia continue their research, Kate is searching Angel's home. Doyle discovers that the demon is afraid of fire, something it and Angel have in common. Angel admits he'll need help and calls Kate. He convinces her to meet him at the bar. Kate asks the bartender to let her know when Angel arrives. He tells her he thinks Angel is in the alley. Kate goes to investigate and the bartender hits her over the head with a bottle. Angel saves Kate before the demon can transfer from the bartender to her. The bartender locks Kate and Angel in the basement. It searches for a new host, as the current body is deteriorating. Kate and Angel escape from the basement and find the creature dragging a woman into the alley. Angel struggles with the demon and throws it on to a burning oil-drum, engulfing the demon in flames. Kate apologises to Angel and admits to searching his home. Angel tells Doyle and Cordelia that as a reward for their hard work he'd like to go out with them. They opt to go home instead and a relieved Angel sits at his desk and turns out the light.

Dudes and Babes: A bar full of them. Most are good-looking and almost all are lonely, vacuous and shallow. Los Angeles in microcosm.

Denial, Thy Name is Kate: Angel quickly works out that his newest ally has problems trusting people. We find out why in **6**, 'Sense and Sensitivity'.

It's a Designer Label!: Cordelia namechecks Calvin Klein. Doyle's huge-collared shirts are a big focus of this (and subsequent) episodes and clash violently with his tan leather jacket. Cordy wears a *very* revealing red boob-tube in the opening scenes and a similar blue one (with flower motif) later. Also, Kate's desperately obvious 'take-me-now' flowery dress and Sharon's bright red top and slit-skirt. As a seeming comment upon the hedonistic yet hollow L.A. club-scene, it's worth mentioning that the bar is overflowing short skirts, curves, big chests and pretty faces (see **Dudes and Babes**).

References: The plot is reminiscent of *The Hidden*, in which a body-swapping, sex-seeking alien mollusc causes mayhem in L.A. while chased by a police detective and a rival alien. More *Batman* references, like Doyle's: 'It's not like you have a signal folks can shine in the sky whenever they need help.' The scene where Angel pulls out his grappling hook and Kate asks 'Who are you?' closely parallels Batman's first meeting with Vicki Vale in Tim Burton's 1989 film. The demon that bursts out of people's chests may have been influenced by *Alien*.

'The International House of Posers' refers to the restaurant chain International House of Pancakes (IHOP), they of the award-winning pancakes, omelettes and other breakfast specialities. Also *Mission: Impossible* ('Your visions are kind of lame. They should send you one of those self-destructing tapes that come with a dossier'), *Cagney and Lacey*, classic 50s cop show *The Naked City*, *Peter Pan*, Patricia McLachlin's novel 'Sarah, Plain and Tall' (or the Glenn Close movie version), Ken and Barbie dolls and Zack Screech, a character from *Saved by the Bell*.

Geographical locations mentioned include Barstow (a town in the Mojave Desert).

The Charisma Show: Cordelia's incompetently drawn cards for Angel Investigations don't look much like an angel but, despite Kate's assertion at the end, they aren't a lobster either. Plus, Cordy's sales pitch when giving out the cards: 'Are you troubled? Or is that just your lazy eye? Anyway, call us, we are *very* discreet.' Her reaction to Doyle picking up her bra in the apartment is great: 'That is *so* high school. Cordelia wears bras. *Ooo*, she has *girlie-parts*.'

L.A.-Speak: Cordelia: 'See *jazz-hands* over there? Mama's boy. Peter-Pan complex? Self-absorbed closet-dud, with a big "the-world-owes-me" chip on her shoulder. Check out Sarah, plain and tall? Has, or comes from, big money.'

Troublemaker: 'Nobody's talking to you, *wipe*.'

Kate: 'Way-to-come-off like a drunken-slut. Slut's better than a hypocrite, right?' Angel: 'Kind of hard on yourself.' Kate: 'That's me. *Self-flagellating-hypocrite-slut*.'

Guy: 'I was pretty much a *spaz* in high school. A real "something is out there" geek, with the gang of geek toy minions.'

Cordelia: 'It moves from body to body. And when it leaves one for the next, not going to *gag* here, the first one goes *kaplooey* pretty fast.' Doyle: 'Curdles like cream on a hot day.' Cordy: 'I believe I covered that with non-dairy *kaplooey*?'

Not Exactly a Haven for the Bruthas: The only black face with a line of dialogue is working behind the bar.

Cigarettes and Alcohol: Kate refers to daiquiri, a cocktail of rum, lime and sugar. Most of the episode takes place in a bar where Sharon seems to be drinking red wine while Angel, inevitably, orders a coke.

Sex and Drugs and Rock'n'Roll: Angel asks where Doyle learned his computer skills. Cordelia suggests, 'Downloading pictures of naked women?' Doyle agrees this is 'more or less accurate'.

Angel on the demon: 'It eviscerates its victims as it moves from body to body and it may only be able to do it after some kind of a sex-act, exchange of fluids kind-of-thing.' The entire episode is marbled with impotence metaphors.

'You May Remember Me from Such Films and TV Series as . . .': German-born Elisabeth Rohm is best known for *One Life to Live*, in which she played Dorothy Hayes, and *Eureka Street*. Obi Ndefo was Bodie in *Dawson's Creek* and has made guest appearances in both *Star Trek: Deep Space 9* and *Voyager* as well as *3rd Rock From the Sun*. Johnny Messner was Rob Layne in the long-running soap *The Guiding Light*. Jennifer Tung played an ensign in *Star Trek: Insurrection* and was one of the stunt team on *Armageddon*. Tracy Stone appeared in *Malibu Shores* (with Charisma Carpenter) and in movies like *Dead Man on Campus* and *The Sky is Falling*. Ken Rush's movie CV includes *Life of a Gigolo, Paradise Cove* and *The Midnight Hour*.

Don't Give Up the Day Job: Director James A. Contner's previous work includes *Midnight Caller, 21 Jump Street, Wiseguy, The Equalizer, Miami Vice, The Flash, Lois and*

Clark: The New Adventures of Superman, *SeaQuest DSV*, *Hercules: The Legendary Journeys*, *American Gothic*, *Dark Skies*, *The X-Files* and *Charmed*. Before that he was a cinematographer on movies like *Heat*, *Monkey Shines*, *Jaws 3-D*, *The Wiz*, *Superman* and *Times Square*. It's his camerawork on the concert footage in *Rock Show: Wings Over the World* (1976). That's a good *Six-Degrees-of-Kevin-Bacon* question: Paul McCartney to David Boreanaz. In *one*.

Logic, Let Me Introduce You to This Window: Angel and Kate run past a mirror in which Angel's face is visible. Similarly, as Angel walks away from Kate at the end, he passes a car and his reflection is seen in the window. Kate says she searched Angel's apartment (and notes he has 'some pretty weird stuff'). She certainly opens his fridge, so presumably she found the blood in it? Once again, we have stunt men who look nothing like the actors they're supposed to be replacing during the climactic alley brawl.

I Just *Love* Your Accent: Doyle uses the *very* European insult 'git'.

Quote/Unquote: Angel: 'This socialising thing is brutal. I was young once, I used to go to bars. It wasn't anything like this.' Doyle: 'You used to go to *taverns*. Small towns, where everybody used to know each other.' Cordelia: 'Yeah, like high school. It was easy to date there. We all had so much in common. Being monster food every other week, for instance.'

Cordelia: 'A couple of hundred years ago all you had to worry about was a hangover. Today, because of your curse-thingy, you can't sleep with anyone or else you might feel a moment of true happiness, lose your soul, become evil again and kill everyone.' Angel: 'Thanks Cordelia, I always appreciate your perspective.' Cordelia: 'No problem. The last thing I want is to show up at the office and find that I'm working for a homicidal monster.'

Kate: 'You can go to *Hell*.' Angel: 'Been there, done that.'

Notes: 'Are you maybe in need of some ... rescuing?'
Considering how well David Fury writes comedy on *Buffy*,
'Lonely Hearts' spends a lot of time getting surprisingly
few laughs. Fundamentally it's another character-building
exercise and shows evidence of last minute rewriting, while
the payoff is a long time coming and we go down a lot of
blind alleys (literal *and* metaphorical) before we get there.

Angel Investigation's telephone number is 555-0162. The
two newspapers Doyle finds details of the murders in are
the *West Hollywood Courier* and the *Los Angeles Globe
Register*. Doyle explains that the invitation rule for vampires only stays in effect while the owner of the home is
alive (see **1**, 'City Of', **5**, 'Rm W/a Vu', **15**, 'The Prodigal').
We see more of Cordelia's apartment. It's half-painted and
sparsely furnished.

Doyle mentions Piasca, a flesh-eating Indian demon that
enters victims through the mouth and eviscerates from
within. Kate lives close to the D'Oblique, where she is a
regular. She has a hard time trusting people, particularly
'male people' (see **6**, 'Sense and Sensitivity').

Soundtrack: There's a vast array of rave and techno heard
including: Ian Fletcher ('Deadside'), Ultra-Electronic
('Dissonance'), THC ('Girlfish'), Kelly Soce ('Do You
Want Me?'), Sapien ('Neo-Climactic'), Chucho Merchan
('Ballad of Amave'), Mark Cherrie and Ian McKenzie
('Lady Daze'), Chainsuck ('Emily Says'), Vast ('Touched'),
A. Hamilton ('For You') and Helix ('Quango').

Did You Know?: When it comes to the stunts on *Angel*,
David Boreanaz told *The Big Breakfast*: 'I do as many as
I possibly can. Of course the producers don't want me to
... My stuntperson Mike Masser does [about] 80 per cent.'

Joss Whedon Comments: Joss told the *BtVS* posting-board:
'Re: *Angel* [and] sunlight. That's been a problem. It's hard
to light the show and avoid it entirely. Tonight there was
a shot that was colourtimed so that what was supposed to
be pre-dawn came out like post-dawn. Bear with us, we
know it's not all there yet.'

Previously on *Buffy the Vampire Slayer*: 'The Harsh Light of Day', 19 October 1999: Dingoes Ate My Baby play the Bronze with Buffy and Willow watching. Parker Abrahms is also there. Willow notes that Buffy and Parker have been seeing a lot of each other. Buffy admits that she has 'lusty feelings' for him. Parker offers to walk Buffy back to her room at the university. Oz and Devon load the instruments on to Oz's van and Willow is left alone. Harmony Kendall appears and she and Willow reminisce about graduation and Willow says Harmony hasn't changed. But she *has* – into a vampire. She tries to bite Willow but Oz saves her. Harmony pouts, saying that her boyfriend will be mad that Willow was mean to her.

Parker asks Buffy about the scar on her neck, caused by Angel at graduation. Buffy attributes it to an angry puppy. She asks if *he* has any scars, but he claims that his are all psychological, stemming from his father's death. Parker explains how the trauma taught him to live for now. Oz and Willow tell Buffy that Harmony is a vampire. Harmony, meanwhile, heads underground to her boyfriend . . . Spike. He and his crew are trying to dig their way into a crypt.

Buffy and Parker arrive at a party and run into Spike and Harmony out on the hunt. Buffy chases them and Harmony tells her that Drusilla left Spike for a fungus demon. She also blurts out that Buffy will be sorry when they have 'the Gem of Amara'. Spike is annoyed at Harmony's inability to keep her mouth shut and drags her away. Xander is shelving books at Giles' when Anya arrives. She asks Xander where their relationship is going. Xander is confused, as he was unaware that they *had* a relationship. He tries to explain that these things develop on their own. Anya explains that she wants to have sexual intercourse so that she can get Xander out of her mind. Afterwards Anya tells Xander that she is over him now, but gets upset when he says, 'OK.'

Buffy calls Giles who promises to do the necessary research, though he always thought that the Gem of Amara (a 'vampire holy grail' that renders the wearer invincible) was a myth. Buffy and Parker spend the night together. Next morning Parker tells Buffy that he will call her later. Buffy finds Giles waiting in her room. She says that she was studying all night, but changes her mind and tells Giles that she's an adult and it's none of his business where she was. Giles isn't interested anyway. He has found some information about the Gem, which may exist after all. Buffy asks Giles and Willow to investigate while she seeks Spike before he gets his hands on the Gem. Spike, meanwhile, has found the crypt. Spike puts on a necklace, thinking it's the Gem. He doesn't feel any different, so he touches a cross to make sure, but it burns him. A fed-up Spike grabs a stake and shoves it into Harmony, but it doesn't kill her. Harmony starts hitting at Spike, who notices a ring on her finger.

Buffy is wandering the campus when she spots Parker giving a girl his 'live for now' speech. Buffy wonders why he didn't call, but he doesn't understand why she thinks it's a big deal. She asks if she did something wrong but he says no, it was fun. 'Is that all it was?' Buffy asks. Parker's not sure what else it was supposed to be. Buffy apologises. As Parker walks away, Spike appears and punches an off-guard Buffy. He comments on how nice it is to be out in the daylight and the two fight. Willow, Oz and Giles arrive at the crypt and find Harmony, who whines that 'being a vampire sucks'. Buffy and Spike are still fighting when Xander finds them and is sent flying by Spike who tries to upset Buffy by bringing up the subject of Angel. Buffy manages to wrestle the ring from his finger. He starts to burn, but makes it into a sewer just in time.

Buffy tells her friends that she wants Angel to have the ring. Oz has a gig in L.A. and will drop it off. Buffy and Willow discuss Parker. Willow says that Parker is a 'poophead'. Buffy agrees, but wonders why he doesn't want her. Buffy takes a walk by herself, as do Anya and Harmony, all sad for their own private reasons.

3
In the Dark

US Transmission Date: 19 October 1999
UK Transmission Date: 21 January 2000 (Sky)

Writer: Douglas Petrie
Director: Bruce Seth Green
Cast: James Marsters (Spike),
Seth Green (Daniel 'Oz' Osborne) Kevin West (Marcus),
Malia Mathis (Rachel), Machael Yayweli (Lenny),
Ric Sarabia (Vendor), Tom Rosales (Manny the Pig),
Gil Combs (Bouncer), Buck McDancer (Dealer),
Jenni Blong (Young Woman)

In a dark alley, a woman is running for her life, pursued by her drug-crazed boyfriend. Lenny threatens to kill Rachel, but Angel comes to her rescue. Spike looks down on Angel from a nearby rooftop, providing a hilarious commentary which ends on an ominous note as Spike promises Angel a 'gruesome, horrible death'. Oz arrives at Angel Investigations. He and Cordelia do some (limited) catching up. Oz offers Angel the Gem of Amara, telling him that Buffy wanted Angel to have it. Doyle explains to Cordelia what the ring does, rendering a vampire 'unkillable'. Doyle, Cordelia and Oz depart for a restaurant, leaving Angel who decides to hide it in the sewer. Rachel calls and tells Angel that the police have released Lenny. Angel promises to help. As Angel leaves he is confronted in the garage by Spike, who wants the ring. Angel tells Cordelia to stay at Doyle's place where she will be safer. Doyle is worried about Spike and Cordelia confirms that he should be.

Angel arrives at Rachel's apartment. She says she loves Lenny, but Angel points out that her love is going to get her killed. His advice is to have faith in herself. Cordy tells Doyle about Spike's past atrocities and Doyle is able to give Angel a lead from one of his contacts, Manny the Pig.

Angel makes his way through a number of seedy venues until he finds Spike, but it's a trap and Angel is chained up by Spike's accomplice. Angel is tortured by Marcus, a vampire with a flair for inflicting pain. He asks Angel the same question over and over again: 'What do you want?' Spike viciously taunts Angel, but grows bored and decides to try to find the Gem himself by searching Angel's apartment. He finds Cordelia and Doyle and makes a deal; give him the ring and he'll trade it for Angel. Angel finally answers Marcus' question, admitting that he wants forgiveness. Cordelia and Doyle search for the ring, Doyle using his demon powers to sniff out its location while Cordy isn't looking. They keep their end of the bargain, Doyle tossing the ring to the ground. As Spike moves to retrieve it, Oz crashes in with his van. Cordelia and Doyle free Angel and they speed away. But Marcus, to Spike's dismay, has liberated the ring and now stands in the sunlight.

While Spike is railing against his bad choice of partners, Marcus is enjoying a stroll on a crowded pier, focusing on a group of scouts. Angel is in need of medical attention, but he demands that Oz turn the van round; Marcus must be stopped from feeding. They arrive just in time to save the children. Angel launches himself into the sunlight. He bursts into flames as he tackles Marcus and the two vampires plunge off the pier into the Pacific. Angel and Marcus fight viciously and Angel manages to push Marcus on to a jagged wooden plank, ripping the ring from his finger and killing his torturer. Angel dons the ring and emerges from the shelter of the pier, amazed at the beauty of the sun and revived by the ring's power.

Doyle and Angel watch Angel's first sunset in over two hundred years. It's likely to be his last, he says, as in a noble gesture, he smashes the Gem of Amara.

Dudes and Babes: Rippling bicep-alert. Again. (See **1**, 'City Of'.)

It's a Designer Label!: Cordelia mentions the late fashion designer Gianni Versace. We'll pass quickly over Rachel's *Urban Tramp* look and on to Cordelia's jogging pants. Oz's purple sunglasses are worthy of a second glance.

References: 'The Angel-mobile' (see **Quote/Unquote**) is yet another *Batman* reference (the fifth in three episodes for those keeping count; and that's ignoring the visual stuff). 'I think the trick is laying off the ale before you start quoting *Angela's Ashes* and weeping like a baby-man' concerns Frank McCourt's novel about a family moving from America to Ireland. There are namechecks for Matthew McConaughey (*A Time to Kill*, *Amistad*, *Dazed and Confused*), Barney, Betty and Bam-Bam Rubble from *The Flinstones* and Johnny Storm the Human Torch (from *The Fantastic Four*). 'The Johnny Depp once-over' refers to the hotel-wrecking antics of this author's favourite actor, celebrity *Fast Show* fan and occasional Oasis slide-guitarist, the star of *21 Jump Street*, *Cry-Baby*, *Edward Scissorhands*, *Ed Wood*, *Donnie Brasco*, *Sleepy Hollow* and the forthcoming *From Hell*.

Spike's 'Lucy, I'm home!' was Desi Arnaz's catchphrase in *I Love Lucy*. Cordelia's 'See girl in distress. See Angel save girl from druggy-stalker-boyfriend' speech follows the format of the *Dick and Jane* books. Spike preferring Mozart's 'older, funnier symphonies' is a misquote from Woody Allen's *Stardust Memories*.

Oz's van interior includes posters for US grunge-act Filter and the seminal Nick Cave and the Bad Seeds LP 'The Good Son'. The two movies showing at the Orpheus Cinema that Oz's van passes are *The Sixth Sense* and *Deep Blue Sea*. Marcus quotes *Hamlet*: 'There is nothing either bad or good but thinking makes it so.' Geographical references include 'that freaky church on Sunset', 'a joint on Third called the Orbit Room', and 'Peterson's Fishery between Seward and Westminster'. When searching for the ring Cordelia notes: 'It's not in the freezer and it's not in the toilet tank. In the movies it's always in one of those places.'

Bitch!: Spike's miaow-moment comes when he tells Cordelia, 'You look smashing. Did you lose weight?' Cordy confirms that she's been using the gym before realising that she's been patronised.

Cordelia, on Doyle's apartment: 'I couldn't get comfortable in here if the floor was lined with mink. How can you live like this?' Doyle: 'I didn't until last week. Then I saw what *you* did with *your* place and I just had to call my decorator.' (See **2**, 'Lonely Hearts'.)

Spike: 'It's called addiction, Angel. We all have it. I believe yours is named *Slutty the Vampire Slayer*.'

'West Hollywood'?: See **Quote/Unquote** re: 'nancy boy hair gel', 'magnificent *pouf*' and Rachel understanding Angel because she has a 'nephew who is gay'. Does anyone get the impression that the subtext is rapidly becoming the text?

The Charisma Show: Cordelia realises that Frankie Tripod isn't a three-legged demon, but rather a nickname for a man with a very large penis.

L.A.-Speak: Cordelia, on Doyle: 'He [air quotes] works here.' And: '*No way*. My apartment is nowhere near this *yucky*. It smells like bong-water in here.'

Doyle: 'Can we concentrate on the *mother-lode* Angel just hit?' And: 'Think of it, man. Poolside tanning, bargain matinées, plus I know a couple of strip-clubs that have a fabulous luncheon buffet . . . I've heard.' And: 'What, a C note? I absolutely paid that back.' And: 'I bet he's out *hangin'-ten* right about now, out on the sandy shore at Malibu. Wind in his hair, bikini babes a-whistlin'.'

Rachel: 'I just start to *jones* for him. The way he *jones's* for *rock*.'

Spike 'Caught me fair and square, white hat. I guess there is nothing to do now but go quietly and pay my debt to society.' And: 'Do you two need to be alone, or can we go on to the "ouchy" part?' And: 'To coin a popular Sunnydale phrase: "*Duh*".'

Cigarettes and Alcohol: Rachel stubs out her cigarette on a used dinner plate. Disgusting.

Sex and Drugs and Rock'n'Roll: Rachel refers to 'rock' (the street name for crack-cocaine, see **L.A.-Speak**). Oz listens to KLA-Rock, 'L.A.'s only modern alternative' station.

'You May Remember Me from Such Films and TV Series as ...': Seth Green's movies include *Stephen King's It*, *Radio Days*, *Can't Hardly Wait*, *Idle Hands*, *Enemy of the State*, *Knockabout Guys*, *Austin Powers: International Man of Mystery* and *Austin Powers: The Spy Who Shagged Me* (as Scott Evil) and *My Stepmother is an Alien* (as Alyson Hannigan's little boyfriend). He played a very Oz-like character in *The X-Files* episode 'Deep Throat' and he provides the voice for Chris Griffin in *Family Guy*. Seth is a *great* actor and his (usually understated) contribution to *Buffy* can't be praised highly enough. 'He can *own* a scene he has no lines in,' notes Joss Whedon. James Marsters isn't from London, though the accent is good enough to fool the most discriminating UK fans. He's actually from Greendale, California and, aside from *Buffy*, he's also been seen (using his 'real' voice) in a guest slot on *Millennium* and, briefly, the movie *House on Haunted Hill*. Kevin West's movie CV includes *Super Mario Bros*, *Indecent Proposal* and the wonderfully named *Killer Tomatoes From France!* Jenni Blong has small roles in *Cry-Baby* and *200 Cigarettes*.

Don't Give Up the Day Job: Doug Petrie wrote the 1996 movie *Harriet The Spy* along with episodes of *Clarissa Explains It All*. No relation to his actor near-namesake, director Bruce Seth Green's TV work includes series like *Knight Rider*, *Airwolf*, *MacGyver*, *She-Wolf of London*, *V*, *SeaQuest DSV*, *Xena: Warrior Princess*, *TJ Hooker*, *Hercules: The Legendary Journeys*, *American Gothic* and *Jack & Jill* as well as numerous episodes of *Buffy*.

Despite a noted appearance as Richard Nixon in *Hot Shots: Part Deux*, Buck 'Dallas' McDancer's usual role is that of stuntman, having worked on numerous films including *Scarface*, *Legal Eagles*, *In the Line of Fire*, *Airheads*, *Vampire in Brooklyn* and *Star Trek: Insurrection*. Aside from acting (in movies as diverse as *8 Heads in a Duffel Bag* and *Short Circuit 2*), Ric Sarabia is the frontman of L.A.-based funk-rap band Tastes Like Chicken.

Logic, Let Me Introduce You to This Window: When Cordelia prints an invoice, the printer has paper in it for front-shots, but from the back the tray seems empty. As Angel and Spike fight around Angel's car, reflections of both can be seen in the windows.

I Just *Love* Your Accent: *Yer-man* Doyle conforms to 'drunken Oyrishmen' stereotypes by 'going to celebrate with a drink down the pub'. Cordelia helpfully adds: 'He'd celebrate the opening of a mailbox with a drink at the pub.' Guinness, no doubt? *Begorrah*.

Spike notes: '*Ooh*, the Mick's got spine. Maybe I'll snap it in two.' Cordelia refers to Spike as 'little cockney'.

Quote/Unquote: Spike's opening commentary. The funniest thing on TV in *years*: '[Rachel voice] How can I thank you, you mysterious black-clad hunk of a night-thing? [Angel voice] No need, little lady, your tears of gratitude are enough for me. You see, I was once a badass vampire, but love and a pesky curse defanged me. Now I'm just a big, fluffy puppy with bad teeth. No, not the hair! Never the hair! [Rachel voice] But there must be some way I can show my appreciation? [Angel voice] No, helping those in need's my job, and working up a load of sexual tension and prancing away like a magnificent *pouf* is truly thanks enough. [Rachel voice] I understand. I have a nephew who is gay, so . . . [Angel voice] Say no more. Evil's still afoot. And I'm almost out of that nancy-boy hair-gel I like so much. Quickly, to the Angel-mobile, away.'

Oz asks if 'Detective' Angel has a hat and a gun? Cordelia replies: 'Just fangs.'

Doyle: 'All I'm saying is that if we're ever going to take that cruise to the Bahamas together, we're going to need a lot more clients of means.' Cordelia: 'And an alternate-reality in which you're Matthew McConaughey.'

Spike, as Marcus sticks a skewer into Angel: 'Someone's having shish-kebab.'

Cordelia: 'This isn't a needle in a haystack, this is a needle in Kansas.'

Notes: 'I don't know about you, but I had a nice day. Except for the bulk of it, where I was nearly tortured to death.' A sequel to *Buffy*: 'The Harsh Light of Day' that is, by turns, hilarious (Spike's opening narration) and extremely graphic. Those without *very* strong stomachs might want to avoid some of the Marcus/Angel torture sequences. Truly wonderful final scenes, however, and the episode is conceptually a cornerstone of the series with Angel facing his darkest corner and emerging triumphant.

Angel performs t'ai-chi exercises (see *Buffy*: 'Band Candy', 'Revelations'). He refers to Doyle's mother and indicates that they have met, or at least spoken (see 7, 'The Bachelor Party'). Doyle, in demon form, has the ability to smell out the location of inanimate objects (or superpowerful rings, anyway). Oz knows basic sixth-grade first aid.

When Oz arrives, Cordelia's 'catching up' involves asking how the Bronze is ('the same') and the Scooby Gang ('they're good'). She later asks about Buffy and if she is 'still the brave-little-Slayer or is she moping around in the dark like nobody around here'. ('She's . . . Buffy,' notes Oz.) Oz sums up the plot of 'The Harsh Light of Day' thus: 'Your buddy Spike dug up Sunnydale looking for it [the Gem]. He got a fistful of Buffy and left it behind. She wanted to be sure it was in good hands.' Spike's version of events is somewhat different: 'Speaking of little Buff, I ran into her recently. Your name didn't come up. Although she has been awful busy jumping the bones of the first lunkhead that came along. Good-looking fellah. Used her shamelessly. She *is* cute when she's hurting.'

Cordelia tells Doyle that Spike has 'nearly done Buffy in a few times', and mentions that he claimed to have killed two Slayers (see *Buffy*: 'School Hard'). She condenses the complex plot of the *Buffy* episodes 'Surprise' and 'Innocence' into: 'One time he and Dru raised this demon that burned people from the inside. It was this whole weird thing with an arm in a box.' This *is* accurate.

The Gem of Amara 'renders its wearer one hundred per cent unkillable if he's a vampire'. Doyle notes that this includes stakes, fire and (best of all) sunlight. Spike says Marcus is 'an expert. Some say artist, but I've never been comfortable with labels. He's a bloody king of torture ... Beneath the cool exterior, you'll find he's rather shy. Except with kids ... [He] likes to eat. And other nasty things.' Spike confirms that Angel sired him (see *Buffy*: 'School Hard').

Soundtrack: Mozart's *Symphony No. 41*. Unfortunately, Spike can't tell his Mozart from his Brahms.

Jane Espenson's Comments: Asked on the *BtVS* Posting Board about the writing processes on *Buffy* and *Angel*, writer Jane Espenson fascinatingly spelled out what happens to an average script: 'Joss and the whole staff work out the story for each episode together and in detail. In theory. In actuality, we all sit and pretend we're being helpful while Joss works out the whole story. Then the writer for that episode writes a "beat sheet", then a "full outline", based on that work. An outline is usually fourteen pages of single-spaced text in which each scene is described [as per] what Joss worked out. What the writer has added at this point is an indication of the shape of the scene – the order the information comes out in, some more specifics about what each character thinks and expresses during the scene, how it transitions into the next scenes, a few sample jokes. Joss gives the writer notes on the outline. He nixes bad things, adds good things, makes sure it's on track. Then the writer writes the first draft. From fourteen pages you go to approximately 50–55 pages of fun-filled description and dialogue. It may sound like this doesn't leave much room for individual creativity – after all, the writer knows exactly what will happen in each scene – but in fact there are many ways to write each scene and the writer has to pick the best way. Then Joss gives notes on the first draft. These can be minor or enormously detailed, or "This scene? Make it better." It takes several days usually for the writer to implement the changes he asks for, because it [can] require rethinking in a big way. There may be further drafts after that, time permitting. Eventually,

Joss takes the script away from the writer into his lair of genius and does his own rewrite. Again, [it can be] minor or enormous. Then it gets filmed. So I laugh when people say that one of us has better "plotting" than another or that Joss wouldn't have let a character say that if he'd written the episode. It *all* goes through the big guy and it's all better for it . . . When Joss writes an episode, Joss writes an episode *himself*. It's a beautiful process of aloneness. Actually quite inspiring.'

4
I Fall to Pieces

US Transmission Date: 26 October 1999
UK Transmission Date: 28 January 2000 (Sky)

Writers: Joss Whedon, David Greenwalt
Director: Vern Gillum

Cast: Tushka Bergen (Melissa Burns),
Andy Umberger (Dr Ronald Meltzer),
Carlos Carrasco (Dr Vinpur Narpudan),
Brent Sexton (Dead Cop),
Garikayi Mutambarawa (Intern), Kent Davis (John),
Jan Bartlett (Penny), Patricia Gillum (Woman Patient)

Cordelia complains to Doyle about their lack of funds. Doyle points out that Angel is more interested in helping clients than charging them. When Angel arrives he tells them he's not comfortable asking for money. Doyle has a vision about a woman called Melissa Burns who is at work when she receives flowers; the card is signed by someone named Ronald. Upset, Melissa steps into the restroom, where she swallows some tranquillisers. Leaving work, Melissa is approached by Angel. He explains that he aids people when the police can't. She thanks him but drives away. Back at the office, Angel asks Cordelia and Doyle if he could be scaring clients away. He suggests that Cordy talk with Melissa. Cordelia agrees but not until she's a paying client. Doyle reminds them their work isn't all about money.

Melissa has stopped at an ATM machine, but her card won't work. Ronald appears and explains that he changed her PIN number to the date they first met. He asks her about the tranquillisers she took earlier in the day. Melissa warns him to leave her alone, but Ronald reminds her that they're in love. Melissa calls Angel Investigations. She tells Angel, Doyle and Cordelia about Ronald Meltzer, a neurosurgeon she dated once and who is now stalking her. She says that Ronald can somehow see her, even when she's alone. Melissa is preparing for bed while Ronald sits in his office minus one eye. The detached eye is watching her as she undresses. Angel visits Kate Lockley and tells her about his client and her stalker. Kate pulls the file on Melissa and Meltzer. His lawyers, Wolfram & Hart, filed a restraining order against *her*. Angel expresses his concern and Kate assigns a policeman to watch her building. Angel visits Meltzer's office where he discovers a book with a personal inscription from the author, Vinpur Narpudan. Ronald catches Angel, who introduces himself under an alias, claiming his wife has a tumour and that she'll die without an immediate operation. Angel makes it clear he'll pay whatever is necessary. Angel confesses to Cordelia that he knows how Meltzer thinks but can't fathom how he's able to see Melissa. Angel researches Vinpur Narpudan, e-mails him asking for help and they meet. Narpudan tells Angel that he introduced Meltzer to psychic surgeons and yogis who could shut down their somatic systems. Meltzer surpassed them, which prompted Narpudan to stop teaching.

Outside Melissa's apartment while she sleeps, Ronald stands in the bushes. A policeman spots him and tells him to put up his hands. Ronald raises his arms but his hands are missing. They are crawling into Melissa's bed and she screams. The policeman rushes to her aid. Melissa lets him in and the detached hands strangle him. Kate questions Angel about how Meltzer killed the officer. He doesn't show up on the security cameras. Angel assures her that Meltzer is the killer and that his fingerprints will reveal all. Doyle asks Angel how they're going to deal with Meltzer. Angel explains Meltzer's detached parts can't reattach if deprived of blood and oxygen. Doyle seals up all possible entry points in an effort to keep Meltzer from gaining access to Melissa. Using his alias, Angel goes to see Meltzer in his office. Meltzer incapacitates Angel with a paralytic drug. Doyle is still sealing every way into Angel's home while Melissa gets some sleep. One of Meltzer's hands pushes its way through a sealed vent, while one of his eyes watches Doyle and Cordelia. They hear the scraping noise and Doyle investigates. He sees fingers coming up through the grille in the floor. But it's a diversion to allow Meltzer entry. Meltzer grabs Cordelia and shoves her into a closet while Doyle is pushed into a storage shaft. Melissa tries to escape but Meltzer blocks her way. Angel bursts in and goes for Meltzer whose teeth fly from his mouth and bite Angel's arm. Angel and Meltzer fight and Angel pins Meltzer's hand to the floor with a scalpel before knocking his head off with a baseball bat, killing him. The next day, Cordelia asks Angel about Meltzer. He assures her that the parts are buried in concrete. Melissa thanks them and Angel, embarrassed, reminds her of the bill which she happily pays.

Dudes and Babes: Cordelia, on men: 'Either you like them and they don't like you. Or you can't stand them, which just guarantees that they're gonna hover around and never go away.' Doyle (trying not to hover): 'I hate guys like that.'

Denial, Thy Name is Ronald: 'Doctor Stalker' just won't take 'no' for an answer.

It's a Designer Label!: Cordelia notes that she has certain needs, for 'designer . . . things'. She wears a white T-shirt and, later, a fetching purple dress. Angel asks: 'Am I intimidating?' Cordelia: 'As vampires go, you're pretty cuddly. Maybe you might want to think about mixing up the black-on-black look.' Next scene, he's changed into a cream sweater.

References: The title comes from Patsy Cline's 1962 hit (it's the song a heartbroken Xander listens to after Buffy rejects him in *Buffy*: 'Prophecy Girl'). Influences on a story about a detached hand with a life of its own range from *The Addams Family* and *Dr Terror's House of Horror* to *The Hands of Orlac*, *The Beast with Five Fingers*, *The Hand* and *Evil Dead 2*. Escapologist Harry Houdini is mentioned, as is OJ Simpson. Kate notes that Wolfram & Hart are 'the law firm that Johnny Cochran is too ethical to join'. Also featured, a quote from Walter Scott's poem *Flodden Field* ('what a tangled web') and a hilarious reference to Barbara Streisand's 'People' (from *Funny Girl*).

Bitch!: Cordelia's in sympathetic mode for most of the time, but she does tell Doyle: 'You're a lot smarter than you look. Of course you look like a retard.'

'West Hollywood'?: Doyle on Angel: 'He likes playing the hero. Walking off into the dark, his long coat flowing behind him in that mysterious and attractive way.' Cordelia: 'Is this a private moment? I could leave you alone.' Doyle: 'I'm not saying *I'm* attracted . . .' Then, later, after Angel leaves in exactly this fashion: 'OK, maybe I'm a *little* attracted.'

The Charisma Show: We see Cordelia doing investigations *and* cracking pithy one-liners. Angel: 'I'm not comfortable asking people for money.' Cordelia (angrily): 'Then get over it. I mean that in a *sensitive* way.' Her brilliant assessment of Meltzer is: 'It's just so unfair. Here's this poor girl. She hooks up with a doctor. That's supposed to be a good thing. You should be able to call home and say: "Hey, mom, guess what? I've met a doctor." Not, "Guess what? I met a psycho and he's stalking me and oh, by the way, his hands and feet come off and he's not even in the circus." ' Plus her triumphant: 'See, you *can* save damsel *and* make decent money. Is this a great country or what?'

L.A.-Speak: Angel: 'I'm in private security . . .' Melissa: 'And you're walking around in underground garages telling people this *because . . .*?'

Doyle: 'Protect and serve. It's *entirely* my bag.'

Cordelia: 'Just between us what's the real *dish* on this guy?'

Cordelia: 'You *so* don't want this guy fixated on you. What is stalking nowadays, the third most popular sport among men?' Angel: '*Fourth*, after Luge.'

Melissa: 'I think you gave up on being loved a long time ago and now you're just another creep who gets off on pain.'

Cigarettes and Alcohol: Doyle asks for a single malt Scotch after his vision. Whatever Angel gives him, it tastes more like 'polymalt'. Doyle puts whisky in Melissa's tea to help her sleep.

Sex and Drugs and Rock'n'Roll: Melissa is taking the tranquilliser Xanitab. Meltzer prescribed a Calcium-Selenium supplement for her.

Meltzer describes Angel as a 'vacuous L.A. pretty boy'.

'You May Remember Me from Such Films and TV Series as . . .': Tushka Bergen played Alice Hastings in the 1999 TV movie *Journey to the Centre of the Earth*. Her films include *Culture*, *Voices* and *Barcelona*. On TV she appeared in *The Others*, *Fantasy Island* and the fantastically weird 'The Dig' episode of *Bergerac*. Andy Umberger is well known to *Buffy* fans as the vengeance demon D'Hoffryn in 'Doppelgängland' and 'Something Blue'. He's also been in *West Wing* and *NYPD Blue*. Carlos Carrasco's film credits include *The Fisher King*, *Crocodile Dundee II* and *Across the Line*. He also appears in several episodes of *Star Trek: Deep Space 9*.

Don't Give Up the Day Job: Director Vern Gillum has worked on *Baywatch*, *Space: Above and Beyond*, *Sliders* and *Brimstone*.

Logic, Let Me Introduce You to This Window: In the opening scene, Cordelia has the invoice in her left hand. The camera switches angle and it moves to the right. When Angel spies on Ronald in his office, he walks past a chrome light switch cover on which his reflection can be seen. Angel drinks coffee, despite the fact that in *Buffy*: 'The Prom' he told Joyce Summers that he didn't because it makes him jittery. When Angel goes to see Kate, he leaves wearing the cream sweater, but arrives wearing the black one he had on earlier.

As Meltzer catches Angel in his office, Angel is holding a book. Yet when he turns the book is gone. If Angel has no heartbeat, why does the poison affect him? How is Ronald able to change Melissa's bank PIN number? Cordelia asks Doyle if he's ever had a relationship and he replies, 'Not me personally. But I've read ...' Two episodes later we find out that this isn't true (see **7**, 'The Bachelor Party').

I Just *Love* Your Accent: Doyle tells Melissa, 'Drink up, love, it's all over.' Say 'love' to the average American and they either think you're coming on to them, or that you're a hippy. He also calls Cordelia 'Princess' without getting his nose broken, which is an achievement.

Quote/Unquote: Cordelia's slogan for Angel Investigations: 'We help the hopeless.'

Doyle: 'Protecting young women such as yourself? Yeah, there've been four. And *three* of them are very much alive.'

Kate: 'This guy could go to jail tomorrow and still kill her in her dreams every night. I've put a few of these creeps away and the hardest thing is to know that he's still winning. She's still afraid. He took her power away and no one can get it back but her.'

Notes: 'Flesh, anytime you want to stop crawling is OK with me.' A study of voyeurism that just about manages to avoid being, itself, voyeuristic by focusing on empowerment. A *lot* of old horror clichés are thrown about with abandon (see **References**) and much of the acting and dialogue are indifferent. However, the 'False-Teeth-of-Death' raise the episode to the level of high camp. And *what* an opening shot of the sun rising over Los Angeles.

Cordelia, on Doyle's visions: 'Last time [they] led to a sex-changing, body-switching, tear-your-innards-out demon, right? I guess they don't call you for their everyday cases' refers to the events of **2**, 'Lonely Hearts'. Doyle mentions an Aunt Tudy who seems rather a large woman. Angel uses the alias Brian Jensen when visiting Meltzer. The book that Angel steals from Meltzer's office is *Anything's Possible* by Vinpur Narpudan. The inscription reads: 'To Ronald. Thanks for having the "nerve" to believe. Fondly, Vin.' The magazine in the hospital cafeteria is *The Journal of Diagnostic Orthopædic Neuropathy*.

Joss Whedon's Comments: Joss has confirmed that 'I Fall to Pieces' started life as a *Buffy* story idea: 'The fellow whose limbs came apart I originally thought [of] as a *Buffy* thing but it didn't seem in place in the *Buffy* world and when we talked about a story on stalking it made perfect sense to have it on *Angel*.'

Changes: As Tim Minear told *The Watcher's Web*: 'Initially, *Angel* was conceived as more of an anthology show, with the emotional emphasis on the "guest" characters' problems. You can see this in early stories like the woman being stalked in **4**, "I Fall to Pieces". As we found our legs, we discovered that our core of regular characters seemed to be where our, and in turn our audience's, interest was. I think this is clear by the time we got to **17**, "Eternity". Everything that happens in that story springs out of our characters. Watching the core group interact is where the real emotional action is. I think that will shape the future.'

5
Rm W/a Vu

US Transmission Date: 2 November 1999
UK Transmission Date: 4 Febuary 2000 (Sky)

Teleplay: Jane Espenson
Story: David Greenwalt, Jane Espenson
Director: Scott McGillis

Cast: Beth Grant (Maude Pearson),
Marcus Redmond (Griff), Denney Pierce (Vic),
Greg Collins (Keith), Corey Klemow (Young Man),
Lara McGrath (Manager), B.J. Porter (Dennis Pearson),
Lyle Kanouse (Disgusting Man[8])

Cordelia can't understand why she wasn't chosen for her latest role and Doyle commiserates. The phone interrupts but it's only her friend Aura from Sunnydale. Doyle asks Angel about Cordelia's past and Angel tells Doyle her 'riches to rags' story. Cordelia, meanwhile, arrives at her awful apartment. Finding the place to be crawling with bugs, Cordelia calls Doyle, but he's otherwise engaged, 'entertaining' a demon acquaintance. The demon has shown up to collect a debt, but Doyle isn't willing to pay and escapes.

Angel is having a shower. An insistent knock makes him answer the door clad only in a towel. Cordelia thrusts her suitcases into Angel's arms, telling him that she's moving in until she can find a place of her own. Doyle arrives and finds Cordy drying her hair. Angel emerges from his bedroom, clad in a bathrobe and boxers. After a disagreement over who put peanut butter in the bed, Cordelia goes to get dressed. Doyle is angry over what he thinks is a tryst between Angel and Cordelia, but Angel explains that he slept on the couch. Cordelia tells Doyle that his 'cousin'

---

[8] Uncredited.

called. Doyle says he would've appreciated a bit of warning. Angel breaks up the disagreement and tells Doyle that he has a visitor and Doyle heads out the back way. Suspicious, Angel is waiting at the top of the stairs; Doyle resents being ambushed. Angel grills Doyle and promises to lend a hand if Doyle will find Cordelia an apartment. Doyle convinces Cordelia that his 'guy' can find her a great place. Angel visits Doyle's apartment, looking for clues. The Kailiff demon, Griff, finds Angel and grabs him by the throat. Meanwhile, Doyle takes Cordelia to the apartment his guy found. Cordelia thinks it's perfect and agrees to move in.

Angel threatens information out of Griff. Angel gives his word that Doyle will pay his debts. The demon pledges Doyle's safety in return. Angel confronts Doyle with the news that he has to pay up. Doyle is not happy at the interference, but grudgingly admits that Angel probably saved his life. Cordelia is asleep in bed but is awakened by the radio, a whispering voice and drawers slamming shut. She insists that she's not afraid – as her bed rises off the floor – though she sits up all night and is awake when the sun rises and the bed hits the floor. She goes about her morning routine but has an encounter with the ghost of an elderly woman. The ghostly shenanigans end abruptly as Doyle and Angel arrive. Cordelia doesn't want them to know about the ghost, but as scissors and trophies go flying, her friends see the evidence of the haunting. They haul her out, screaming that she'll die before giving up the apartment. That, it seems, would suit the ghost fine.

Angel and Doyle research Cordelia's new residence. Angel tries convincing Cordy that it's only a place to live, but she insists she needs the place to become herself again as part of a redeeming process for the horrible person she was in Sunnydale. They discover the building was owned by Maude Pearson who died of a heart attack in 1946 on the same day that her son disappeared. Since her death wasn't violent, there is some doubt that Maude is the ghost. Cordelia disagrees, telling Angel and Doyle that her apartment has a 'little old lady smell of violets and

Aspercreme' and that they should do a cleansing spell. Doyle goes to fetch the ingredients. Angel cautions Cordelia to stay at the office as he leaves to seek further information from Kate. Later that night, Cordelia receives a call from Angel instructing her to meet him at her apartment. But when she arrives, she finds the ghost tricked her. Angel and Kate investigate the apartment. The son, Dennis, was involved with a woman and had planned to elope, but Maude was against the marriage. The investigating officer deemed Mrs Pearson's death suspicious because of the enmity between mother and son, even though the coroner pronounced the cause of death as heart failure. Angel and Kate discover a long list of suicides that took place in that apartment over the years. Worried, Angel calls the office but Doyle answers instead of Cordelia. Doyle plays back a message with Angel's voice telling Cordy to go home. As Cordelia confronts Mrs Pearson, trying to defend herself from the ghost's attack, Angel and Doyle race to her rescue. Cordelia is strung up by a wire noose, but Angel and Doyle arrive in time to save her. Cordelia is hysterical and Angel tries in vain to calm her. As they reach the door, Griff and two other demons arrive intent on killing Doyle. Mrs Pearson unwittingly helps Angel and Doyle to fight the demons as objects are hurled around the room. The ghost traps Cordelia in the bedroom and continues to taunt and insult her, but goes too far when she calls Cordelia 'a bitch'. Cordelia gives Mrs Pearson a dose of her own medicine. The demons are defeated. Cordelia seems to be rid of the ghost until, possessed, she makes a hole in the wall revealing a skeleton. Mrs Pearson walled up her son before collapsing. Dennis's spirit takes vengeance against his mother. Angel promises Doyle long-term help in exchange for his life story. Doyle agrees, but asks for time. Cordelia, meanwhile, is on the phone to Aura. She explains that she shares with a roommate, but it's all right since she hardly ever sees him. Dennis seems happy to have Cordelia sharing his house, as she catches up on dirt from Sunnydale.

Dreaming (as *Buffy* Often Proves) is Free: The flashback to Maude walling up her son is one of the scariest the series has done because the dialogue is so bland and casual.

Dudes and Babes: Boreanaz appears almost naked covered only by a small towel. *Very* popular with people of all sexualities, interestingly.

Denial, Thy Name is Maude: Spending 40 years chasing off every female in the vicinity isn't the most balanced of actions, even for a ghost.

It's a Designer Label!: Cordelia's suitcases are from Louis Vuitton's collection. She wears Nike trainers. Even Angel's boxer shorts are black. Cordelia confirms what we've all suspected for some time, Angel wears mousse.

References: The episode title is written in the style of a classified newspaper advert for an apartment. *A Room With a View*, from which this is a shortened form, is a Merchant-Ivory film adapted from E.M. Forster's novel about the British abroad. There's yet another *Batman* reference (Cordelia says her rival for an acting job looked like 'Catwoman taking out the cat-trash'). The credit card commercial Doyle talks about seems to be a Mastercard ad that ends with something that cannot be defined by money. Also, *Casper The Friendly Ghost*, *Poltergeist* ('You see a light? Go towards it'), Patrick Swayze and his performance in *Ghost*, Elton John's 'The Bitch is Back' and the acting brothers Dave Paymer (*Get Shorty, City Slickers, Murphy Brown*) and Steve Paymer (*Mad About You*).

Bitch!: Maude calls Cordelia a 'stupid little bitch'. Cordelia replies: 'I'm not a snivelling whiny little cry-Buffy. I'm the nastiest girl in Sunnydale history. I take crap from no one . . . Back off Polygrip. You think you're bad? All mean and haunty? Picking on poor pathetic Cordy? Well, get ready to haul your wrinkly translucent ass out of this place because, lady, *the bitch is back*.'

The Charisma Show: 'I'm a girl from The Projects.' Without a doubt, this is *the* episode for Charisma fans.

Cordelia: 'I am *not* giving up this apartment.' Angel: 'It's haunted.' Cordelia: 'It's *rent controlled*.' And: 'This is easy. Little Old Lady ghost, probably hanging around because she thinks she left the iron on.' And, best of all: 'You're gonna pack your little ghost bags and *get the hell out of my house*.'

L.A.-Speak: Doyle on Cordelia: 'She's really something, isn't she? It's like wrestling a tiger just to get to know her.'

Demon: '*Screw you*.'

Doyle on the story of his life: 'Quite a tale it is, too. Full of ribald adventure and beautiful damsels with loose morals . . .'

A Haven for the Bruthas?: A black demon is in evidence, which is only fair in an ethnically diverse melting-pot like L.A.

Cigarettes and Diet Root-Beer: Cordelia drinks diet root-beer judging from the can Dennis moves around her coffee table.

Sex and Drugs and Rock'n'Roll: Since Angel doesn't eat (see **8**, 'I Will Remember You') it *must* have been Cordelia who got the peanut butter on the bedclothes.

'You May Remember Me from Such Films and TV Series as . . .': Beth Grant was Helen in *Speed*, while her numerous other movies include *Doctor Doolittle*, *A Time to Kill*, *Too Wong Foo Thanks For Everything Julie Newmar*, *The Dark Half*, *Flatliners*, *Child's Play 2* and *Rain Man*. On TV, she's appeared in *Malcolm in the Middle* and *Friends* and provided some of the voices on *King of the Hill*. Marcus Redmond played Detective Kevin in *Fight Club* and Raymond Alexander in *Doogie Howser, M.D.* Greg Collins gets lots of roles in big budget movies, normally playing cops. He's in *Enemy of the State*, *Armageddon*, *Godzilla*, *Con Air*, *Independence Day*, *The Rock* and *Police Academy 6: City Under Siege*. Corey Klemow was Joe Martindale in *Spiders* and Ross in *Rubbernecking*. Lyle Kanouse appeared in *Kate's Addiction*.

Don't Give Up the Day Job: Award-winning *Buffy* writer/ producer Jane Espenson ('Band Candy', 'Earshot', 'The Harsh Light of Day', 'Pangs', 'A New Man' and 'Superstar' among others) is a sitcom veteran who has written for *Dinosaurs, Ellen* and *Star Trek: Deep Space 9*. Although he has acted in both *Lawnmower Man* and *Terminator 2: Judgment Day*, Denney Pierce is primarily a stuntman with credits on *American History X, Anaconda, Primal Fear, Last Man Standing, Village of the Damned, Sneakers, The Abyss* and *1969*.

There's a Ghost in My House (or Two . . .): Dennis Pearson: suffocated to death by being walled up by his insane mother to stop him eloping, his spirit is bound to the apartment. He is able to manifest his face by pressing into surfaces and he can also move objects and change TV channels. He seems harmless and Cordelia takes something of a shine to him. His mom, on the other hand . . .

Logic, Let Me Introduce You to This Window: When Doyle enters the offices, he puts his key in the lock and opens the door, but we never see the lock turn. The second hand on his watch isn't moving when he looks at it. When Cordelia and Doyle are in Angel's apartment, the can of Chock Full o' Nuts is facing in different directions from one shot to the next. There are two different models of Philco refrigerators used in Angel's apartment. The one in this episode is squarish with the maker's name across the upper part of the door. The other model (seen in other episodes) is rounded, with the name near the handle. When Angel rings the office from the station, not only doesn't he wait for the coin to drop, but he seemingly dials too many numbers. The noose used to hang Cordelia disappears and reappears several times.

When Cordelia is giving her audition to Doyle she brushes her hair behind her ears. During an angle switch it moves back to its original position. When the ghost face peers through the wall there is a lamp on the table to one side of it which disappears in subsequent shots. As Angel and Doyle arrive at the apartment, it's obviously afternoon. How did Angel get there without bursting into flames, especially as Doyle walks in and closes the drapes? One of the Kailiff demons shoots a tile on the fireplace, but later the tile is intact. Angel is hit in the head with a flying book during the cleansing scene (that could have been deliberate, though it looks rather painful for poor David). There is no chain lock on Cordy's old apartment door, yet there was one in **2**, 'Lonely Hearts'. When Angel tells Doyle about the Cordettes, he is reading a book. From one angle, his hand is on the desk. In another, it's resting on his leg. There's a red neon sign flashing and a fire escape outside the window of Doyle's apartment. The front shot of the building shows a fire escape, but no neon sign. Footsteps can be heard within the office when Doyle shows Angel and Cordelia what he's found on the computer. When Cordelia walks into the bedroom in the new apartment, there is one large picture over the bed; that night, there are two small pictures. Vampires can, seemingly, be invited into a home even if they are nowhere near the home at the time (and the home isn't even yet purchased). As Cordelia notes, the rules are getting all screwed up.

I Just *Love* Your Accent: Doyle asks Cordelia if anybody rang the firm asking about him. 'Your cousin called, with one of those names from your part of England.'

Quote/Unquote: Angel, on Aura: 'I think she's one of Cordelia's group. People called them *The Cordettes*. A bunch of girls from wealthy families. They ruled the high school. Decided what was in, who was popular. It was like the Soviet Secret Police if they cared a lot about shoes.'

Cordelia: 'My urination just hasn't been public enough lately.'

Kate: 'Thing about detectives is that they have résumés and business licences and last names. Pop stars and Popes, those are the one-name guys.' Angel: 'You got me. I'm the Pope.'

Doyle: 'What about friendship and family and all those things that are priceless like they say in that credit card commercial?'

Notes: 'Yeh, well, she pissed me off.' Jane Espenson again proves she's one of the best writers of comedy *and* character-based drama on television. Often at the same time. This *House That Bled to Death* variant is brilliantly assembled, with a great line of dialogue every thirty seconds and some genuine scares amid the Cordelia-induced hilarity. The series standard themes of guilt and redemption continue with Cordelia the focus this time (see **1**, 'City Of', **3**, 'In the Dark', **9**, 'Hero'). Unsurprisingly, it's Charisma's favourite episode, and *Angel*'s first 24-carat classic.

There is a painting by the sliding door in Angel's apartment of a woman playing a flute. Angel says that Cordelia can't type or file, which we knew anyway. The stations that appear on Cordelia's 'haunted radio' are 107.9FM and 1400AM. Cordelia's latest audition is for trash bags. The names in her phone book under 'D' are: Tom D, Doyle, Danielle, and two entries for David (one crossed out). Doyle's phone number is 555-0189. Doyle notes that Cordelia's high school diploma is 'all burned'. 'It was a rough ceremony,' says Cordy referring to the events of *Buffy*: 'Graduation Day'. One of her five trophies 'with some of the shiny worn off' is 'Queen of the Winter Ball'. Cordelia's new address is 212 Pearson Arms. Doyle claims to play badminton. He always meant to learn Latin but never did.

Presumably Aura is the same girl who found the 'extreme dead guy' in her locker in *Buffy*: 'Welcome to the Hellmouth'. When Cordy is discussing 'who's wearing what in Sunnydale' and hears about a girl who 'never did have any taste . . . She is *so* nasty', Aura *could* be telling her about their old friend Harmony Kendall and which vampire she's hanging out with in *Buffy*: 'The Harsh Light of Day', 'The Initiative' and 'Pangs'.

The three suicides mentioned as occurring in apartment 212 were: Margo Dressner, 3 October 1959, Jenny Kim, 18

October 1965 and Natalie Davis, 7 March 1994. The newspaper Doyle finds the report of the death of Maude Pearson in is the *Los Angeles Globe Register*, one of the same papers seen in **2**, 'Lonely Hearts' (see **11**, 'Somnambulist').

Soundtrack: The Mills Brothers' 1940s classic 'You Always Hurt the One You Love' is heard along with Beethoven's Ninth Symphony. This seems to be a favourite of Angel's as he hummed it in *Buffy*: 'Killed by Death'. Maybe he's a fan of *A Clockwork Orange* which also uses it. Also worthy of praise is the excellent soundtrack; dramatic in places and funny in others and, as such, a perfect metaphor for the episode.

Did You Know?: As the ghost says, 'This is my house,' and Cordelia gets up and runs away from the camera, the tattoo on Charisma Carpenter's back can be briefly glimpsed. Readers can see it in much greater detail on the cover of the October 1999 edition of *FHM* magazine.

Jane Espenson's Comments: 'How scripts are assigned. Usually it kind of rotates. Whoever has had the longest break writes the next one. But if one person pitched a specific idea, they usually get to write it (like my "Band Candy"). Or if a specific story calls for a specific kind of writing strength – Marti [Noxon] tends to get the big love relationship stories. And then sometimes a writer's personal schedule will dictate which episodes they're available for . . . As for Angel dripping wet in a towel, actually, first I wrote the scene with him reading a book, fully clothed. Then I thought, hey, not a particularly cinematic choice. What might work better? Dripping wet and naked just suggested itself . . . I think it's a little better than the whole book thing. But America didn't get to hear all the funny lines I wrote about *Wuthering Heights*.'

6
Sense and Sensitivity

US Transmission Date: 9 November 1999
UK Transmission Date: 11 Febuary 2000 (Sky)

Writer: Tim Minear
Director: James A. Contner

Cast: John Capodice (Tony Papazian),
Ron Marasco (Allen Lloyd), Alex Skuby (Harlan),
Kevin Will (Heath), Ken Abraham (Spivey),
Jimmy Shubert (Johnny Red),
Ken Grantham (Lieutenant),
Adam Donshik (Uniform Cop #1),
Kevin E. West (Uniform Cop #2),
Wilson Bell (Uniform Cop #3),
Colin Patrick Lynch (Beat Cop),
Steve Schirripa (Henchman),
Christopher Paul Hart (Traffic Cop)

Kate arrests a man named Spivey and spends hours
interrogating him. County Supervisor Caffrey has been
murdered and Kate is convinced Spivey knows where
suspected killer Tony Papazian is hiding. Spivey and Kate
come to blows and her fellow detectives pull her from the
room. Angel is in the sewer, battling a two-headed demon
with tentacles. Cordelia and Doyle arrive, providing Angel
with a sword to slay the creature. Angel instructs his
colleagues to cut off its heads and limbs, ensuring it doesn't
come back to life 'again'. Indignant, Cordy berates him
over his insensitivity. The duo return to the office, covered
in slime. Angel begins to tell Cordelia something, but she
says that she doesn't want to hear anything until he
enquires about the completion of their task. The discussion
is interrupted as Kate arrives and shows Angel photographs of Tony Papazian, explaining her sources have
dried up. Angel offers to help but Kate cautions him, she

only wants him to locate Tony. Back at the precinct, Kate
sees her father, who is about to retire from the force. Their
conversation is strained and awkward. Kate is called to the
phone. Angel says he has located Tony at San Pedro pier.
Realising that Tony may escape by boat before Kate
arrives, Angel dons a tourist disguise and joins Tony and
his henchman. Annoyed by Angel's presence, Tony orders
his man to get rid of Angel and a fight takes place. Kate
arrives in time to arrest Tony, but she chastises Angel,
pointing out that he could have been hurt. Tony makes a
phone call to his lawyers, Wolfram & Hart. He tells them
that Kate is the thorn in his side and he wants her
removed, permanently. Papazian's lawyer, Lee Mercer,
threatens to charge the police with brutality. Cordelia tells
Angel that it's nice to have a simple case for a change. But
Angel expresses his concern that it may not be over. Doyle
confirms Angel's suspicions. Johnny Red told Doyle that
Papazian is planning something. Kate goes to a bar where
fellow officers congratulate her on the arrest. She sits with
her father who says that Papazian could get off on a
technicality. Kate is shown a memo that orders all
personnel to attend a sensitivity course due to her handling
of the Papazian case. The next day, Kate and her
colleagues are in class, listening to Allen Lloyd. Allen
hands one officer a wooden staff, which he calls the talking
stick. Whoever holds the stick is given the freedom to
express their true feelings, without judgement from his
peers. When the officer begins to open up, Kate makes a
glib comment. Allen hands Kate the stick, telling her he
knows she's been hurt. Angel and Doyle question Johnny
about Papazian who, he says, is out to get Kate. Angel
goes to warn Kate where she apologises to him about the
previous night, then asks him to accompany her to a
retirement party. The Wolfram & Hart lawyer visits
Lloyd's home. He enquires about the sessions. Lloyd
reassures him that by the following day he should see
results. Kate tells Angel that she has a fear of public
speaking. She greets her father and introduces Angel. Kate
begins her speech by praising her father's years of service,

but then reveals much about their private lives. She begins to cry, telling everyone her father never told her she was pretty. This sparks an outpouring of emotions from the crowd and fights begin to break out. Angel takes Kate to his office. Cordelia arrives, to find Angel and Doyle babysitting Kate who is babbling about Angel's intense eyes. Angel asks Kate about the sensitivity training and she shows him the memo. Angel goes to Lloyd's home. He discovers the talking stick being used in some type of magic but Allen attacks Angel with the stick.

At the station officers are releasing prisoners because of the effects of the stick. Kate escapes from Angel's office and searches for her father. Angel rushes to the station where Cordelia and Doyle have followed Kate. Angel pulls his friends into a hug. He becomes emotional as he admits that he threatened Lloyd with violence. Lloyd explained that Tony hired him to neutralise the police so he could kill Kate. Angel feels that Cordelia and Doyle judge him when he becomes a vampire. Frustrated, Doyle attempts to enter the station but the police have locked the door. Inside, Kate's partner is declaring his love for her. Cordelia and Doyle force Angel to break into the basement. Tony goes after Kate with a gun, but Angel arrives and tries to talk Tony out of confrontation. Finally Angel knocks Tony out. At Wolfram & Hart his lawyer tells Tony that he's become a risk and they refuse to represent him. Angel checks on Kate. Everything seems to be back to normal. Kate tells Angel that they suspect the drinks at the party were spiked. Kate's father tells her she embarrassed him at the party and she's never to mention the incident again.

Dudes and Babes: Judging from Harlan's comment, Kate must have a strong bladder as she never needs to 'pee' during interrogation. Kate's uninhibited view of Doyle and Cordelia's relationship: 'Where's the truth? He's hiding behind Mr Humour. Look at Doyle, really look at him, what do you see?' Cordelia: 'A bad double-poly blend?' Kate: 'That's defence, Cordelia. Maybe you should open your heart to a new possibility.' Doyle: 'Hey, you know, she's starting to make some sense . . .' Kate wants to picture Angel in his underwear.

Denial, Thy Name is Kate: 'I'm hearing a *lot* of denial.' As Lloyd very perceptively notes, genuine emotion makes Kate uncomfortable. Her 'inappropriate sarcasm' masks anger. She's been hurt before, and she's afraid of being hurt again.

Denial, Thy Name is Trevor: 'In my day we didn't need any damn sensitivity,' says Trevor and that becomes clearer as Kate tells her colleagues about her childhood. 'He forgot how to be anything but a cop a long time ago. Maybe that's why I became a cop too. After Mom died, you stopped. It was like you couldn't stand the sight of me. Her face, her eyes looking up at you. But big girls don't cry, right? You said, *gone's gone* and there is no use wallowing. Worms and dirt and nothing, for ever. Not one word about a better place. You couldn't even tell a scared little girl a beautiful lie. God, I wanted to drink with you. I wanted you to laugh with me just once, the way you laughed with Jimmy, or Frank . . . My best friend, Joanne, her mom was soft and she smelled like macaroni and cheese and she'd pick me up on her lap and she would rock me. She said that she wanted to keep to herself. She said that I was good and sweet. Everybody said I was. Do you realise that you've never told me that I'm pretty? Not once in my life?' But his ultimate denial comes at the end: 'You make an idiot out of yourself, embarrass me in front of the guys. You don't bring that up ever again. As far as I'm concerned it didn't happen.'

It's a Designer Label!: Cordelia has a pair of new orange sandals which Angel fails to notice, but Doyle does. Her other clothes include a white and red top and demin skirt. We must mention the cool end of Angel's wardrobe, that royal blue sweater. And the non-cool end . . . the Hawaiian shirt. Kate's blue dress at the retirement party is gorgeous.

References: The title is a misquotation of Jane Austen's *Sense and Sensibility*. The planet Mongo is mentioned (the home of Emperor Ming in *Flash Gordon*), along with Jar Jar Binks (from *Star Wars Episode 1: The Phantom Menace*), Frankie Valli and the Four Season's 'Big Girls Don't Cry', Conan O'Brien's chatshow *Last Night*, *Armageddon* ('asteroids are hurtling towards the earth'), *Clueless* and Dr Laura Schlessinger (New York author and controversial radio host). 'Mr and Mrs Spock need to mind-meld' is a reference to *Star Trek*, of course. 'Makes Mark Fuhrman look like *Gentle Ben*' refers to the police detective who was accused of racism during the OJ Simpson trial and the sickly 1970s TV series about a bear.

Los Angeles area locations mentioned include: Stockholm, San Fernando Valley and Burbank, Long Beach, San Pedro and Carlsbad.

Bitch!: Kate: 'I don't want to come off as insensitive, but if either of you tries to stop me I'm gonna have to blow you the crap away, because I've got to go find my daddy.' She later tells Papazian: 'I am not a bitch. I'm just protected.'

'West Hollywood'?: Trevor tells Angel he's relieved to see Kate out with a man. He was starting to think she leaned in another direction. Papazian calls Angel 'a nancy boy' (see **3**, 'In the Dark').

The Charisma Show: Charisma gets a great bunch of lines here including: 'Am I wrong in thinking that a "please" and "thank you" is generally considered good form when requesting a dismemberment?' and 'You *do* remember leaving us in the sewer with a giant calamari?'

L.A.-Speak: Spivey: '*Bite me.*'

Cordelia: 'Do you think that tentacle spew comes out with dry cleaning?' And 'Hey. What's your *damage*?' And 'You stink of *whammy*.'

Angel: 'I wanted to, you know, thank you so much for going through those coroner reports, because I can imagine how not fun it is to read about, you know, coroner stuff.' Cordelia: '*Lame.*'

Angel: 'What've you got?' Cordelia: 'The *weebies*. This guy clearly has anger management issues.'

Papazian: 'Who's the *mook*?' And 'Nobody beats me, baby, especially not a stone-bitch like you.'

Cigarettes and Alcohol: Internal Affairs blame the outbreak of sensitivity on spiked alcohol in the Blue Bar. Kate drinks a beer with her father and a white wine at the retirement party. Trevor Lockley, on the other hand, seems to enjoy shots of neat vodka.

'You May Remember Me from Such Films as ...': Ken Grantham's movies include *Peggy Sue Got Married*, *Tucker: The Man and His Dream*, *Sibling Rivalry* and *Class Action*. Colin Patrick Lynch has appeared in *Hot Shots!* and *Terminator 2: Judgment Day*.

Don't Give Up the Day Job: Writer/producer Tim Minear's previous credits include *The X-Files* (co-scripting the classic 'Kitsunegari' with Vince Gilligan) and *Lois and Clark: The New Adventures of Superman*. 'Chris Carter got a hold of a spec *X-Files* script I'd written,' he told Rob Francis. 'Chris invited me to join the writing staff before my tenure at *Lois and Clark* was up. *The X-Files* was a dream come true for me. It was the one show I watched religiously. It's very rare that a writer gets a gig on the show he sampled. I was the first in that show's history. Ken Horton's assistant, Kim Metcalf, introduced me to *Buffy*. She told me, 'I want you to work with Joss.' Mutant Enemy always seemed to be lurking around the corner.'

Logic, Let Me Introduce You to This Window: In the scene where Kate is chasing Spivey, he throws his bag on top of the car, but in later shots the bag is gone. During the fight between Kate and Spivey, he opens a car door. When the camera changes angle, it's closed. Angel drinks coffee in this episode (see **4**, 'I Fall to Pieces'). Why does a vampire need night-vision equipment? Where does Angel get the Hawaiian shirt and hat from? Does he carry disguises in the car? When Kate first sees her father at the police station, she is holding books, but when she reaches the counter, they've disappeared. As Kate gives her speech she goes from having no purse and her arms at her side to clutching a purse with one hand on her hip. How did Angel gain entry to Allen Lloyd's house? Yet again, Angel's image is captured on video (see **1**, 'City Of', **19**, 'Sanctuary').

Quote/Unquote: Kate: 'You have the right to remain silent. But I wouldn't recommend it.'

Spivey: 'I heard it was suicide.' Kate: 'Supervisor Caffrey shot himself.' Spivey: 'It happens.' Kate: 'In the back of the head. Wrapped himself in plastic and he locked himself in the trunk of his car?' Spivey: 'He'd been depressed.'

Lieutenant: 'Your need for catharsis is not the issue here.'

Angel: 'My parents were great. Tasted a lot like chicken.'

Notes: 'I'd like to apologise for having treated you so shabbily, so I wrote a poem about it. "I saw a leaf and I did cry . . ." ' Two parts *Goodfellas*, one part absurdist-comedy. This hits all of the wrong notes and yet, somehow, manages to stay on course for most of the episode, thanks largely to fine performances from the regulars (Boreanaz is on particularly good form). Nice to see the series taking some format risks and, mostly, succeeding.

Angel uses the alias 'Herb Saunders from Baltimore'. He confirms that he doesn't have a pulse. After Cordelia breaks into the police station, there's another shot of the tattoo on Charisma's back as she wipes her hands on her trousers (see **5**, 'Rm W/a Vu').

Kate is stationed at the LAPD Metro Precinct. Her badge number is 3747 and her extension is 229. She has been awarded a number of Commendations, including the Medal of Valour. Kate's father is Trevor Lockley, a corporal in the LAPD, badge number 6873. His retirement party is held at the Blue Bar. The memo on sensitivity training is dated 9 November 1999.

Soundtrack: The songs heard in the bar are by soul legend Solomon Burke, 'Everybody Needs Somebody to Love' and the much less famous 'Baby'.

Did You Know?: In an extraordinary interview with *FHM*, Charisma Carpenter revealed much detail about her early days in Las Vegas ('the weirdest thing was that we had a normal life – there are school districts, stores, churches. Everyone thinks of The Strip when you say "Vegas", but it's a really normal town') and her schooldays ('I was a social butterfly . . . My problem was that I had boys on the brain all the time – my hormones were going wild'). She talked candidly about getting into trouble for taking her father's Corvette without permission ('I took a whuppin' for that') being 'tortured' by her elder brother and his friend ('on a red-hot day they made us stand barefoot on the asphalt') and about her time as a cheerleader ('I was the best. I took it to the '*Ooomph*' degree. And I can still do the splits').

7
The Bachelor Party

US Transmission Date: 16 November 1999
UK Transmission Date: 18 Febuary 2000 (Sky)

Writer: Tracey Stern
Director: David Straiton

Cast: Kristin Dattilo (Harry),
Carlos Jacott (Richard Howard Straley), Ted Kairys (Ben),
Chris Tallman (Nick), Brad Blaisdell (Uncle John),
Robert Hillis (Pierce), Lauri Johnson (Aunt Martha),
Kristen Lowman (Rachel), David Polcyn (Russ)

Doyle tries to persuade Angel to have some fun at a sports bar. Angel is content with his book. Cordelia is going on a date with an upwardly mobile trader. Her friends are protective and question her date, Pierce, about his prospects and their plans for the night. Cordelia drags Pierce away, saying 'Don't wait up.' Doyle laments that Cordelia won't ever fall for someone like him. He picks up Angel's book and a picture of Buffy falls out. Doyle shows his approval with a wolf whistle, but his appreciation is ended by the vision of a young man being held by vampires. Angel and Doyle find the nest, saving the man's life in the process. Angel takes the victim home, so Doyle heads back to the office, unaware that a vampire is following him.

At Le Petit Renard, Cordelia is bored by Pierce's market-talk. Afterwards Pierce offers to walk Cordelia to her car but as a vampire attacks, he drives off leaving Cordelia to fend for herself. Doyle bravely fights off the vampire, saving Cordelia, who is impressed by Doyle's 'hidden depths'. She realises that she 'wants more to a man than rich and handsome', she wants 'brave and interesting' as well. Deciding that Doyle deserves a reward for saving her, she is about to invite him out for a mochaccino when a woman appears in the doorway. The stranger is introduced to Cordelia as Doyle's wife, Harry. Harry apologises to Doyle for the surprise visit. Angel arrives and is introduced to Richard Straley, Harry's fiancé. Angel takes Cordelia out of the room to give them privacy and Harry suggests that Richard wait for her in the car. Harry hands Doyle divorce papers and asks for his signature saying that she doesn't want to hurt him. Doyle tells Angel that he and Harry married young and how happy they were until Doyle came into his 'inheritance' from his demon father. A surprise to both of them, the marriage fell apart. Doyle bears Harry no ill will and he admits that maybe Richard will be good for her. Both Angel and Doyle have some doubts about him and Doyle asks Angel to keep him under surveillance. Angel watches as Richard exchanges a package with someone in a car. Angel follows Richard to his family's restaurant where Richard hides the package in the fridge. Angel sees Richard's demon face and bursts through a window. Harry stops the struggle, saying she knows that her fiancé is a demon. Harry says she encouraged Doyle to embrace his demon-half, but he was the one who couldn't accept it, and that was ultimately the cause of their failed marriage. Doyle is shocked that Harry would marry another demon, but in a moment of clarity he admits that Harry knows her own mind. He signs the divorce papers and gives them to Harry, accepting an invitation to Richard's bachelor party. At the Straley house, the family is discussing the agenda for the upcoming festivities, including, but not limited to, the ritual eating of the first husband's brains. Angel and Doyle arrive at the restaurant for the party. Richard is surprised that Doyle brought Angel. Cordy and Harry go to the wedding shower in the Straley home. Cordelia is shocked to learn that Doyle was a third-grade teacher and a volunteer in a soup kitchen. At the party, Angel becomes suspicious of Richard's brothers. Everyone is distracted by the arrival of a stripper. Doyle finally gives his blessing on the marriage without understanding the true nature of his consent. Angel sees Uncle John performing a blood ritual. He calls Cordelia and asks for help from Harry, who is an ethnodemonologist, in translating the spell from Aratuscan. She promises to try to find the translation. Angel is discovered by the family and they fight. Overpowered by the demons, Angel is hurled from the window. Richard announces to the rest of his family that Doyle has given his blessing. They imprison Doyle and Uncle John pulls out the ritual knife. Harry and Cordelia discover the meaning of the incantation and the tradition that goes with it, 'ingesting the first love'. Doyle tries to convince Richard that his brains are not worth eating. Angel smashes in the door wearing his vampire face and fights the demons as Doyle embraces his demon side and breaks free of his prison. Cordy and Harry arrive at the restaurant and Harry stops the fight. She confronts Richard about the ritual and her fiancé admits that he was going to eat Doyle's brains. Not wanting to base her marriage on a lie she gives him back his ring and walks out. Cordelia tries to cheer up Doyle, telling him that 'nice guys don't always finish last'. Doyle's pleasure is brutally cut short by another vision. Buffy Summers is fighting for her life.

Dudes and Babes: After Cordelia compliments Doyle on his bravery: 'You think you could say that again without so much shock in your voice? You're stepping on my moment of manliness here.'

Denial, Thy Name is Doyle: Although she was initially 'freaked' by Doyle's assimilation of his father's genes, Harry learned to accept it and encouraged Doyle to explore his inheritance. It was Doyle himself who couldn't face his demon aspect and wrecked the marriage.

It's a Designer Label!: Cordelia calls Pierce 'Mr Armani'. She also mentions Tiffany & Co, one of America's leading jewellery retailers. Cordy's black evening dress and matching shawl are, in Pierce's words, 'Wow'. Also in the *phwoar!* department, Cordy's black jogging vest, the shiny pinky-purple trousers of the female vampires and the stripper with the blue feather boa. Mark down Doyle's hideous bright orange shirt as a 'fashion crime'.

References: The episode shares its name (and some – mostly aesthetic – details) with a Tom Hanks movie. 'They have trivia games on the Internet now,' refers to the NTN game network which provides interactive sports games for services like AOL. Also referenced, a misquote from *Gone With the Wind* ('tomorrow is another day'), Primal Scream's 'Movin' On Up', the 'Spelling Bee' competition, *Pulp Fiction* ('pumpkin', 'hon bun'), USA For Africa's 'We Are The World', the US Green Card, 'Pictionary', the sports network ESPN and (obliquely) *A Hard Day's Night* ('A book!'), Kentucky Fried Chicken and Bob Hope's 'Thanks for the Memories'.

Bitch!: Cordelia: 'I swore when I went down that road with Xander Harris, I'd rather be dead then date a fixer-upper again.'

Cordelia, on Pierce: 'All I could think about was if this wimp ever saw a monster he'd probably throw a shoe at it and run like a weasel. Turns out the shoe part was giving him too much credit.'

Doyle, on Richard: 'He's a demon? And she's all signed on to be Mrs Demon? Tell me again how ugly he is?'

The Charisma Show: 'I think it, I say it. That's my way,' could be Cordelia's catch-phrase. She asks: 'Doyle taught third grade? The kind with children? Are you sure he wasn't just held back and used that as his cover story?'

L.A.-Speak: Pierce: 'I'm not really sure about this neighbourhood.' Vampire: 'You're right, it's crappy.'

Doyle: 'That wasn't . . .' Cordelia: '. . . An incredible *spaz attack*? Good.'

Angel: 'Where are you?' Cordelia: 'In the netherworld known as the 818 area code.'

Not Exactly a Haven for the Demon Bruthas: Once a nomadic tribe with violent leanings, they gave up those orthodox teachings and language (Aratuscan) at the turn of the century. They appear to be a peaceful clan that has totally assimilated into human society. However, they still follow some of the ancient ways. When an Ano-movic demon marries a divorcée, the brains of the prior spouse to the newly betrothed woman must be eaten during a ritual performed by a family elder. This is said to bring good luck on the new union.

Cigarettes and Alcohol: Doyle admits to Angel that what Harry used to tell him is right – the booze does him no good. He even refuses (initially) to drink whisky with Angel, but he does share a toast to Harry with Richard.

Sex and Drugs and Rock'n'Roll: Stripper alert.

'You May Remember Me from Such Pop Videos as . . .': Despite a long TV career guesting on series as diverse as *Parker Lewis Can't Lose*, *21 Jump Street*, *Friends* and *Ally McBeal*, Kristin Dattilo's main claim to fame is the leading role in Aerosmith's 1990 video 'Janie's Got A Gun'.

'You May Remember Me from Such Films and TV Series as . . .': Carlos Jacott was tremendous as the agent in *Being John Malkovich* and also appears in *She's All That*, *The Last Days of Disco* and *Grosse Pointe Blank*. He was Ramon the Pool Guy in *Seinfeld* while *Buffy* fans will remember him as Ken in 'Anne'. Brad Blaisdell played

Mike the Bartender in *Three's Company* and can also be seen in episodes of *Happy Days*, *E.R.* and *Caroline in the City* and in the movies *Inspector Gadget* and *The Rat Pack*. Kristen Lowman played Mrs Henderson in *Problem Child* and has been in *Frasier*.

Logic, Let Me Introduce You to This Window: When Pierce and Cordelia are having dinner, watch the background. A waitress approaches the lady behind Cordelia twice. During the bachelor party, Angel walks into the kitchen and his reflection can be seen in the window. His reflection is also seen on the glass shutters in his office. If Harry and Doyle have not seen each other or spoken in four years, how did Harry find Doyle at Angel Investigations? Doyle's cross pops in and out of his T-shirt at regular intervals. Richard's red demon make-up can be spotted ending above his wrists in one scene.

I Just *Love* Your Accent: When Doyle sees a picture of Buffy, he asks Angel how he thinks she would feel about a man with an Irish accent.

Motors: Cordelia's date, Pierce, along with lots of money, a house in Montecito and a place in the hills with a pool, also possesses a Mercedes CLK 320.

Quote/Unquote: Doyle: 'You're marrying that guy?' Harry: 'I know it's wild, huh? I'm definitely the Ying to his Yang, but it works. He's got a good heart, Francis, just like you.' Doyle: 'Yeah, maybe, but the container? Can I get a side of *bland* with that bland?'

Uncle John reading from the party itinerary: 'First we greet the man of the hour. Then we drink. We bring out the food. Then we drink. Then comes the stripper, darts, then we have the ritual eating of the first husband's brains. And then charades.' Ben: 'Wait. What was that? Charades?' Nick: 'I don't know about that . . .'

Uncle John: 'He's going to eat the guy's brains with a shrimp fork?' Nick: 'Pardon me if our ancient ancestors didn't leave behind any former-husband-brain-eating forks.' Uncle John: 'Get a soup spoon, you moron.'

Harry: 'You know how I feel about these barbaric Ano-movician customs.' Nick: 'You're nothing but a *racist*.'

Notes: 'I'm only going to ask you this once, Richard, and I expect a straight answer. Were you or were you not intending to eat my ex-husband's brains?' A mostly amusing episode which fills in much background detail on Doyle. Nice characterisation and an impressive bar-room brawl at the end; however, they can't disguise a *very* thin plot. Good performances all round, though, particularly Charisma and Kristin Dattilo's unlikely but effective double act.

Doyle married Harriet before he was twenty. The marriage began to go wrong after he reached his twenty-first birthday and inherited his father's demon aspect. They haven't seen each other for four years. Doyle never met his father, and his mother (see **3**, 'In the Dark') didn't tell him about his demon side. Doyle wears a Celtic cross around his neck. According to Harry, Doyle was a third-grade teacher and a volunteer worker at a food bank which was where they met. The only money in Doyle's family was 'underneath the couch cushions'. He says that the duck served in La Petit Reynard is dry, indicating that he's visited this very exclusive restaurant.

Since the break-up, Harry has visited Kiribati, Togo and Uzbekistan. She met Richard while researching North American demon clans. The white board in Angel's office during the opening scene reads: 'Order cards, water, coffee. 818-555-1961. 10:00AM.'

Soundtrack: Although there are no actual songs in this episode, four pieces of instrumental music can be heard: 'Come Correct' (by C.Tory/Z.Harmon) from *Transition Music Sampler: Urban Songs and Instrumentals*, Paul Trudeau's 'Don't Do It', 'Retro Pop' from *Killer Tracks Music Library* and Diana Terranova's 'Come On 2000'.

Critique: *Xposé*'s Brian Barratt was impressed with this episode noting that 'Writer Stern brilliantly trades off cosy

feelings of domestic mundanity: the demons seem un-
threatening to the point of being dull. The twist: They can't
comprehend anything out of the ordinary in chomping on
somebody's frontal lobe.'

Previously on *Buffy The Vampire Slayer*: 'Pangs', 23
November 1999: As Buffy slays a vampire, she looks
around uneasily, believing that someone is watching her.
Someone is . . . Angel. Buffy, Willow and Anya watch the
building of the new campus Cultural Centre. Xander is
doing construction for the site and Anya is turned on by
watching him dig. The Professor of Anthropology makes a
speech about all cultures working together. Willow thinks
that the Thanksgiving traditions are a farce – a time when
the Pilgrims massacred the Indians and stole their land.
Xander begins to dig, much to Anya's delight and falls
through the ground into a cavern beneath.

Buffy decides that she can have her own Thanksgiving
dinner. Spike, having escaped from the Initiative is cold
and hungry. Riley and crew are looking for him. Forrest
believes that Spike is no threat, since he can't feed due to
his implant. Xander is about to leave for work, but Anya
realises that he's sick and decides to take care of him.

The anthropology professor is looking at an artefact
display, when a hand materialises around a knife in the
display and an Indian appears, killing her. Buffy is at
Giles's, preparing for Thanksgiving. She leaves to get more
food and Angel appears. Giles isn't pleased about Angel
trying to help Buffy without telling her that he's here, but
Angel maintains that it's the only way. He tells Giles that
they should speak to Father Gabriel, a priest whose family
has been in this area since missionary times. Spike tries to
get Harmony to take him in, but she's been reading
self-help books and she claims that she doesn't need Spike
to complete her. He tries to seduce her, but she grabs a
stake and chases him. Buffy and Willow are shopping when
they see Riley Finn. Willow leaves them alone and bumps
into Angel. He explains that he's protecting Buffy, but that
she can't know. Buffy invites Riley to their Thanksgiving

dinner, but he's headed to Iowa for the holiday. Buffy goes
to the church to look for Father Gabriel and finds him
dead. Hus, the Chumash Indian, has killed him and tells
Buffy that she can't stop his vengeance, claiming that she
slaughtered his people, before turning himself into a flock
of birds. Giles points out that Hus has killed innocent
people. Willow says that the Chumash were peaceful until
the Europeans came, spreading diseases, hanging them,
cutting off their ears. Willow thinks that instead of killing
Hus, they should find a way to help him. Giles believes this
is impractical and they argue. Giles takes Willow aside and
they realise that they have both seen Angel. Anya arrives
with a very sick Xander. Willow tells him that the
Chumash suffered from diseases like malaria, smallpox and
syphilis. Xander, particularly disturbed by the latter,
wonders why Buffy hasn't slain him yet. Willow explains
that it's not that simple but Xander says that you don't
talk to vengeance demons, you kill them. This offends
Anya and the gang begin to argue – except Buffy, who
chooses to make pie instead. There's a knock at the door
and they find Spike asking for help. Buffy and Giles refuse
to let him in, but he explains that he can't bite and offers
them information about the Initiative. Elsewhere, Hus
brings forth more warriors to help him. Giles believes that
Hus is targeting authority figures and believes that the
Dean may be at risk. Buffy and Willow debate the morals
of killing the Chumash and Spike thinks it's ridiculous. He
says that conquering nations do that kind of thing and that
there's no point in feeling badly about it. Xander and Giles
agree with him.

Willow, Anya and Xander go to warn the Dean when
they run into Angel whom Xander, like Willow before him,
assumes is evil again. Willow explains that they think Hus
is looking for a leader, but Angel explains that to a
warrior, the leader is the strongest warrior. Giles, Buffy
and Spike are attacked by Hus. Buffy discovers that the
Indians can only be killed with their own weapons, but
before she can put that to the test, Hus turns himself into
a bear. Buffy stabs him, causing the warriors to disappear.

Angel looks at Buffy through the window and leaves. The gang sits down to dinner amid the carnage. Willow says it was like old times. 'Especially with Angel being here,' says Xander. Buffy stares at him.

8
I Will Remember You

US Transmission Date: 23 November 1999
UK Transmission Date: 25 February 2000 (Sky)

Writers: David Greenwalt, Jeannine Renshaw
Director: David Grossman

Cast: David Wald (Maura Demon #1),
Chris Durands (Maura Demon #2)

Cordelia tells Angel that she and Doyle are worried about him after he spent three days in Sunnydale without talking to Buffy. Angel replies that Buffy didn't even know he was there just as she walks into the office. Buffy demands an explanation from Angel. In the next room, Cordy tells Doyle that Buffy and Angel's discussion could last for a while and they should go for a cappuccino. Buffy tells Angel that she can sense when he's around, whether she sees him or not. They agree to keep their distance from one another, but their discussion is interrupted when a demon comes crashing through the window. Buffy and Angel defend themselves before the demon retreats. Pursuing it through the sewers, Angel tells Buffy that he can handle the demon alone, but Buffy insists on helping. Discovering blood on the wall, Angel touches it and tells Buffy that he feels strange. Mistaking his meaning, Buffy says she is confused about her own feelings whenever he's around. He admits having her near is unbearable. Buffy leaves the tunnels to track the demon on the surface, but as soon as she is gone, the demon attacks Angel. It slices open Angel's hand and a fierce struggle commences. Angel stabs the demon, whose blood mixes with his own. A mysterious light appears over the wound and Angel drops to his knees. He hears a pounding heartbeat and cries 'I'm alive!'

Cordelia and Doyle find the mess in Angel's office. Angel walks in and Cordy notices that he used the front entrance. They watch as Angel crosses the room to the window and stands in the direct sunlight. Angel reveals he is human and decides he must eat. He tells Cordy to find Buffy and tell her he's killed the demon, but not to reveal his humanity. Doyle discovers that the creature is a Mohra demon, an assassin who kills warriors like Angel and Buffy. Its blood has regenerative properties, hence Angel becoming mortal again. He questions why this miracle has come about and needs to know if the transformation is permanent. He tells Doyle that he wants to speak with The Powers That Be. Doyle agrees to contact the Oracles and takes Angel to the Gateway for Lost Souls, located beneath a post office. Angel is met by two Oracles. He asks what happened to him and they assure him that he is mortal. Angel shares the news with Doyle. Angel and Buffy are confused by the turn of events and agree that they shouldn't rush into anything, but soon they're in each other's arms, kissing. Doyle and Cordelia are at a bar, Cordy lamenting that she's probably out of a job now that Angel is cured. Doyle is happy that he'll no longer have to endure the horrible pain of his visions just as he experiences another one. Buffy and Angel are in bed, Buffy listening to Angel's heartbeat. They fall asleep in each other's arms. Angel is awakened by Doyle who tells him about his vision; the demon has regenerated and is at a saline plant in Redondo. Angel says he will kill it again. Doyle reminds Angel that he's human and suggests they wake Buffy. Angel refuses, adamant that he has to kill the demon on his own. They find a couple of bodies and the sight of blood sickens Angel. The demon attacks and is too powerful for Angel and Doyle. Back at the office Cordelia tells Buffy that Angel has gone to fight the demon. The demon is about to kill Angel when Buffy arrives. Angel tells Buffy to shatter the jewel imbedded in its forehead, which kills the demon.

Angel returns to the Oracles. He tells them the demon warned him about 'the End of Days'. Angel asks what will happen to the Slayer. They tell him she will die. Angel pleads to exchange his life for hers. He wants things to go back to the way they were. They agree since Angel is willing to make such a sacrifice. They take back the previous 24 hours which only Angel will remember. Angel explains to Buffy what is going to happen and why. Buffy argues but Angel tells her he would be a liability to her. Buffy laments that she can't go on knowing what they could have had. Angel reveals that she won't remember. Buffy says that she will never forget. Buffy and Angel are suddenly back in his office discussing their plan to keep their distance from one another. Buffy turns to leave and the Mohra demon crashes through the office window. Angel smashes the jewel in its forehead, killing it. Buffy says they've covered everything, as Angel glances down at his broken clock. When he looks up, Buffy has walked out of his life.

Dreaming (as *Buffy* Often Proves) is Free: The ultimate dream episode; it never happened.

Dudes and Babes: Buffy looks as great as ever. Plus, naked-Angel alert with Buffy licking ice cream off his chest. That should put paid to all this 'West Hollywood' nonsense.

It's a Designer Label!: Cordelia: 'That's our Buffy.' Doyle: 'She seemed a little . . .' Cordelia: 'Bulgarian in that outfit?' She certainly does (particularly the boots). Cordelia's denim skirt puts in another appearance. Angel's red dressing gown puts in its first. And hopefully last.

A Little Learning is a Dangerous Thing: Buffy knows that Angel's axe is Byzantine. Since when was she an expert on antiques?

References: The title is from a song by Sarah McLachlan. Cordelia mentions 'the director's cut of *Titanic*'. There are references to *The Teenage Mutant Ninja Turtles*, Orson Welles, the US game show *Let's Make a Deal* ('tunnel number one it is') and the contemporaneous Arnold Schwarzenegger movie *End of Days* (which was released the same week that this episode premiered on US television). Angel's line, 'being on the outside, looking in', is very similar to dialogue from the *Forever Knight* episode 'Dying for Fame'.

The pier visible behind Buffy when she is in Santa Monica is Pacific Park.

Bitch!: Cordelia, on Buffy and Angel: 'Let me explain the lore here, OK? They suffer, they fight. That's "business as usual". They get groiny with each other, the world as we know it falls apart.'

Cordelia: 'They didn't even have cookie-dough-fudge-mint-chip when you were alive.' Angel: 'I want some. Can you get that?' Cordelia: 'It'll go straight to your thighs.'

Plus a scene of vintage Buffy/Cordelia 'second grade' bitching.

The Charisma Show: Having Sarah around seems to brings out the best in Charisma.

On Angel: 'Where's the crabby scowl, the morbid gloom?' And, on finding some dust in the office: 'She killed him. Oops. My bad. It's just dust I forgot to sweep under the rug.'

L.A.-Speak: Buffy: 'Oh, boy. I was really *jonesing* for another heartbreaking sewer talk.'

Doyle: 'The Oracles are finicky and unpredictable. You do get in, don't dilly-dally. Ask your questions, get out.'

Buffy: 'That was *unreal*.'

Cigarettes and Alcohol: Doyle seems to be drinking a Margarita in the bar with Cordelia. In the same scene a distinctive white bottle of Malibu can be seen behind the bar.

Sex and Food and Rock'n'Roll: Once Angel announces that he's hungry, he rushes to the refrigerator and eats a PopTart, an apple, a bologna sandwich, a chocolate bar and yoghurt (which he doesn't like). He also asks Cordelia to get him cookie-dough-fudge-mint-chip ice cream, which he and Buffy eat in bed along with crunchy peanut butter (see **5**, 'Rm W/a Vu'). Buffy is also holding a packet of strawberries.

'You May Remember Me from Such Films and TV Series as . . .': Sarah Michelle Gellar is a former child star, appearing in Burger King adverts as a four-year-old and having a starring role in *Swans Crossing*. She won a Daytime Emmy for her role as Kendall Hart in the soap *All My Children*. Her movies include *I Know What You Did Last Summer* (as Helen Shivers), *Cruel Intentions* (as Kathryn Merteuil) and *Scream 2*. And she also plays Buffy Summers in . . . Hang on, you all *know* who *she* is.

Randall Slavin has appeared in *Beethoven's 2nd*, *Marshal Law*, *Primal Fear* and *Generation X*.

Don't Give Up the Day Job: Jeannine Renshaw was initially an actor playing the teacher in *Hook* and appearing in *Home Improvements* before co-creating the series *VR.5*. David Wald is a stuntman with credits on *The Glimmer Man*, *Escape From L.A.*, *Blade* and *Beverly Hills Ninja*. As well as acting in *Mighty Morphin Power Rangers* he was also camera assistant on the movie *976 – Wish*.

Logic, Let Me Introduce You to This Window: Angel's reflection can be seen in the glass door behind Buffy in the pre-title sequence. Angel is very close to the broken window while fighting the demon in the office without any apparent trouble, but he visibly flinches from the light streaming down into the sewer. Buffy has the time to change her outfit between the scenes in Angel's office and chasing the demon into the sewers. Another question asked a few times in *Buffy* (see, for instance, 'Graduation Day' Part 1): How does Angel, whose heart does not beat, bleed?

I Just *Love* Your Accent: 'You have so much to learn little Irish man,' Cordelia tells Doyle.

Quote/Unquote: Female Oracle: 'I like Time. There is so little and so much of it.'

Buffy, on the demon: 'It was rude. We should go kill it.' Angel: 'I'm free.'

Cordelia: 'I've decided not to feel sorry for myself. I'm taking matters into my own hands, organising a little 'going out of business' sale to subsidise the severance package Angel never bothered setting up for me.'

Male Oracle: 'Temporal folds are not to indulge at the whims of lower beings.'

Notes: 'Batten down the hatches, here comes Hurricane Buffy.' An overtly romantic episode with a very illogical (pure fantasy) sub-plot that gives us our first look at representatives of 'The Powers That Be'. Boreanaz and Gellar are, as ever, highly watchable together, but the story tends to replace form and substance with sentimentality, which is occasionally mawkish. It's thus a triumph of style-over-content. In other words, it's fan-fiction. Worse, it's slushy *shipper*-fiction designed to jerk tears and nothing more. Despite the time metaphor, no cigar.

There are several allusions to the events of *Buffy* episodes: Buffy's reference to a 'heartbreaking sewer-talk' concerns 'The Prom', Cordelia asking Angel, 'Did you *do it* with Buffy?' refers to 'Surprise', while the 'It's a long story'/'maybe not *that* long' exchange mirrors a similar sequence in 'Faith, Hope and Trick'. Angel's two gifts to the Oracles are his wristwatch and a Famille rose vase, Ch'ing dynasty, circa 1811. Buffy, ostensibly, came to L.A. to visit her father, Hank (see *Buffy*: 'Welcome to the Hellmouth', 'Nightmares', 'When She Was Bad').

Cordelia tells Doyle that Angel was 'in Sunnydale for three days, tracking her and that *thingumagiggy* you saw in your vision'. A one-line summation of the events of 'Pangs'. She used to have a cat. Doyle reads about the demon from *The Book of Kelsor*. The extract says: 'DEVIL TURN'D. Mohra Demon or ASSASSINS for Darkness. Veins run with the BLOOD of eternity. In what manner, and how zealously he is affected with the moving of the Spirit. With the Holy Sisters desire Copulation (if he would vast quantities of salt to live) . . .' A 'dive on 2nd near Beach' in Santa Monica called the Long Bar is used as a hideout by demons.

Critique: *TV Guide*'s Matt Roush wrote: 'While *The X-Files* only gets more ponderous in its 'mythology' (i.e. the lugubrious season opener), *Buffy the Vampire Slayer* just gets more entertaining, returning to its epic storyline – the tragic Buffy–Angel romance – in a fabulous recent crossover. A newly human Angel, able to smile and fulfil his passion for Buffy (and for postcoital cookie-dough-fudge-mint-chip ice cream), is forced to turn back time, eradicating her memories of their fleeting bliss so only he'll remember. "They've got the forbidden love of all time," says Cordelia. No lie.'

Ian Atkins in *Shivers* added: 'The poignant last protests of Buffy, and Angel's resignation, make the most of these two extremely talented actors in a scene of incredible beauty. Some people may have seen it coming from the off ... but for an episode focusing on the value of those special moments in all our lives, it does a marvellous job.'

Kristine Sutherland, who plays Buffy's mother Joyce on *Buffy the Vampire Slayer* was equally impressed, telling Paul Simpson: 'I caught that episode where Buffy goes to visit [Angel] and they have that one day. I loved it ... When you watched their relationship over the years, there was so much that thwarted it and made it impossible. It was an incredible release for me as an audience person to go there at least once. The romantic in us *does* live.'

9
Hero

US Transmission Date: 30 November 1999
UK Transmission Date: 3 March 2000 (Sky)

Writers: Howard Gordon and Tim Minear
Director: Tucker Gates

Cast: Tony Denman (Rieff),
Anthony Cistaro (Scourge Commander),
Michelle Horn (Rayna), Lee Arenberg (Tiernan),

Sean Gunn (Lucas),
James Henricksen (Elder Lister Demon),
David Bickford (Cargo Inspector),
Christopher Comes (Storm Trooper #2),
Paul O'Brien (Captain), Ashley Taylor (First Mate)

Cordelia narrates a commercial she has devised to an underwhelmed Angel: *The Dark Avenger*. Cordelia tries an 'everyman' approach using Doyle. He agrees to read Cordy's script to camera, but it's a disaster. Angel confides to Doyle that Buffy was in L.A. much longer than five minutes, that he became human and chose to sacrifice that life to continue fighting the good fight. Doyle says he couldn't give up the pleasures of the flesh for duty. Angel tells him that he'll never know until he's tested. There is an apocalypse coming, Angel can feel it and he tells Doyle that they need to prepare. Cordelia is upset that Angel kept something so momentous a secret. Prompted by these sentiments, Doyle begins to tell Cordelia about his demon side, but is interrupted by a vision. Angel and Doyle search a tenement and find a group of terrified demons hiding inside. Angel offers to help them. They say he is 'The Promised One', a saviour mentioned in their prophecies. Their leader explains that they are running from The Scourge, demon-hunters who persecute half-breeds. When Angel asks Doyle who they are, he replies: 'Death.' Doyle once refused to aid members of his own race, the Brachen, fleeing The Scourge, and as a result they were killed. Doyle was burdened with his visions as a penance. He tells Angel that The Scourge are dedicated to their cause, that they won't stop until every half-breed is annihilated. Angel feels they must help the Lister demons escape. Cordelia rents a truck to transport them to a ship and sanctuary on Briole Island. Cordelia is confused that demons are their clients, but Doyle assures her the clan are in need of help.

A young demon, Rieff, absconds, convinced that they will all die. Doyle convinces Rieff to return to his family, assuring him that even if Angel isn't their saviour, he is still a hero. Doyle acts as a decoy to lead The Scourge away from Rieff and, with Angel's help, loses them. Angel then offers his services to The Scourge, saying that although he is a vampire and a half-breed himself, he needs to be cleansed. The Scourge leader accepts Angel's offer. The captain of the *Quintessa* is anxious to leave, but Cordelia assures him that Angel will arrive soon. The demon elder thanks Cordelia for her help and accidentally lets slip Doyle's secret. Angel is present at a meeting of The Scourge with their leader, Tiernan. He unveils a weapon called the Beacon, a light that destroys those with human blood. Tiernan tells his troops to exterminate the half-breeds. When Doyle and Rieff arrive at the ship, Cordelia is angry with Doyle for not telling her about his demon heritage. Doyle says he was afraid of rejection. Cordelia says that being poor and short are much worse than being a half-demon and that he should ask her out. Angel arrives, followed by The Scourge who deploy the Beacon. Angel knows he must stop it from detonating and prepares himself for a suicide mission to disarm the weapon. Doyle knocks Angel out, kisses Cordy goodbye and assumes his demon face, leaping on to the platform where the Beacon is suspended. Angel recovers too late to stop Doyle and watches as his friend uncouples the power supply but is disintegrated in the process.

Angel and Cordelia sit in silence, watching the commercial Doyle filmed: 'Is that it? Am I done?'

Making Adverts (According to Cordelia) Can Be Cheap: Cordelia surreally directs, in voice-over, *The Dark Avenger* advert (complete with 'knife-carrying goon').

It's a Designer Label!: Cordy's blue and red 'tie-around-and-backless' top is abandoned later for a blue-tank-top-and-ponytail look.

References: The narrator for Cordelia's commercial should be: 'That bald *Star Trek* guy or one of the cheaper Baldwins.' References include *Braveheart*, *The Man With Two Brains*, *Mask*, *Very Bad Things*, *Roots*, *Seinfeld* ('yadda, yadda, yadda'), 1 Timothy 6:12 ('fight the good fight'), Alfred Lord Tennyson's 'In Memoriam', *The Love Boat*, *End of Days* (see **8**, 'I Will Remember You'; presumably the events of this episode are what the Oracles were predicting) and, obliquely, Randy Newman's 'Short People'.

'West Hollywood'?: Cordelia, discussing having Angel in *The Dark Avenger* commercial asks: 'Would it kill him to put on some tights and a cape and garner us a little free publicity?' Doyle: 'I don't see Angel putting on tights . . . Oh, now I do and it's really *disturbing*.'

The harbourmaster's brother is called Big Randy and he's known to Angel who may or may not have bitten him. Enough said.

The Charisma Show: The visualisation of Cordelia's advert. One of the funniest things the series has done. She's also got some choice lines, including: 'This may look like a popular brand of breath freshener; it's really a cunningly disguised demon repellent.' And: 'What do you think I am, superficial?'

L.A.-Speak: Cordelia: 'Buffy blows into town and puts you into a permanent funk. And I'm just supposed to stand by and watch our business go belly-up?'

Doyle, on The Scourge: 'They have a big hate-on for us mixed-heritage types. Very into pedigree.'

Cordelia: 'I've rejected you way before now. So, you're half-demon. *Big whoop*. I can't believe you'd think I care about that. I mean, I work for a vampire, *hello*?'

Doyle: 'That *doohickey* – it's fully armed, isn't it?'

Not Exactly a Haven for the Half-Demons: An allegory of the persecution of the Jews and other ethnic and religious groups by the Nazis, this is not the first time that a Howard Gordon script has explored anti-Semitism, his highly rated *X-Files* episode 'Kaddish' in 1997 touching on similar themes.

Cigarettes and Alcohol: Doyle used to smoke but seems to have given up the habit.

'You May Remember Me from Such Films and TV Series as . . .': Tony Denman is Ben Smythe in *Good Vs. Evil* and also appeared in *Fargo*. Anthony Cistaro will be known to fans of *Cheers* as the semi-regular character Henri. He also played Mario in the US TV series *Alright Already*. Michelle Horn played Saghi in two episodes of *Star Trek: Deep Space 9* and provided one of the voices for *Lion King II: Simba's Pride*. Lee Arenberg's movie CV is extensive: *Cradle Will Rock, Johnny Skidmarks, The Apocalypse, Mojave Moon, Car 54, Where Are You?, Robocop 3, Live! From Death Row, Bob Roberts, Whore* and *Meet The Hollowheads* among them. He's played Ferengi characters in both *Star Trek: The Next Generation* and *Star Trek: Deep Space 9* and was Bobby G in *Action*.

Don't Give Up the Day Job: Howard Gordon was executive producer on *The X-Files*, co-writing the episode 'Synchrony' with David Greenwalt in 1997. He has' recently been developing an American TV version of the UK vampire mini-series *Ultraviolet*. Fans of the original (the best example of British telefantasy since *Doctor Who*) await the outcome with some trepidation. Tucker Gates directed episodes of *The X-Files* along with *Roswell, Space: Above and Beyond, Nash Bridges* and, in England, *Cracker*.

Logic, Let Me Introduce You to This Window: When Angel grabs the bike to make his escape from The Scourge, he is wearing one of their uniforms, but when he arrives at the ship he's no longer wearing it. In the Lister hideout, when Cordelia and Doyle are talking, their lips and the sound are not in synch.

Motors: Angel can drive a motorcycle. Cordelia's driving licence seems to include heavy goods vehicles judging by the size of the truck she delivers.

Quote/Unquote: Doyle: 'Angel Investigations is the best. Our rats are low.' Cordelia: 'Rates.' Doyle points to the script: 'It says "rats".'

Doyle: 'Cordy, oppressed demon people here, not getting any safer.' And: 'Too bad we'll never know if this is a face you could learn to love.'

Notes: 'The good fight, yeah? You never know until you've been tested. I get that now.' Ignore the Nazi-subtext and concentrate instead on a trio of staggering performances by the regulars. A hymn to nobility, heroism and self-sacrifice, Doyle and Angel 'fight the good fight', knowing that it will cost one of them their lives. The fan outrage that followed the episode seemed to miss this point entirely. The dramatic intensity of Doyle's prior rejection of his heritage and his subsequent redemption is breath-taking. A noble death ensures that the character won't be forgotten in a hurry.

Angel has a punch bag in his apartment. Doyle says that Harry (see **7**, 'The Bachelor Party') has decided to stay in L.A. Brachen demons have a good sense of direction (see **3**, 'In the Dark') and are, according to Doyle, good at basketball.

Soundtrack: Robert Kral, in a fascinating interview with *The Watcher's Web*, noted: 'A woodwind player, Chris Bleth, comes in each week to supply me with the "human element" to the score. It's really essential in love scenes etc. Samplers are great, but when the soloists come in they bring the music to life. I especially enjoy when we've brought in Elin Carlson for the vocal parts used on **9**, 'Hero' and **15**, "The Prodigal". First there's the spotting session. This is where David Greenwalt, myself and the music editor [Fernand Bos] will sit together and watch the episode through, deciding on where the music should go and any special needs. The sound guys are also present, so there's discussion about dialogue and sound effects as well, which is very handy because it can often affect the music and what to play. I usually write in the order of appearance, which I like because the music develops as it goes along. Sometimes I'll write a theme first that I know will be needed, often fully fledged and orchestrated, then I can go backwards and develop it over the course of the episode. In **9**, "Hero", for example, the theme was fully orchestrated, but the first time you hear it is solo voice with no harmony.'

Did You Know?: Special effects supervisor Loni Peristere told an online web-chat: 'Because it's television I wasn't sure [what I could get away with] but David Greenwalt said: "I want [Doyle's] flesh to melt off and muscle and then bones." That was the original idea but we thought that would be a bit too graphic so we did it in make-up stages.'

Joss Whedon's Comments: Joss maintains, despite persistent fan rumours, that Doyle was only ever intended to be on the show for nine episodes. In an interview with *Eon*, Joss bemoaned that: 'Our big surprise has been ruined. We were gonna take away [Angel's] mentor figure – shake up his life a little bit. Then, of course, it got out as it always does. But, yes, this was our idea from the beginning.' Asked, in another interview, about this ruination and if he would do anything differently in future, Joss noted: 'I honestly don't know how I could because an actor's agent will always start putting him up for stuff. You have an entire crew and extras [who] will sometimes get on the Internet. It's not like the old days, all you need now is one person and everybody in the world can know.' He also told *SFX* that: 'It did cause a lot of fuss. He's a popular guy . . . He wasn't *that* popular before we killed him; something I have to remind people.'

Real Gone Kid: Tim Minear also confirmed: 'We knew very early that we were going to kill off Doyle. All the character development which led up to that moment was written with [his] impending death in mind. The notion to bring in Wesley came later. We never planned for *Angel* to be the Angel/Cordy show. In fact, by the end of the season you'll see that we've been adding characters all year long.'

Around this time, Tim also began to post on to the alt.tv.angel newsgroup. Asked if he was surprised at fan reaction to Doyle's fate, he commented: 'Not a bit. Ever since it was leaked, I've seen the growing trend. We were pretty much expecting this kind of response.' On any possible return for Glenn Quinn, Tim noted: 'Doyle is dead. Glenn Quinn is not. I don't think that doors, particularly on fantasy shows like ours, are ever completely shut. But then, I am not an Oracle.'

Conspiracy Theory: Fuelled by some offhand comments by members of the cast and crew ('the producers felt that his character didn't fit the direction that the show was going in,' David Boreanaz noted, while Howard Gordon told *SFX*: 'If the death of Doyle was in Joss's mind from the beginning, I honestly didn't know'), rumours persist about dark goings-on behind the exit of Glenn Quinn. This is particularly awkward for Boreanaz who remains a close friend of Quinn. 'I see him all the time,' he told Sky, and the pair spent New Year's Eve 1999 together at *Playboy*'s millennium party. When appearing on UK MTV David mentioned that he is learning to play the drums. 'My friend Glenn Quinn is teaching me.' According to *Starlog* magazine, 'Quinn departed under rather murky circumstances. The party line states that Doyle was never intended to be a permanent fixture on the show . . . [Rumours] however, suggest that Quinn was let go after the producers determined that the character had outlived his usefulness.' 'I don't know which is which and I don't ask,' Charisma Carpenter told the magazine. 'All I know is that I am very sad to see Glenn go. Personally, there was a kinship, a friendship that forms when you work that many hours. He was very charismatic and jolly and just an all-around fun person to be with. As far as the characters go, Cordelia and Doyle had such a great relationship. There was a lot of chemistry. My mom said, "I was really sad to see him go because I felt he was going to reach you. It was so compelling."' Quinn himself has maintained a dignified silence concerning his departure, telling *Starburst*: 'It's a personal matter I have chosen not to discuss. I love Doyle and hope they are able to bring him back some day.'

An article in the *Oakland Tribune* noted: 'Quinn was abruptly written out of the show. Creator Joss Whedon says that was always the plan. *Look me in the eye and say that, buddy*. So Whedon actually goes eyeball to eyeball and says "That was always the plan," it's hard to call the guy a fibber. Whedon admits he got quite a bit of hate-mail concerning the decision, but thinks that offing a character keeps the viewers on their toes.' According to Christopher Golden: 'Whatever Joss Whedon says, as far as I'm concerned, that's Gospel.' Ironically, in the week that *Angel* premiered, *TV Guide*'s 'Hollywood Grapevine' featured a piece on Glenn Quinn noting that: 'If things don't work out [on *Angel*], he's covered [having] bought a share in a Hollywood nightclub called Goldfingers.' Perhaps the actor really *did* know from day one.

A Comic Requiem: Issue 6 of the popular Dark Horse monthly *Angel* comic included a piece of scripting worthy of the TV series. Written by Christopher Golden and Tom Sniegoski, part two of 'Earthly Possessions' takes place during the period just before and just after this episode. In a two-page sequence, Doyle is seen fixing a plaque to the wall of the office. Angel asks Doyle to do some investigating: 'I'll talk to all the wrong people,' says Doyle. 'Story of my life.' The next two-page sequence occurs a week later, in the aftermath of Doyle's death. A grief-stricken Cordelia silently reads the inscription on Doyle's plaque:

> *'An Irish Blessing'*
> *May you be in Heaven*
> *half an hour before the*
> *Devil knows you're dead*

'Oh, Doyle,' Cordelia notes sadly. 'You had to be the hero.' See **The Angel Comics**.

10
Parting Gift

US Transmission Date: 14 December 1999
UK Transmission Date: 10 March 2000 (Sky)

Writers: David Fury and Jeannine Renshaw
Director: James A. Contner

Cast: Maury Sterling (Barney),
Jayson Creek (Producer #1), Sean Smith (Producer #2),
Sarah Devlin (Producer #3), Jason Kim (Soon),
Brett Gilbert (Reptilian Demon),
Henry Kingi (Kungai Demon), Lawrence Turner (Hank),
Cheyenne Wilber (Concierge), Dominique Jennings (Mac),
Kotoko Kawamura (Ancient Korean Woman)

Angel returns to the Oracles to ask that they fold time
again and bring Doyle back. They remind Angel that
Doyle died so Angel could continue to save others. Angel
tells them he's blind without Doyle's visions. The Oracles
state, 'For every door that closes, another opens.' A
frightened demon runs down an alley, hotly pursued by a
leather-clad motorcyclist. Missing Doyle, Cordelia is looking for something he left behind in the office. Angel tells
her to take the day off, but she chides him for trying to
push her away. She tells him that she's not going anywhere. The alarm on her watch suddenly goes off and she
remembers that she has an audition. Rushing out, she
nearly collides with the pursued Barney, an empathy
demon. He says that he has heard about Angel and asks
for help. Barney asks, as it's the middle of the afternoon,
why Angel is not in his coffin. Angel is appalled by such
stereotypical piffle. Barney tells Angel his pursuer is
unshakable. Cordelia's audition goes terribly, due to a
sudden vision she experiences. She returns to the office and
kisses Angel. Realising that neither of them experienced
anything from the exchange, Cordy reveals that when she
and Doyle kissed, he must have passed his ability to receive
visions from The Powers That Be. Angel asks what she saw
in her vision but Cordelia's description is vague. She kisses
Barney to see if she can pass *him* the gift, but again she is
unsuccessful. Angel asks Cordelia to stay with their client
while he checks out Barney's apartment. As Angel suspected, the motorcycle is parked outside Barney's lodgings.
Angel discovers demon blood on the apartment door.
Silhouetted in the doorway is Wesley Wyndham-Price
aiming a crossbow at Angel.

Angel bats the crossbow from Wesley's grasp and asks about the Council. Wesley explains he no longer works with them. He is now a rogue demon hunter, on the trail of a creature who has left a trail of mutilated bodies. Angel asks if the demon is Barney. Wesley describes a large and powerful creature. Angel notices fluid dripping on to Wesley's jacket. The demon drops down on to them and they fight before the demon escapes out the window. Cordelia tries to draw a shape she saw in her vision. She can make no sense of it. Barney draws her into conversation, telling her that he senses the pain she's feeling regarding Doyle's loss as Angel and Wesley return. Cordelia kisses Wesley, still trying to pass off Doyle's gift. A startled Wesley allows Angel to tell Barney that Wesley wasn't hunting him. He was actually after the Kungai demon who was intent on stealing Barney's empathic abilities. Wesley provides a description of the demon from one of Angel's books. This reveals that the demon is of Asian origin. Angel decides he should begin his hunt in Koreatown. Wesley insists on accompanying him.

Cordelia is still struggling with her drawing. Barney asks if he can help and Cordelia tells him of her unwanted new ability. Barney tells her that Doyle left her his most valuable possession. She fixes Barney a cup of coffee, while he makes a call to his associate, Hank. He admits he has acquired the Kungai horn, but he thinks he's found something better, a girl with seer eyes. He tells Cordelia that she's a terrible actress, but that *he* is a good actor. Angel finds the dying demon in a massage parlour. The demon has a large wound in his forehead. The demon tries to speak to Angel, who is frustrated that he doesn't understand the language. Wesley tells Angel that he has knowledge of the dialect. Angel points out that the demon is dying, not from the arrow wound Wesley inflicted, but from the removal of his Tak horn. Wesley struggles with the translation but the demon dies. Angel pieces several clues together and realises that he was describing Barney.

Cordelia finds herself gagged and bound. Barney and Hank argue over the value of Cordy's eyes. Wesley blames

himself for Cordelia's abduction as he laments that he is a
fraud and the Council was right to sack him. Angel
discovers Cordy's discarded sketches. He recognises the
shape as a famous sculpture. He tells the self-flagellating
Wesley that to find Cordy they must find the sculpture.
After researching, they find the sculpture was purchased by
a hotel. Wesley remembers the translation of a word the
Kungai demon was repeating: 'Auction'. Barney is at the
hotel, acting as an auctioneer, selling the stolen talents of
various demons. Demons and humans are bidding, including a lawyer representing Wolfram & Hart. Barney points
out that Cordelia is a rare find. Barney is about to drop
the gavel on Cordelia, finalising her sale. In a desperate
attempt to buy time, Cordelia goads the bidders that she's
worth more than they're paying for her. After the auction,
the lawyer tells Barney that her employers are only
interested in the eyes. Barney is about to extract Cordelia's
eyes when Angel and Wesley arrive. While Angel battles
Hank and Barney, Wesley struggles to free Cordelia who
stabs Barney with the Kungai horn. Sitting at Angel's
kitchen table, Cordelia frames her drawing while Angel
cooks breakfast. She tells Angel the drawing is a reminder
that something of Doyle's is still with them. Wesley packs
his bag. He says goodbye, but he stays long enough to
accept Angel's invitation to breakfast.

Denial, Thy Name is Cordelia: The empathy demon Barney
sees through Cordelia's façade. She suspects that she's a
terrible actress and feels a heavy burden of guilt over
Doyle's demise, wondering if things would have been
different if she'd been nicer to him.

It's a Designer Label!: Wesley's leather biker pants are
impressive ('interesting look for you') if not for the wearer.
'They tend to chafe one's . . . legs.' His lightweight cream
suit is much more *him*. Barney says Cordelia is wearing
shoes she can't afford. The green and white dress and
cream blouse she sports to her audition are rather plain,
something that can't be said for the green woollen top-
thing-with-lots-of-holes that crops up during the rest of the

episode. Its practicality is questionable (being so short that it doesn't cover her naked midriff and gives us *another* look at Charisma's tattoo: see **5**, 'Rm W/a Vu, **6**, 'Sense and Sensitivity'). But it's certainly a talking point.

References: Wesley's middle name is a tribute to the king of British science fiction, John Wyndham (1903–1969), author of *The Day of the Triffids*, *The Midwich Cuckoos*, *The Kraken Wakes* and *Random Quest*. Other references include misquotes from Alexander Graham Bell ('for every door that closes, another opens'), Isaiah 48:22 ('no rest for the wicked'), *Macbeth* ('what is done cannot be undone'), plus allusions to the fairytale *The Frog Prince* ('I'll smooch every damn frog in this kingdom'), the Japanese healing art of shiatsu and *Ace Ventura: Pet Detective* ('all-righty then'). The 'grey blobby thing' from Cordelia's vision turns out to be the sculpture *Maiden with Urn* by Van Gieson.

Wesley's 'through storm and rain, heat and famine' is inspired by an inscription on the New York City Post Office which is, in turn, an adaptation of a quote from *The Histories of Herodotus*. Angel Investigations is in a section of Los Angeles County just south of Koreatown.

Bitch!: Cordelia: 'That's one spooky talent you got there. You can just look at me grinding my teeth, sighing, grunting and sense that I'm frustrated? Amazing.'

Barney: 'Why aren't you in your coffin?' Angel: 'I hate that stereotype. You're a demon and you don't know anything about vampires?' Barney: 'Only what I learned from TV.' Angel: 'Vampires don't sleep in coffins. It's a misconception made popular by hack writers and ignorant media. In fact, you know, we can and do move around during the day. As long as we avoid direct sunlight.'

The Charisma Show: Cordelia, discovering that her 'gift' came via Doyle's kiss, spends the episode desperately kissing anybody within kissing distance in the hope that it will vanish. She gets some great lines too: Barney: 'Can I help?' Cordelia: 'Not unless you can explain to me why I have to suffer skull-splitting migraines, getting visions so vague they require closed-captioning.' And: 'I didn't ask for this responsibility, unlike some people, who shall remain lifeless.' And: 'I'm really not a seer. I only had a vision once and I'm pretty sure it was just something I ate.'

Also, some top comedy in her trying to continue her incompetent, emotion-filled audition for Stain-Be-Gone while having a vision ('*GRASS STAINS!*').

L.A.-Speak: Cordelia: 'Well, thanks for that insight, Mr Emotional Radar.'

Domestic Matters: At some point in his life, Angel learned to cook. After late-night sessions 'stalking great lurking evil', he prepares a breakfast of toast and eggs, served with glasses of orange juice. Cordy brews the office's coffee in an old-fashioned pot, using Maxwell House.

Sex and Drugs and Rock'n'Roll: Cordelia is horrified by the 'gift' that Doyle's kiss has given her: 'Why couldn't it have been mono or herpes?'

'You May Remember Me from Such Pop Videos as . . .': Alexis Denisof can be seen in the video for George Harrison's 'Got My Mind Set On You'.

'You May Remember Me from Such Films and TV Series as . . .': Alexis later played Richard Sharpe's love rival, Johnny Rossendale, in *Sharpe* and appeared in *Rogue Trader*, *First Knight* (as Sir Gaheris) and *True Blue* before landing the role of Wesley on *Buffy the Vampire Slayer*. Recently, he portrayed an American hitman in the Vic Reeves/Bob Mortimer remake of *Randall and Hopkirk (Deceased)*. Maury Sterling was Vaughan Lerner in *Alright Already*. Jayson Creek can be seen in the movie *Domination*.

Don't Give Up the Day Job: Henry Kingi has acted in *Vampires*, *Barb Wire* and *Predator 2* but is best known for a thirty-year career as a stuntman in movies as diverse as *F/X – Murder By Illusion*, *Die Hard*, *Patriot Games*, *From Dusk Till Dawn*, *Dante's Peak*, *Lost World: Jurassic Park*, *Batman and Robin*, *US Marshals*, *Armageddon*, *Lethal*

Weapon 4, *Blade* and *End of Days*. On TV he was the stunt co-ordinator on *The Bionic Woman*.

Logic, Let Me Introduce You to This Window: The initial shot of Angel in his office with Barney shows his hands in his lap. The shot over his shoulder has his fingers steepled beneath his chin. When Angel hands Cordelia a pencil and pad to sketch her vision, one shot shows the pencil and pad together in Angel's left hand. The next has the pencil in his right hand and the pad in his left. David Boreanaz seems to be laughing during the scene where he knocks the crossbow from Wesley's hands. He also appears to be prompted from off-screen when he speaks Korean.

As Angel is startled by the demon in the bathhouse, he spins around. In the next shot he is still in the process of turning. In Angel's apartment, when Barney slaps Cordelia, you can see his hand doesn't connect with her face.

I Just *Love* Your Accent: It's good to have Wesley back, especially as he's 'on the trail of a particularly nasty bugger'. But, 'Butcher an innocent girl, will you? I'm going to thrash you within an inch of your life. And then I'm going to take that inch.' Oh dear, just as we were starting to think that somebody had finally got the right idea about how we speak in England. As Angel notes, 'Easy, tiger.'

Motors: Wesley drives a 'Big Dog' motorcycle. Say no more.

Quote/Unquote: Barney: 'You should know right away before there's any misunderstanding, I'm a demon.' Angel: 'I appreciate the candour.'

Barney's advice to Cordelia on overcoming nerves: 'I'm sensing a little performance anxiety here. Little trick: picture everybody ...' Cordelia: 'In their underwear?' Barney: 'I was going to say dead. But hey, if that underwear thing works for you ...'

Wesley: 'A lone wolf such as myself never works with anyone ... I'm a rogue demon hunter.' Cordelia: 'What's a rogue demon?'

Notes: 'We get at least an extra thousand if the seer's eyes are intact.' Although he doesn't appear anywhere except the credits, Glenn Quinn's presence is all over this episode. A story about loss, redemption and friendship, 'Parting Gift' moves *Angel* in a new direction without sacrificing the set-up of the previous episodes. The reintroduction of Wesley is well handled (and *very* funny) and there are some terrific moments like the strange menagerie of creatures at the auction and the marvellous breakfast cameo at the end.

Angel speaks Korean. Wesley speaks a smattering of the oriental language of Kungai demons. He was unaware that his former date, Cordelia (see *Buffy*: 'The Prom'), is working for Angel. Angel and Cordelia last saw Wesley in 'Graduation Day' Part 2, the episode in which Cordelia and Wesley kissed. Cordelia's memories of Doyle: 'He drank too much and his taste in clothing was like a Greek tragedy. And he could be really sweet sometimes. He was half demon. A secret he kept from me for, like, ever. I guess that's the reason he sometimes smelled weird?'

Wesley mentions that he was sacked by The Watchers' Council after Buffy would no longer take orders from them (in the aftermath of 'Graduation Day' Part 2, presumably). Wesley refers to the two Slayers assigned to him. One [Faith] 'turned evil and now vegetates in a coma' (this is the first definitive statement in either *Buffy* or *Angel* to confirm that Faith is still alive. See **18**, 'Five by Five', **19**, 'Sanctuary') and the other, Buffy, 'is a renegade'. The Byzantine axe Angel carries is the same one Cordelia wanted to sell in **8**, 'I Will Remember You'.

Popular fan theory: Doyle didn't actually intend to pass his powers to Cordy with the kiss in **9**, 'Hero' – he just snogged her because he knew he was going to die. It was actually The Powers That Be who did the passing. It's less noble, perhaps, but much more human and touching than Doyle giving the object of his affections a gift she doesn't want.

Alexis Sold: Although born in the US, Alexis Denisof had done most of his work in Britain and, seemingly, has an old friend to thank for the part of Wesley. 'They were looking for somebody "who thinks he's Pierce Brosnan but is actually George Lazenby",' Tony Head told Paul Simpson and Ruth Thomas in an interview for *Dream-Watch*. Head, the erudite British Watcher Rupert Giles on *Buffy*, suggested Alexis with whom he had worked in a 1993 theatre production of *Rope* in Chichester. 'He played one of the two guys who did the murder and he was fantastic, as indeed they've found on *Angel*. I'm hoping to get a little guest spot in *Angel* because I'd love to do some more work with Alexis. I had one scene with David [in the *Buffy* episode 'Pangs'] which was really nice. I miss the tension between the characters. It's nice to keep it alive. We've talked about it, but it's probably going to be next season . . .'

David Fury's Comments: Speaking to the Canadian Film Centre in Toronto, Fury answered questions regarding upcoming events on *Angel*: 'I enjoy Wesley. I reintroduced the character on *Angel* with my script **10**, 'Parting Gift'. It's fun to write him. There are dimensions to the character that are slowly being introduced. There's more to Wesley than people think.'

11
Somnambulist

US Transmission Date: 18 January 2000
UK Transmission Date: 17 March 2000 (Sky)

Writer: Tim Minear
Director: Rick Kolbe

Cast: Jeremy Renner (Penn),
Nick McCallum (Skateboard Kid),
Kimberleigh Aarn (Precinct Clerk),
Paul Webster (Uniform #1),
Brian Di Rito (Task Force Member #1)

A woman is stalked and killed in the L.A. night. Her murderer carves a cross on her cheek with a steel thimble. Dropping the body to the ground, the vampire raises his head. Angelus.

Angel awakens from his terrifying nightmare. But was it ...? At the crime scene, Kate Lockley examines the woman's injuries. Kate tells an officer that this is victim number three. Wesley arrives at Angel Investigations and hands Cordelia the mail, including the morning paper. Cordy returns everything to him, explaining it's not theirs, but the dentist's next door. Wesley sees the headlines and seems distracted. Angel emerges obviously in a bad mood, snapping at Cordelia. Unseen, Wesley hovers in the hallway watching Angel closely. Angel meets Kate at the police station and she admits she's working on a perplexing case, showing Angel the crime scene photos. After Angel leaves, Kate shares the killer's profile with her fellow officers. Alarmingly, the profile fits Angel perfectly. Angel restlessly prowls the city streets. Preparing to leave the office, Cordelia opens the door and is startled by Wesley who is armed with a stake. Cordy chastises him for entering Angel's office with the weapon in hand. Wesley explains that during his time as Watcher, he did extensive research on Angel. He says that Angelus carved a cross into the cheek of his victims before killing them. Cordelia tells Wesley to leave, saying that Angel is her friend and there's nothing he can say that will make her turn on him. At that moment Angel walks in and tells Cordy that Wesley is right. Wesley shoves a cross in Angel's face. Angel laughs, grabbing Wesley and taunting him that if he wanted to, he could easily kill him. Releasing Wesley, Angel tells them he has no memory of committing the crimes, but he's been having killing dreams. Dreams that he enjoyed. Wesley suggests Angel may be sleepwalking. Angel instructs his friends to chain him in his bed.

A woman flees a stalker. However, this woman is in eighteenth-century dress and is running down a cobbled street. Her attacker grabs her, carves the cross into her cheek, feeds, and then drops the body to the ground.

Angelus stands over her body. Angel is dreaming again, but jerks awake as Cordelia rushes in with the morning paper, gleefully informing him that there's been another murder. Angel is in the clear. Disagreeing, Angel flatly states that he did it. Another male vampire accompanied him, one Angelus sired. The dead woman was the young vampire's sister. He and Angelus decide his next kill should be his father. Angelus encourages Penn to kill his family, telling him that family blood is always the sweetest.

Penn, in his apartment in modern day Los Angeles, reads the newspaper about his crimes. One wall is covered with clippings. Angel, Wesley and Cordy discuss Penn's history. Wesley suggests Penn is trying to draw Angel out. Wesley warns Angel that he can't tell Kate about Penn, but Angel reasons that Kate could lead them to the vampire. Angel asks her about the investigation. He realises there's a familiar pattern to the murders. He asks Kate if she trusts him and Kate replies that she does. Angel pins a drawing of Penn to the wall, then gives Kate a description of his next victim. This proves to be accurate and Penn is spotted by the police before he can kill again. When the officers pull their guns, Penn escapes by leaping up to a second-storey window of an abandoned warehouse. Angel and Wesley, hearing the call for back-up, speed to the scene. Angel watches Kate enter the building. Intent on getting to Penn first, Angel scrambles up the warehouse's walls. Inside, Kate discovers that her weapon is useless against Penn but Angel drops through the ceiling, landing between them. Penn is pleased to see his mentor and invites Angel to join him in a drink. Angel informs Penn he's come to kill him and the two vampires fight as an incredulous Kate looks on before Penn escapes. Kate tells Angel that she shot Penn three times. Pulling her gun, she holds it inches from Angel's chest, asking if she shoots, will he too get up. When she asks Angel who he is, he tells her she already knows. Angel grabs the cross she's wearing, clutching it in his fist. Kate watches as Angel's hand begins to burn.

Kate goes over files from past decades that match the current spate of murders. At Angel Investigations,

Cordelia greets a client who tells her that the police referred him and begins to pump her for information about Kate and Angel. Cordelia notices his long black coat hanging on the back of the chair and realises he is Penn. She opens the blinds as Angel arrives and she passes him a stake as he apologises to Penn for making him a vampire. Angel accuses Penn of getting back at his father through the centuries by continuing to re-create the murders of his family. Before Angel can stake Penn, Wesley inadvertently provides Penn with a hostage as he warns Angel that he'll do something more inventive next time before escaping. Angel visits Kate. She tells him that she's researched him and Penn. She says she believes everything and pointedly calls him Angelus. Kate refuses to let him in, blaming him for murders because he's responsible for creating Penn. Angel says nothing in his defence. Threatening to stake him the next time she sees him, Kate slams the door in his face. Angel, Cordelia and Wesley discover that Penn stays at the same hotel every time he's in the area. Angel and Wesley break into Penn's apartment where they discover that Penn is planning an attack on some schoolchildren. Kate shows her fellow officers a picture of Angel. She tells them the killer may try to contact Angel, or he may even be the killer's next target. Penn suddenly speaks from the back of the room, telling Kate the drawing of him is a terrible likeness. Officers try to restrain Penn but he effortlessly tosses them aside and grabs Kate. Wesley and Angel are pulling into the underground garage, as all police units are leaving. Angel tells Wesley that Penn is there. Angel goes in search of Penn as he drags Kate through the tunnels. Penn is disappointed that Angel didn't fall for his decoy plan. Kate takes advantage of Penn's distraction and throws holy water in his face. Penn confronts Angel, telling him he was re-creating the murders in an effort to please his real father, Angelus. As Angel and Penn fight, Kate finds a piece of wood. Penn holds Angel in front of him, using him as a shield. Kate points the stake at Angel and drives it into him, angling it so the point passes through him and into Penn's heart.

Cordelia tells Angel that she's had a vision. Realising that he's upset, she tells him that his dreams weren't real. Angel reminds her that the beast is still within him. Cordelia replies that The Powers That Be didn't send the message to Angelus, they sent them to him. Angel laments that he could go bad again and, being a true friend, Cordelia assures him that if he does, she'll kill him.

Dreaming (as *Buffy* Often Proves) is Free: Given the subject matter it's remarkable that the episode doesn't make more of Angel's dreams. The ones we see are very literal with none of the surrealism we've come to expect from *Buffy*. The implication that Angel has a psychic link to Penn (and others he has sired) gives a context to this.

Denial, Thy Name is Penn: Angel correctly guesses that Penn has spent the last 200 years acting out the thrill of his first kills – those of his family. Penn's search for a father figure to please inevitably leads him back to his sire.

It's a Designer Label!: Cordelia has a mother-of-pearl bracelet. She wears some great gear including a striking red dress, a pink blouse and a white vest-style T-shirt. Angel seems to sleep in his day clothes and we discover that even his socks are black. Kate's chunky white sweater doesn't flatter her.

References: Angel: 'I taught him well' and Cordelia: 'A real *Psycho*-Wan Kenobi' combine the Hitchcock classic with *Star Wars*. 'Gallagher's changed his act more times than this dude has in the last two centuries' concerns an American stand-up comedian who is famous for his physical comedy often involving watermelons. Also referred to: Stephen King's *Apt Pupil* and the Angie Dickinson series *Police Woman*. 'Somnambulist' also features elements of two *Forever Knight* episodes: 'Bad Blood', in which Nick Knight had the chance to stop Jack the Ripper (who was also a product of his sire, LaCroix), and 'Blackwing', in which Nick dreams he is murdering women before the murders take place in real life.

Three of the areas targeted for the manhunt are Compton, Downey and Norwalk.

Bitch!: Kate: 'Thanks for the offer, but I don't need your help. I know what to do. Drive a stake right through the son-of-a-bitch's heart. And when that happens, I suggest you don't be there because the next time we meet, I'll do the same to you.'

The Charisma Show: Loads of great lines. On Wesley's stake: 'Kind of rude coming into a vampire's place of business with one of those, don't you think? Could be misinterpreted.' And: 'Great news, sports fans. There's been another killing. Maybe not so great news for the, you know, dead person. At least now we know that Mister "I'm so tortured" didn't do it.' And: 'You look half-dead. Which for someone who's completely dead, would be kind of neat.' And, best of all: 'My glamorous L.A. life. I get to make the coffee *and* chain the boss to the bed. Gotta join a union.'

L.A.-Speak: Cordelia: 'For a guy who's two hundred plus, you're not usually with-the-bags.' And: 'You wanted to compare *skinnies* on the current "evil happenings"?' And: 'No go. The DMV is *totally* stalker-phobic.' And: 'Jeez, Wesley. *Hover much?*'
Cordelia: 'That's our Angel, dour, sure, but not afraid to get personally involved in his work. And you're totally pumping me for information, aren't you? ... Oh crap. You're him. *He*. The guy. *Apt-Pupil*-boy.'
Kid: '*Hey, dude.*'

Cigarettes and Alcohol: The skateboard kid wants Penn to buy him beer from a liquor store.

Sex and Drugs and Rock'n'Roll: Wesley: 'Whilst executing my duties as Watcher in Sunnydale I did extensive research. Specifically on Angel, given his uncomfortable proximity to the Slayer.' Cordelia: 'He looked pretty comfortable to me.'

'You May Remember Me from Such Films and TV Series as ...': Jeremy Renner plays Ted Nida in the TV version of *The Net*. He was also Jack in the pilot episode of *Zoe, Duncan, Jack & Jane*. Kimberleigh Aarn appeared in *Bonfire of the Vanities* and *Presumed Innocent*.

Don't Give Up the Day Job: Director Rick Kolbe has a hugely impressive television CV including work on *Millennium*, *JAG*, *Star Trek: Voyager*, *Tales of the Gold Monkey*, *Star Trek: The Next Generation* (including the finale 'All Good Things'), *Magnum PI*, *Battlestar Galactica*, *CHiPS* and *The Rockford Files*.

Logic, Let Me Introduce You to This Window: As Penn and Angel stand over Penn's sister's body, their breath can be seen (see **15**, 'The Prodigal'). During the first fight between them, Penn grabs Angel by the shirt. The camera angle changes and he's holding Angel's coat instead. When Penn refers to Angel not meeting him in Italy he says he waited 'until the nineteenth century'. Angel gives his reason as getting held up in Rumania, which took place in 1898, so Penn must mean the *twentieth* century? Kate has never worn a cross on-screen, so it's convenient for her to be not only wearing one here, but fiddling with it so prominently. Angel leaves for the police station wearing a grey sweater, but when he arrives it's changed to a black shirt. When Kate arrives at the crime scene, she gets out of the car without latex gloves. We see her reach the police tape, the camera cuts to a frontal view and she has one glove on.

Angel is wearing the black leather trench coat when he comes through the ceiling at the warehouse; it gets covered in dust and plaster. He's wearing it in the next scene at the offices and it's as clean as a whistle. Do vampires sweat? Penn wipes perspiration from his face as he holds Wesley hostage. Kate tells Angel that she's read all about him. In *Buffy*: 'Angel', Giles says that he could find no mention of Angelus in the texts, but he did in *The Watchers' Diaries*. Kate's line, 'a demon with the face of an angel', is exactly what Giles reads in the *Buffy* episode. With The Council's desire for secrecy it seems somewhat remiss that they've let this vital publication into the public domain. When Kate is lying on the floor in the warehouse, her cross is inside her sweater, but when she gets up, it's on the outside.

How strong do you have to be to shove a blunted piece of wood through *two people*? How does Angel know Kate's address? Once again, Angel's photograph is taken despite cameras using mirrors as part of their focusing mechanism (see **1**, 'City Of').

I Just *Love* Your Accent: Wesley says, 'You'd be locked up faster than Lady Hamilton's virtue,' referring to Emily Lyon (1765–1815), the wife of Sir William Hamilton and the lover of Admiral Horatio Nelson. The Irish accents in this episode are woeful, though Boreanaz's is *slightly* better than Jeremy Renner's.

Quote/Unquote: Kate profiles the killer: 'Our suspect will be a white male. To the observer he will not seem a monster. His victims put up little or no struggle, so it's likely that he is charming, attractive, but at his core he is a loner. Possibly a dual personality who, once the crime has been committed, retains no memory of the act. He will not view his victims as subhuman, rather it's himself that he views as something other than human, more than human, a superior species. Stalking his prey, getting to know them. It's unlikely that he'll be married though he may have recently come off a long-term relationship that ended badly. We look for a precipitating event in cases such as this and a painful break-up is always at the top of the list. Prior to failing this relationship may have marked an inactive period in our suspect's life. He would have regarded it as a lifeline, his salvation, but once ended, it resulted in his recidivism. What is not in question is his experience. He's been doing this for a very long time, and he will do it again.'

Cordelia: 'I don't care how many files you have on all the horrible things he did back in the powdered-wig days. He's good now and he's my friend and nothing you or anyone else can say will make me turn on a friend.' Angel: 'Cordelia, he's right.' Cordelia, to Wesley: 'You stake him and I'll cut his head off.'

Wesley: 'Where did you get the police radio?' Angel: 'Police car.' Wesley: 'Oh dear.'

Angel: 'People change.' Penn: 'We're not *people*.'

Angel: 'I'm sorry for what I did to you, Penn, for what I turned you into.' Penn: 'First-class killer? An artist? A bold re-interpreter of the form?' Angel: 'Try cheesy hack. Look at you. You've been getting back at your father for over two hundred years. It's pathetic and clichéd. Probably got a killer shrine on your wall, huh? News clippings, magazine articles, maybe a few candles? You are *so* prosaic.'

Penn: 'You approved of me in ways my mortal father never did. You're my real father, Angelus.' Angel: 'Fine. You're grounded.'

Cordelia: 'You're not him, Angel. Not any more. The name I got in my vision, the message didn't come for Angelus, it came for you. And you have to trust that whoever that The Powers That Be be ... are ... is ... Anyway, they know the difference.'

Notes: 'I believe in Los Angeles. It's the city of dreams, a mystical oasis, built from a desert. But even sunny-blond-L.A. has its trashy dark roots.' The best episode of *Angel*'s first season, as Angel's past (in the shape of one of those he sired) comes back to haunt him. A multi-layered story, with a great part in it for Elisabeth Rohm and some memorable set-pieces. The Cordelia/Wesley double-act continues to delight, while the opening and final scenes are worthy of considerable praise. The continuity with various *Buffy* episodes is good too (see **15**, 'The Prodigal').

Angel says that he has a link which allows him to see through Penn's eyes while he's sleeping. (Presumably this ability exists for all those he has sired, including Spike and Drusilla?) Penn displays superhuman speed and agility, more than any vampire previously seen. Penn's family were Puritans, and he was sired by Angelus in the late 1700s. His first kill was his sister and for two hundred years he has relived his first nights as a vampire over and over again, enacting the kills as serial murders. He was in Los Angeles in 1929 and 1963, returning each time to the same spot. In 1929 it was the Regents Gardens Hotel and in 1963 it was the Cloverwood Apartments. He may also have been responsible for deaths in Boston in 1908. In current day L.A., he has been dubbed 'the Pope' by the tabloid press due to his 'signature': a cross carved into the victim's cheek. His four victims are: Reggie Sparks, a crossing guard; Jinny Markem, tenth grader; Jessica Halpern, 25, a waitress; and a nameless woman.

Penn: 'What's in Rumania?', Angel: 'Gypsies' refers to the events of 1898 seen in *Buffy*: 'Becoming' Part 1 (see **18**, 'Five by Five'). The dreams Angel has are a lot like those induced by The First Evil in *Buffy*: 'Amends'. Angel tells Penn, 'It *has* to end.' He used a very similar line to Drusilla in *Buffy*: 'Lie to Me'. It's something of a catch-phrase for Angel; he also used a variation to the Tahlmer demon in **2**, 'Lonely Hearts'. Angel Investigations is next to the business premises of Dr Folger, a dentist (see **22**, 'To Shanshu in L.A.'). The office has a water cooler.

The newspaper Wesley finds is the *Los Angeles Globe*, the same paper in which Cordelia and Wesley find references to Penn in 1929 and 1963 (is it a sister paper of the *Los Angeles Globe Register*? See **2**, 'Lonely Hearts', **5**, 'Rm W/a Vu'). Among the headlines in 1963 are 'US Delegation Attend Meet' and 'Europe Secret Pact Expected This Week'. The 1929 paper, deliciously, includes 'Wall St Confident As Stocks Surge'. In Wesley's extensive file on Angel a briefly glimpsed clipping had a headline involving President Roosevelt. L.A. has an occult book store called the Ancient Eye, which contains books on Angel's past, including an illustration of him feeding.

Alexis Denisof is added to the title-sequence with this episode, with clips from **10**, 'Parting Gift', **12**, 'Expecting' and **13**, 'She'.

Soundtrack: 'Leave You Far Behind' by Lunatic Calm.

Did You Know?: Perhaps unsurprisingly Charisma Carpenter hated her name (inspired by a brand of Avon perfume) when she was at school: 'How can you call yourself

Charisma when you go to a [strict private] school and your mom dresses you in pink hot-pants?' she asked *TV Guide*'s Jennifer Graham. 'They looked at me like I was Satan!' To James Brady, of *Parade*, she confessed that she called herself Chrissy for several years: 'It took me until I was thirteen to go by my real name.' After graduating, Charisma worked 'in my dad's San Diego restaurant, did property management and clerked at a video store. After doing those "bread and butter" jobs, I went back to school to study teaching. I never intended to be an actress.' Following a move to Los Angeles to visit a boyfriend, and at the time of the 1992 riots, she landed a job waitressing at Mirabelle's restaurant on Sunset Boulevard. 'I was the waitress from hell.' There, she got a theatrical agent and began hitting the audition trail which ultimately landed her in over twenty major commercials including a two-year stint as the 'Secret Antiperspirant' girl. 'Being on commercials is funny because no one ever recognises you. They just come up and say, 'Did I go to school with you?'' '

Tim Minear's Comments: From *The Watcher's Web*, on the writing of 'Somnambulist': 'Someone came up with the concept: "A serial killer [using] Angel's old M.O. It turns out it's a vampire he created in his heyday." We sat together in the writer's room with a big board. We beat out the story points scene by scene, creating the teaser and acts one-through-four. We sharpened and defined the elements (at first Angel thinks he's doing the murders in his sleep). Joss is involved in everything from concept to final approved story. The writer of the particular episode will then go off and flesh out the story. He or she will get notes on that outline and make some (hopefully minor) changes, then the writer will get the green light to go to script. 11,"Somnambulist" was actually my first script. 6, "Sense and Sensitivity" was the second I wrote, though the first produced. I like good old-fashioned ripping yarns. And I think "Somnambulist" is very funny, actually.'

12
Expecting

US Transmission Date: 25 January 2000
UK Transmission Date: 24 March 2000 (Sky)

Writer: Howard Gordon
Director: David Semel

Cast: Daphnee Duplaix (Sarina),
Ken Marino (Wilson Christopher),
Josh Randall (Bartender),
Doug Tompos (Doctor Wasserman),
Louisette Geiss (Emily), Julie Quinn (Pregnant Woman),
Maggie Connelly (Nurse), Steven Roy (Jason)

Cordelia prepares for a night out with some friends while explaining her unique filing system to a baffled Angel. Wesley has a new axe that he's eager to try out. Sarina and Emily arrive. When the girls compliment Wesley on his axe, he inadvertently plunges it into the wall. Sarina says that Cordy is going on her third date with Wilson Christopher just as Cordelia suffers a vision. She tells Angel and Wesley that an egg is about to hatch and writes an address, then she and her friends leave. Angel and Wesley locate the house and Angel kicks in the front door; Wesley rushes in only to find an elderly couple. Claiming to be termite exterminators, Angel and Wesley embarrassingly back out of the house and find that the source of their quest is next door. After a messy battle they successfully kill the hatchling before it can escape. The girls are at an elite club Lounge La Brea. Cordelia and Wilson are getting along fabulously. Later in the evening, Wilson drives Cordy home. When he kisses her good-night, Cordelia invites him inside. She turns the lights down but Phantom Dennis turns them back up. Cordy explains that it's bad wiring, and retreats to the kitchen. Once alone, she tells Dennis to behave. Wilson finds her talking to herself and she admits to having a ghost. Wilson kisses her and they end up going to bed together. The next morning, Cordelia wakes to discover that she's alone, and very late for work. Throwing back the covers she finds herself extremely pregnant. Worried by Cordelia's non-appearance, Angel and Wesley arrive at her apartment. They find Cordelia still in bed. Cordy tells them she's ready to wake up from her bad dream now. Angel assures her they have come to help and asks her to call Wilson, but the number has been disconnected. Angel suspects that Wilson is a demon who can only reproduce by impregnating human women. He tells Wesley to take Cordelia for a prenatal exam while he goes in search of the father. Wesley tells the doctor he and Cordy have just moved from England. An ultrasound scan is performed and they discover at least six heartbeats. Extracting some amniotic fluid, a nurse watches in horror as the syringe cracks and the fluid burns a hole in the floor. The Lounge La Brea bartender tells Angel that Sarina may know Wilson's whereabouts. At her apartment Angel finds a very pregnant Sarina who admits that she knew something wasn't right with the guys they were dating.

Cordelia tells Wesley there are seven babies and they are trying to communicate with her. Rationalising that Angel and Doyle are not human, she tries to reassure herself. Angel tells Wesley that he suspects there are more women in the same condition. Wilson and his buddies hang out at an elite gun club, he says, and he intends to locate them and find out how to terminate the pregnancies. Angel finds Wilson at the club. Wilson refuses to provide Angel with any information but Angel says that he knows what is going on. A demon has permeated them with his life-force and they impregnate unsuspecting women in exchange for wealth. Wilson shoots Angel. Enraged, Angel attacks, quickly defeating his opponents.

Wesley is researching the demon when Cordelia knocks him unconscious saying that no one is going to hurt her babies. Cordelia takes the tunnels to a chemical plant. Several other women, including Sarina, are also there. Angel calls Wesley who explains that Cordy became violent. Angel believes that Cordelia has a telepathic link with the demon and that she's probably on her way to an industrial park in Reseda, where Wilson and his friends built a shrine. Wesley surmises that the telepathic link between the women and the demon is what's keeping the unborn offspring alive. Angel asks if Wesley's a good shot.

The women move to a large birthing pool. Wesley sternly instructs them to come out, warning Cordelia that if she doesn't she'll die. The huge demon emerges and demands to know who the intruder is. Wesley announces that he's a rogue demon hunter and reminds the demon of the story of David and Goliath. Angel appears rolling a tank of liquid nitrogen which he hurls towards the demon. Wesley then shoots the tank, the nitrogen freezing the demon solid. Cordelia and the others feel their babies dying inside them. Cordy shatters the frozen demon with a pulley.

Cordy arrives back at work and assures Angel and Wesley that she's stronger than the demon surrogates thought. She admits that she's learned that there are two people whom she can trust with her life.

Dudes and Babes: Cordelia's friends Emily and Sarina are gorgeous while the bar sequences include lots of girls in short skirts. Wilson and his hunky chums surely don't need a demon's help to attract the ladies?

It's a Designer Label!: What on earth is Cordelia wearing in the opening scenes? It looks like a green bra with a triangular dangly bit at the front.

References: Cordelia's nickname for her ghostly flatmate, Phantom Dennis, seems to be a pun on the title of *Star Wars: Episode 1 – The Phantom Menace. Rosemary's Baby*, *I Don't Want To Be Born*, *The Unborn*, *Demon Seed* and *To The Devil . . . A Daughter* are obvious recurring riffs, given the subject matter, while aspects of the story bear a resemblance to *The Midwich Cuckoos*. Also referenced: The Joker from *Batman*, the film version of *Evita* (and its star, Madonna), *The Dating Game*, KC and the Sunshine

Band's 'Shake Your Booty' and the biblical story of David and Goliath.

Bitch!: Wilson: 'This is a private club, featured word, *private.*' Angel: 'You don't talk to me, I'll kick your ass. Featured word, *ass.*'

'West Hollywood'?: Cordelia's girlfriends jump to conclusions about Wes and Angel. 'The good ones are always gay.' Wesley notes: 'I didn't mean "doxy" in a sexually promiscuous sense. You don't think sticking the axe in the wall put them off?' Angel: 'That was charming.' Wesley: 'What about the fact they thought we were gay?' Angel: 'Adds mystery.'

The Charisma Show: Like 5, 'Rm W/a Vu', this is primarily Cordelia's story and Charisma has the opportunity to display the range of her talent, being both funny and dramatic. Some of her exchanges with Angel are among the series' finest: 'Have you talked to Wilson?' Cordelia: 'What would I say to him? "I had a really great time and I think you left something at my place"?' Angel: 'You're not alone.' Cordelia: 'That's sort of the problem, isn't it?'

L.A.-Speak: Cordelia: 'You're photographing all these gorgeous, famous people. *Where's the insecure?*'

Sarina: 'Sometimes the guys were like, jumpy. But this town, you know? Everything is fake. Things are weird and you stop asking questions.' And: 'Jase, *moolah!*'

Angel: 'I'm starting to get the big picture here. You guys proxy for big daddy demon.'

Cigarettes and Alcohol: Sarina drinks (heavily) from a bottle of wine.

Sex and Drugs and Rock'n'Roll: The Hacksaw Beast is described as an inner earth and procrea-parasitic demon. It is humanoid but much bigger than a human and very hard to kill. The young are fed and maintained by a telepathic link to their parent in the early stages of development. This telepathic influence also extends to the surrogate mothers to control them.

Sarina's line 'nice axe', is *loaded* with innuendo. Cordelia assures Angel that the sex she had with Wilson was 'safe'. This is the first episode to explicitly deal with sexual intercourse.

'You May Remember Me from Such Centrefolds as . . .': Daphnee Duplaix was *Playboy*'s 'Playmate of the Month' for July 1997.

'You May Remember Me from Such TV Series as . . .': Ken Marino played Steve in the US remake of *Men Behaving Badly*.

Don't Give Up the Day Job: Away from acting, Josh Randall was a grip on movies like *Pure Danger* and *Skyscraper* while Steven Roy was best boy on *Electra* and an electrician on *Street Law*. Director David Semel's previous work includes episodes of *Dawson's Creek* and *The Love Boat: The Next Wave*.

There's a Ghost in My House: 'Dennis, knock it off. This is the one guy I've actually liked in a long time and if you keep killing the mood, I'll kill you. All right, empty threat, you being a ghost and already dead and all. But I'll do something worse. I'll play *Evita* around the clock. The one with Madonna.'

In one of the most touching moments of the season, a tearful Cordelia sitting in bed is firstly offered a tissue by Phantom Dennis and then tucked in.

Logic, Let Me Introduce You to This Window: When Angel bribes the bartender, the reflection of his hands can be seen on the bar. Sarina's apartment building uses the same hall set as Barney's in **10**, 'Parting Gift'. When the syringe drops to the floor, it has no writing on it, but another shot shows writing on the tube. The light is visible in the office fridge even after its door is closed. During the gun-club fight, part of the wall comes off; Angel steps on it and you can hear the polyfoam crunch. Where does Cordelia get her maternity denims from?

When Cordelia drinks the blood, some dribbles from her mouth and she wipes it with her sleeve yet there's no blood on her overalls or her sleeve in later scenes. Someone coughs as Angel enters the Lounge La Brea.

I Just *Love* Your Accent: Wesley is compared to Hugh Grant. He says: 'No one is more fond of Cordelia than I, but if she wants to go *gadabouting* with those *doxies* . . .' Blimey, that's a bit judgemental. Plus he's the only English person to use the phrase 'trendy hot spot' since 1975. Cordelia says that compared to her old apartment the new one is Buckingham Palace. Angel and Wesley breaking into the wrong house is *very* reminiscent of a sequence in the 1978 'Hard Men' episode of the British police series *The Sweeney* but that's most likely a coincidence as few Americans have even heard of it.

Quote/Unquote: Bartender: 'You're the boyfriend?' Angel: 'No. I'm family.'

Angel: 'Why is Mrs Benson filed under "P"?' Cordelia: 'Because she's from France. Remember what a pain she was?' Angel: 'It made me wanna drink a lot.' Cordelia: 'That's the French for ya.'

Wesley's heroic moment: 'I'm here to fight you, sir. To the death. Preferably yours.'

Cordelia: 'I've learned men are evil. Oh, wait. I knew that. I learned that L.A. is full of self-serving phoneys. Nope, had that one down too. Sex is bad?' Angel: 'We all knew that.' Cordelia: 'I learned that I have two people I trust absolutely with my life and that part's new.'

Notes: 'You're afraid of what's inside of me.' Derivative, but a lot of fun, 'Expecting' takes a potentially ludicrous situation and creates an amusing and at times touching story from it.

Angel says that bright light hurts his eyes and that he doesn't hum (although we saw Angelus do so in *Buffy*: 'Killed By Death'). He knows that Wilson is human, probably from his smell (see **1**, 'City Of'). The sword Angel uses to kill the Tahval demon appears to be the one Doyle gave him to kill the sewer beast in **6**, 'Sense and Sensitivity'.

Wesley claims to have some allergies, but we don't believe a word of it. Wesley and Cordelia pose as a married couple using the alias of Mr and Mrs Penborne when they visit the gynaecologist. Wesley has a new Bavarian hunting axe. Cordelia refers to coming to L.A. as like 'skydiving without a parachute except for the smashing your body to bits part. Actually, no, it was like that, too.'

Soundtrack: Splashdown's 'Games You Play' and an unknown title by the band Royal Crown Review.

Joss Whedon's Comments: Asked by *DreamWatch* about the more experimental episodes of *Buffy* and *Angel* and how they compare to those done by other series, Joss confessed: 'I don't want to do things that are just a wink to the audience. I thought the *X-Files/Cops* thing ['X-COPS'] made sense, it actually worked in a weird way. But *Felicity* did *The Twilight Zone*, *Chicago Hope* did a musical show and I don't want to be one of those shows that is self-indulgent. The great thing about *Buffy* and *Angel* is that they are so baroque, strange and fantastical that you can get away with those things so, whether it be a musical episode, which everybody always talks about, it makes perfect sense in the *Buffy*-universe. The episode that I did at the end of this season [*Buffy*: 'Restless'] is all dreams and it is unbelievably bizarre, but it's in a world where it makes sense. As long as we don't start getting cutesy [or] stupid, we have opportunities to go to new places.'

13
She

US Transmission Date: 8 February 2000
UK Transmission Date: 31 March 2000 (Sky)

Writers: David Greenwalt, Marti Noxon
Director: David Greenwalt

Cast: Bai Ling (Jhiera), Colby French (Tay),
Heather Stephens (Captured Demon Girl),
Sean Gunn (Palm Ridge Spa Worker),
Tracy Costello (Laura), Andre L. Roberson (Diego),
P.J. Marino (Peter Wilkers), Honor Bliss (Girl),
Chris Durand (Demon Henchman #1),
Alison Simpson (Demon Girl #1),
Lucas Dudley (Security Guard)

Cordelia is having a party at her apartment. Wesley dances, embarrassingly, while an uncomfortable Angel looks on. One of Cordy's friends, Laura, asks Angel if he'd like to dance. Angel declines and, feeling awkward, moves to the seemingly deserted kitchen. A chair slides back from the table as Phantom Dennis offers Angel a seat and a beer.

At an ice factory a man guards a coffin-like box. Hearing sounds from within he opens it. What he finds inside terrifies him. At the office Cordelia complains about Angel's lack of social skills. Cordelia has a vision about the factory and Angel and Wesley find a burned corpse with a security company business card in the dead man's pocket. Angel meets Tay who claims to be from another dimension, sent to retrieve an entity that has crossed over. He warns Angel not to interfere. Back at Angel Investigations, Angel gives Wesley a sketch of Tay. Wesley suggests that he travelled to their dimension via a portal. Wesley and Cordy research, while Angel checks out the Security Company, breaking into their offices. He finds an invoice from the Jericho Ice Company but is attacked by a beautiful but powerful woman. She questions Angel about his identity and who's paying him to hunt 'them'. Angel explains that he's looking for someone who burns people alive. She drives off and Angel follows in his car. Angel calls Cordelia on his cellphone. Cordy reports that four other bodies were burned in a similar manner. Angel follows the woman to an art gallery. She finds a guard and tells him that a man wearing a black coat is following her. Angel poses as a guide while the guards search for him in vain. Wesley has found something on the Vigories of Oden Tal. He tells Cordelia that in their dimension women are slaves.

Angel follows the woman to the storage area. When they confront one another she realises Angel is a vampire, and tells him he must leave as a portal opens and a naked girl falls through. Tay and five henchmen burst in, telling Angel the two women belong to them. Angel attacks Tay while his men grab the girl and drag her to a car. Angel asks the woman what will happen to the girl. She replies that she will be 'unmade'. Tay takes the kidnapped girl to a warehouse and removes the ridge between her shoulder blades.

The woman, Jhiera, explains that she was helping the girl escape their homeland. In Oden Tal, the female passion centre, the Ko, is located in the ridge between their shoulders. Upon removing the Ko, males control the females. Jhiera is the first of her kind to escape and says it took her months to learn to control her power. Angel asks who burned the guard at the ice factory and Jhiera admits it was one of her girls. Angel says he will help Jhiera but the killing must stop. Jhiera says she doesn't need his help. Wesley and Cordelia sneak into the warehouse where they overhear Tay telling the kidnapped girl that she's going home. Tay tells his men that their mission is not over until they have captured Jhiera.

Jhiera arrives at the Palm Springs Spa, where a man is guarding three girls lying in tubs filled with ice. She warns him that they need to move the girls. He suggests a place in the desert. Wesley and Cordelia overhear Tay being told the location of the girls. They find Angel and go to the Palm Springs Spa. Angel finds Jhiera with the girls in the spa room and warns her that Tay is on his way. Wesley and Cordelia get the girls out while Angel and Jhiera leap from the shadows and attack Tay's men. Tay threatens to kill Wesley and Cordelia if the girls aren't returned to him. Jhiera simply says, 'Then, they'll die,' and walks out. Cordy and Wesley simultaneously attack their captors and the fight resumes. Outside Tay and one of his men grab

Jhiera and are about to remove her Ko when Angel comes to her rescue. Jhiera runs to the truck and drives off with her precious cargo. Angel releases Tay and warns him that if he continues to track the women, he'll gain another enemy. Later Jhiera visits Angel and tells him the girls are safe.

Dreaming (as *Buffy* Often Proves) is Free: Cordelia says Wesley awoke her from a dream about a 'Going Out of Business' sale at Neiman's. Not so much free, then, as *cheap*.

Dudes and Babes: For the fellahs, Cordelia's party. Check out the *skirt*. The extremely short dress worn by the girl following Jhiera up the steps to the art gallery deserves a few seconds of your time. And speaking of Jhiera, those leather pants ... Cordelia's friend Laura has a masters degree in fine arts and runs her own 'selling sandwiches from a cart' business.

The ladies, on the other hand, may like to ponder on yet another appearance of Boreanaz topless for no adequate reason. It's also worth keeping your finger on the 'pause' button during the sequence where the portal opens for the first time. The wind effects are so strong, they blow David's shirt up and reveal his belly button.

It's a Designer Label!: Orange shirt alert. The fashion store Neiman-Marcus in mentioned (see **1**, 'City Of'). Wesley's 'great sweater' is the talk of the party. Unfortunately, he doesn't know who knitted it and this loses him the chance of a date. Cordelia's multi-coloured party dress is wonderful, while her extremely tight jeans and black boots get a lot of screen time.

References: The title is from H. Rider Haggard's eponymous 1886 novel. In the episode's best scene Angel describes the 1862 painting *La Musique Aux Tuileries* by French Impressionist Edouard Manet (1832–1883). 'On the left one spies the painter himself. In the middle distance is the poet and critic Baudelaire, a friend of the artist. Now, Baudelaire, interesting fellow. In his poem *Le Vampyr* he wrote: "Thou who abruptly as a knife didst come into my heart." He strongly believed that evil forces surrounded mankind and some even speculated that the poem was about a real vampire. Oh, and Baudelaire was actually a little taller and a lot drunker than he is depicted here.' The implication being that Angel knew symbolist poet Charles Baudelaire (1821–1867), the author of *Les Fleurs Du Mal*, and that *Le Vampyr* is about Angel himself. Also referenced: *Carrie*, English novelist Nancy Mitford (1904–1973), Steve and David Paymer (see **5**, 'Rm W/a Vu') and the Sizzler steakhouse restaurant chain.

During the car-tailing sequence, the marquee on the Los Angeles Theater is for the movie *Heartbreaker*. And just as we were all starting to think they'd given up on the obvious visual references to *Batman*, watch Angel jumping off the roof of the security firm.

Bitch!: Cordelia to Wesley: 'Grovelling isn't just a way of life for you, it's an art.'

And, to Jhiera: 'Look who's here. Can I get you something? Knife to our throat so you can run away?'

'West Hollywood'?: Wesley hugging Angel?

The Charisma Show: On Angel's mood at the party: 'I'm so glad you came. You know how parties are, you're always worried that no one's going to suck the energy out of the room like a giant black hole of boring despair. But there you were in the clinch.' On Laura: 'It's not like Laura's going to throw you down on the living room floor and tear off all of your . . . Well, actually, Laura . . .' On her vision: 'Exploding eyeballs. Did I mention I hate this gig?'

L.A.-Speak: Cordelia: 'Gross. Oh, *eww* is all.' And: 'A *hottie*, huh? I guess she's that all right. What with the *sizzle*?' And: 'Stop kissing butt.'

Spa Guy: '*Excellent*. Just when I need the artistic eye of a Goddess.' And: 'They're *chillin*'. The little sisters are fine.' And: 'Man, that's *lame*.' And: 'My shaman has a place in the desert. He never could turn away scantily clad women in distress, from any dimension.' Can we say 'scene-stealing'?

Not Exactly a Haven for the Sisters: Like *Buffy*'s 'Beauty and the Beast' (also a Marti Noxon script), this episode (with its castration metaphor) tries to make big statements but ends up full of stereotypes and dangerously obvious solutions. Complex issues about empowerment are turned into something not far short of penis-envy here.

Cigarettes and Alcohol: 'Let the consumption of cold things begin.' There's a link between Angel drinking beer at Cordelia's party and the security man at the ice factory also having a can. After Cordelia's vision she holds a glass of something to her throbbing temple. It *could* be iced water, but it may just as easily be neat vodka.

Cordelia: 'Can I get you some blood or anything?' Angel: 'I'm good.'

Sex and Drugs and Rock'n'Roll: The Vigories are from another dimension called Oden Tal. The males are fierce warriors. The females have raised ridges running down either cheek, violet eyes and a row of ridges on their back. These are called the Ko. This area contains their personality and passion. When they come of age, the Ko controls their physical and sexual power and signals when they are aroused. Initially, there is a period where the Ko manifests itself as heat and intense strength. At first the girls cannot control this power and need to be cooled constantly. With practice they can use the power at will. When the Ko is removed they become docile. Females are enslaved by the males who cut off their Ko.

Cordelia: 'Diego, *pants on!*'

Wesley: 'What say a couple of brooding demon hunters start chatting up some of the fillies?' Wesley says the thing he enjoyed most about the party was 'the tiny Reubens and the shrimp puffs'. A man of taste, clearly.

'You May Remember Me from Such Films as . . .': Bai Ling was one of *People* magazine's '50 Most Beautiful People in the World in 1998'. She played Tuptim in *Anna and the*

King and Miss East in *Wild Wild West*. She can also be seen in *Nixon* and *The Crow*. Heather Stephens's movies include *Clubland* and *Dante's Peak* while Lucas Dudley appears in *Solo* and *Letters From a Killer*.

Don't Give Up the Day Job: Alison Simpson is a dancer who can be seen in *The Big Lebowski*. She also appeared in *Man on the Moon*. Chris Durand is probably best known for playing Michael Meyers in *Halloween H20: Twenty Years Later* but his stuntwork is visible in *Soldier*, *Slappy and the Stinkers*, *Scream 2*, *The Mask* and *Maniac Cop 2* and *3*.

There's a Ghost in My House: Angel: 'Hi, Dennis. How are you doing? Still dead? I know the feeling.'

Logic, Let Me Introduce You to This Window: Are vampires pan-dimensional? If not, how does Jhiera know what one is? Angel appears to be in direct sunlight on more than one occasion.

I Just *Love* Your Accent: Wesley: 'I feel rather chipper myself. That was quite a soirée last night.' In **12**, 'Expecting', Wesley blamed the crumbling of his stiff-upper-lip on allergies, this time it's 'something in my eye'. *Sure.*

Motors: Angel's licence plate is NKD 714. Jhiera drives a red Dodge Durango.

Quote/Unquote: Angel: 'The quiet reserved thing, don't you think it makes me, kinda cool?' Cordelia (points at Wesley): '*He* was cooler.' Angel: 'Now I'm depressed.'

Notes: 'Call me old-fashioned, but I can't allow tourists to go around torching locals.' A real disappointment. 'She', with its heavy-handed moralising and lack of interesting characters, is paced with all of the tension of the snapped elastic band. And it's *annoyingly* P.C. The hole where the rain got in this season, clearly. Wesley's three (count 'em) pratfalls during the episode are an insult to both the character (who is, ironically, just starting to find his feet) and the audience (who are trying hard to like him). Plus, it's difficult to escape a nagging suspicion that this is actually a rejected *Deep Space 9* script with its 'dimensional portals'.

Angel tells Cordelia about his period in Hell (see *Buffy*: 'Becoming' Part 2, 'Anne', 'Faith, Hope and Trick') for the first time. He notes that: 'In Hell you tend to know a lot of the people,' unlike Cordelia's party. He says he has two modes with people: 'bite' or 'avoid'. The cellphone that Cordelia gave Angel is a Motorola Digital. The date it displays is 12 January 2000. Angel believes that cellphones were invented by a 'bored warlock'. Cordelia thinks that 'a guy who knows how to use an ancient scythian short bow' should be able to figure out how to use a phone. Cordelia uses the *Los Angeles Globe-Register* (see **2**, 'Lonely Hearts', **5**, 'Rm W/a Vu', **11**, 'Somnambulist') to research four similar killings in the last eleven months. When Angel tells Jhiera that 'gypsies have a strange sense of humour', this is not only a reference to his curse (see *Buffy*: 'Becoming' Part 2 and **18**, 'Five by Five') but also a line from the *Angel Demo Reel*. Angel's grappling hook puts in a first appearance since **2**, 'Lonely Hearts'. Wesley officially joins the firm in this episode. The invoice lists the number for the ice factory as 555-0197.

Soundtrack: 'Strangelove Addiction' by Supreme Beings of Leisure, 'In Time' by Morphic Field and 'Light Years On' by 60 Channels. The music Angel and Wesley (ahem) 'dance' to is called 'Pure Roots' from *Non-Stop Music Library*.

Did You Know?: David Boreanaz has a phobia about chickens. Poor lamb! Charisma, on the other hand, suffers from a phobia of tarantulas. That's much more understandable.

You Dancin'?: Highlight of the episode is the sequence where Wesley dances (love Angel's little smirk while watching him) and then Angel imagines what his own efforts at grooving would be like. And in case you miss it first time around, the sequence is repeated beneath the closing credits. It's so funny you'll have trouble staying upright and will temporarily forget what a thoroughly rotten episode this is.

14
I've Got You Under My Skin

US Transmission Date: 15 February 2000
UK Transmission Date: 7 April 2000 (Sky)

Teleplay: Jeannine Renshaw
Story: David Greenwalt, Jeannine Renshaw
Director: Robert David Price

Cast: Will Kempe (Seth Anderson),
Katy Boyer (Paige Anderson),
Anthony Cistaro (Ethros Demon),
Jesse James (Ryan Anderson),
Ashley Edner (Stephanie Anderson),
Patience Cleveland (Nun), Jerry Lambert (Rick The Clerk)

Wesley shows Angel an ornate knife for use in killing Kek demons. Angel reminds Wesley that they are extinct. Cordelia uses the knife to cut the brownie she has cooked for them. Angel accidentally calls Wesley, Doyle.

In a suburban home a boy, Ryan, and his sister are fighting. Their parents tell them it's time for bed. Once the children are tucked in, their father padlocks the door. Cordelia asks Angel about Doyle and Angel admits he feels responsible for his death. Cordelia has a vision of Ryan. Wesley and Angel drive to his home as he escapes from his room and rushes into the road in front of an oncoming car. Angel saves Ryan, hurting himself in the process. Ryan's father, Seth, comes running from the house. He chastises the boy as Paige, his mother, joins them. Paige thanks Angel and noticing his injury, invites him inside. Paige cleans the wound as Angel questions them about Ryan. Seth is evasive. Outside, Wesley searches the grounds and discovers a suspicious fluid around the foundation of the house. Paige says she collects angels when Angel tells her his name and she invites him for dinner the following evening. Joining Wesley, Angel tells him all is not well in the house. Wesley produces a phial of the glowing liquid. Angel recognises it as Plakticine. Someone inside is possessed by a demon.

Cordelia discovers that the family have moved from city to city for several years. She asks Wesley about the fluid and he tells her it's excrement from an Ethros demon. Wesley and Angel decide they need an exorcist. Cordy asks, who is it that needs exorcising? Angel mentions the father and Wesley tells them a father doesn't need to be possessed to terrify his children. Wesley suggests they reveal the demon by feeding it Psylis Eucalipsis powder. Angel returns to the home with freshly baked brownies. After the meal, while Paige gets Angel's brownies, Angel plays with Ryan and his sister, Stephanie. Paige gives everyone a brownie and Angel watches as they all eat them. Ryan's face contorts as Angel explains the boy is possessed by a demon. Seth asks what Angel needs. He calls Wesley, who admits he's having trouble finding a priest to perform the exorcism. Angel escorts the family to his apartment. Angel cautions everyone not to break the circle, no matter how much Ryan pleads for them to come to him. Angel and Wesley go to a Catholic church where a nun senses the demon within Angel. Angel admits that he is what she thinks he is but says that he is trying to help someone. The nun warns them that an Ethros demon is even more dangerous than Angel.

Ryan begs Paige to release him. Cordelia assures them that Angel and Wesley will return shortly. Wesley tells Angel their only option is for him to perform the exorcism. Angel agrees, but vows to be at his side. Ryan is lying in bed, his face green. Wesley and Angel return as Paige breaks the circle of powder. Ryan grabs her around the throat as Angel and Wesley are trapped in the elevator. They climb out and Wesley begins the exorcism pouring binding powder around the bed. Angel hands him a Bible before backing out of the room. Cordelia says that an Ethros demon can be trapped in an Ethros box, without which it will leap into the nearest living person. Angel sends her to *Rick's Magick-N-Stuff* for a box. Wesley is taunted by the demon who says that the Council fired him because he was inadequate and that his father knew he never lived up to his potential, even after being locked under the stairs. Wesley falters and Angel enters the room. The demon tells Angel that Wesley is planning to kill him.

Angel tells Wesley that the exorcism is too dangerous. The kitchen begins to tremble and a bag of Ryan's marbles scatters across the table, forming the words, 'Save Me'. Wesley tells Angel that they don't have a choice. They hear Doyle's voice coming from the bedroom. Ryan taunts Angel, telling him Doyle is talking to him. Enraged Angel wraps a cloth around his hand and picks up a cross. Cordelia returns with the box. Brushing past her, Angel presses the cross on to Ryan's chest. The demon explodes from the boy in a flash of light and shoots towards the box held by Wesley and Cordelia. The demon smashes through the box and disappears. Wesley follows a trail of Plakticine through the apartment. He tells Angel the demon has escaped. Angel speculates the demon is tired and will need to regenerate before possessing someone again. Wesley and Angel easily track the demon by the Plakticine to some caves. Wesley taunts the creature about not getting the boy's soul. The demon asks, 'What soul?' It tells Wesley and Angel that it found no conscience, no fear, just a black void within Ryan. Angel realises that it was the demon that sent the 'Save Me' message. Wesley solemnly reminds Angel that Ryan is back with his family as Angel kills the demon to put it out of its misery.

After Seth and Paige are asleep, Ryan sneaks into their bedroom and takes matches off the night table, then he pours gasoline around his sister's bed setting the room ablaze. Seth and Paige escape from their bedroom but the fire has spread and they can't reach Stephanie. Angel jumps through the window and rescues Stephanie. Kate puts Ryan into police care.

Denial, Thy Name is Paige: One of the worst cases witnessed since Joyce Summers. Poor Paige just doesn't want to admit that her son is a murdering monster, does she?

It's a Designer Label!: Cordelia suggests that Wesley wears too much cologne. Definitely 'West Hollywood', then? Cordelia's white trainers and pink roll-neck sweater put in debut appearances.

References: 'I remember the children's rhyme. How come they're all full of death and cradles falling and mice getting tails cut off? The whole thing needs a ratings system,' is Cordelia's rant about nursery rhymes (specifically *Rock A-Bye, Baby* and *Three Blind Mice*). Cordelia twice refers to *The Exorcist* ('head spins around?' and 'I wonder if I should put plastic down. Are you expecting any big vomiting here because I saw the movie?' confirming an earlier observation that Cordelia had seen the movie in *Buffy*: 'I Only Have Eyes For You') and it's an obvious influence on the plot. Wesley says he owns two Thighmasters (the second was a free gift accompanying his *Buns of Steel* – a popular workout video). Also referenced: *The Bad Seed* and a misquote from Evelyn Waugh's *A Handful of Dust* ('I'll show you *fear*'). The title of the episode is taken from the Cole Porter song made famous by Frank Sinatra. Cordelia's 'Kill, kill, kill' is a line from The Doors' 'The End'. The cards that Ryan and Stephanie have look like Pokémon trading cards.

L.A.-Speak: Cordelia: 'You don't have to be *Joe-Stoic* about his dying. I know that you have this unflappable vibe working for you, but you don't have to do that for me.' Angel: 'I'm not unflappable.' Cordelia: 'Great, so *flap*.'

Cordy: 'No one could have said "demon poo" before I touched it?' And: '*Jeez*, we got it. Circle, angry, kill, kill, kill. Go to church already.'

Cigarettes and Alcohol: Seth Anderson smokes. Angel says that this doesn't bother him.

Sex and Drugs and Chocolate Brownies: Cordelia's recipe for chocolate brownies was handed down to her by her mother (who got it from *her* housekeeper). And she's improvised a little. Wesley is less than enthusiastic about the results. Angel's attempts are more successful, at least in confirming the presence of a demon in the Anderson household.

'You May Remember Me from Such Films and TV Series as . . .': Will Kempe was Rick Von Sloneker in *The Last Days of Disco*, Acid Sid in *Pledge Night* and Legs Diamond in *Hit the Dutchman*. Katy Boyer appears in *The Lost World: Jurassic Park* and, on TV, in *Babylon 5*, *Beauty and the Beast* and *Silk Stalkings*. Jesse James can be seen in *Gods and Monsters*, *Message in a Bottle* and the excellent *X-Files* episode 'The Uninvited'. Nine-year-old Ashley Edner has also been in *The X-Files* and plays Kelly in *Malcolm in the Middle*. She's also done voice-artist work on *Hanging On* and *Lion King II: Simba's Pride*. By contrast, Patience Cleveland played Miss Hanson in the 1960s classic series *Green Acres* and also appeared in *Psycho II*.

Don't Give Up the Day Job: Jerry Lambert is also a composer, his music being heard in *Texas Chainsaw Massacre 2* and *Hidden Agenda*, though his most famous work is the theme song to *It's Garry Shandling's Show*.

Logic, Let Me Introduce You to This Window: Angel tells Paige, 'I'm not a big bleeder.' As noted on several occasions he shouldn't be a bleeder *at all*, as his heart doesn't beat. Why didn't the car that almost ran over Ryan stop? Angel's reflection is visible on his desk in the opening scene. If holy objects like crosses and holy water burn a vampire, then why is Angel able to hold a copy of the Bible without bursting into flames? There are bars on Stephanie's windows early in the episode, yet when Angel saves her from the fire, they're gone.

I Just *Love* Your Accent: Wesley's scarred relationship with his father is dealt with. (It has some parallels with Angel's relationship with *his* father. See **15**, 'The Prodigal'). 'A father doesn't have to be possessed to terrorise his children' is a telling statement and explains a lot about Wesley's personality.

Quote/Unquote: Angel: 'Cordelia, just put down the very sharp knife.'

Stephanie: 'Angel's funny'. Seth (dryly): 'He hides it well.'

Nun: 'You would come into a place of worship?' Angel: 'I'm not what you think.'

Ethros: 'Do you know what the most frightening thing in the world is? Nothing. That's what I found in the boy. No conscience, no fear, no humanity, just a black void . . . That boy's mind was the blackest Hell I've ever known. When he slept, I could whisper in him. I tried to get him to end his life, even if it meant ending mine. I had given up hope. I know you bring death. I do not fear it. The only thing I have ever feared is in that house.'

Notes: 'I like to think of myself as possessing . . .' An interesting little filler. There's a nice set-up that initially suggests the subject will be child-abuse and then switches to something more supernatural that throws the viewer. The *Exorcist* set-pieces are well handled and the child actors do a good job, but the whole thing is rather uninvolving, despite some background detail on Wesley.

Angel uses the alias Angel Jones. He tells Cordelia that Rick's *Magick-N-Stuff* is between a yoghurt shop and the Doggie Dunk on the corner of Melrose and Robertson.

Although Ethros demons have a physical body, they can possess people. They have a tendency for mass murder and try to corrupt the souls of those they possess. They can scan the surface thoughts of those near them, imitate voices and possess a level of telekinetic power. They secrete a green fluid called plakticine. The possessed victims have enhanced strength and can manifest a demonic appearance. If the host of an Ethros demon ingests eucalyptus powder they show their demon aspect. When an Ethros is cast out it immediately seeks another body. The demon is expelled with such force that the newly inhabited rarely survive. When wounded, an Ethros demon seeks primordial volcanic basalt to aid its regeneration. In order to trap an Ethros demon an Ethros box must be used, an item made of 600 species of virgin woods hand-crafted by blind Tibetan monks. Lizzie Borden (1860–1927) was suspected of murdering her stepmother and father in a sensational trial in Massachusetts in 1892. Despite a wealth of circumstantial evidence, she was acquitted. Wesley suggests that she was possessed by an Ethros demon.

Did You Know?: During Charisma Carpenter's time as a cheerleader in San Diego she and two male friends were at the beach one night when they were attacked by an armed man. He ordered Charisma to tie up her friends with the clear intention that he would rape her. With astonishing bravery and a gun held to her head, Charisma refused and, in the ensuing commotion, she and her friends were able to fight off the man who fled, shooting and wounding one of the men. Their witness statements eventually led to the arrest of the man, a San Diego police sergeant and serial rapist. A dramatisation of the incident was filmed by the Discovery Channel's *The Justice Files*, with an interview with Charisma herself.

15
The Prodigal

US Transmission Date: 22 February 2000
UK Transmission Date: 14 April 2000 (Sky)

Writer: Tim Minear
Director: Bruce Seth Green

Cast: J. Kenneth Campbell (Angel's Father),
Henri Lubatti (Suit 1),
Frank Potter (Uniformed Delivery Man),
Eliza Szonert (Chambermaid),
Bob Fimlani (Groundskeeper),

Christine Hendricks (Barmaid),
John Maynard (Uniformed Worker),
Glenda Morgan Brown (Angel's Mother),
Mark Ginther (Head Demon Guy),
John Patrick Clerkin (Black Robed Priest),
Mike Vendrell (Suit 2)

Galway, 1753. From the shadows of the doorway, Angel calls out to a serving girl, Anna, attempting to entice her inside. She asks 'Master Liam' why he stays in the shadows. He complains that the sun hurts his eyes, as someone angrily throws him into the light. Liam's father accuses him of trying to corrupt the girl, calls him a layabout and a scoundrel and declares that he's ashamed to claim him as his son.

Los Angeles, the present day. Angel battles a demon in an underground railway tunnel. Kate arrives as Angel kills the demon. Kate is still wary of Angel and is angry that witnesses' descriptions of the demon are vague. Angel notices Kate's father and asks her why he's there. She rationalises that he must have heard the call on the police scanner and came to check up on her. Kate tells Angel that she wants their relationship to be strictly business. Wesley discovers that the dead demon is a Kwaini, a peaceful, non-violent race. Angel speculates that someone must have caused it to become violent. Kate tells Angel that she doesn't like discussing demons and asks that he refer to them as 'evil things'. Angel tries to explain that this particular evil thing wasn't *evil*. Angel trails a deliveryman who leads him to an apartment building where he is handed a package by Trevor Lockley. Angel asks Trevor what is in the package, but the old man says that he doesn't know what Angel is talking about.

Liam leaves home, his father telling him that he's a disappointment. He goes to a tavern where he meets the alluring Darla. She makes him a vampire. Kate meets her father, Trevor, for lunch. He asks her about Angel, and whether she's seeing him. Kate tells him that Angel isn't her type. She also reveals that Angel is a private investigator. Wesley runs tests on the Kwaini demon and discovers a drug in the demon's system. Wesley and Angel decide the demon was after someone on the train who had the drug. Cordy arrives having tailed the deliveryman to Kel's Exotic Auto Shop. Trevor arrives at the shop to warn the drug distributors that Angel is investigating their operation. After he leaves, a demon orders his men to kill both Angel and Trevor.

Liam's family and friends gather at his graveside. That night, Darla comes to the grave and watches as Angelus claws his way out of the ground, welcoming him to her world. She tells him he can have anyone he wants and he tells her that he'll start with the village. Angel and Wesley argue about whether to warn Trevor about the demons he's dealing with when two Kwaini demons attack them. Angel calls Kate to warn her that Trevor is in danger. Trevor answers a knock at his door finding two men from the auto shop.

Liam's father is nailing the windows shut in the house, unaware that his son stands in the doorway. The father says that a demon cannot enter unless it's been invited but Angelus says that he *was* invited, pointing to his dead sister who thought he was an angel. Angelus taunts his father, then kills him. The men ask Trevor if he's told Kate about their business dealings. Angel arrives and asks Trevor to invite him in, but Trevor refuses as he's attacked by the two men, who reveal themselves as vampires. Angel helplessly watches as they kill Trevor. Once dead, Angel enters and kills one of the vampires. The other escapes as Kate finds her father. Angel prepares to do battle as Wesley asks him what happened to his cautious plan. Angel curtly replies that he's moved to plan B. Kate walks into the auto shop, shooting anyone who stands in her way but is surrounded by the demon and several henchmen. Angel steps from the shadows and a battle begins, which ends with Angel and Kate killing the demons. Angel tries to talk to Kate but she tells him that her father was human and he knows nothing about being human.

Darla looks at the bodies of Angelus's parents and sister. He tells her that he's won, proving to his father who was the more powerful. Darla tells Angelus that now his father is dead, he can never approve of him. Angel watches from a crypt as Kate visits her father's grave.

Denial, Thy Name is Liam's Father: The relationship between father and son is best described as strained. 'It's a son I wished for, a man. Instead, God gave me you. A terrible disappointment,' Liam is told. 'A more dutiful son you couldn't have asked for. My whole life you've told me in word, in glance, what it is you required of me and I've lived down to your every expectation, now haven't I?' he replies.

When Angelus tells Darla that by killing his father he has 'won', his sire tells him that his victory took moments, but that his father's defeat of *him* will last a lifetime. Angelus is horrified: 'He can't defeat me now.' Darla notes: 'Nor can he ever approve of you, in this world or any other. What we once were informs all that we have become. The same love will infect our hearts, even if they no longer beat. Simple death won't change that.' Angelus asks if the death of his family is the work of love. 'Darling boy,' says Darla. 'Still so very young.' (Compare this with Angel's half-spoken assertion that a vampire's personality after death isn't *that* far removed from what it was like before in *Buffy*: 'Doppelgängland'.)

It's a Designer Label!: Cordelia's 'undercover' get-up (blonde wig, dark glasses, long pink overcoat) is spectacular. Also notable, her short multicoloured top and her red trousers in the opening scene. Where does she get the money for all of these designer label clothes?

References: The title is from the parable of The Prodigal Son told in Luke 15. There's an allusion to the belief that garlic will repel vampires. 'Fools rush in' is from Alexander Pope's *An Essay on Criticism*. The full line is, of course, 'Fools rush in where angels fear to tread.' Also referenced: The Lord's Prayer.

Bitch!: Wesley: 'A deliberate cautious approach would be the most sensible plan. Fools rush in . . .' Cordelia: 'No, he wants you to stay here.'

'West Hollywood'?: Trevor, on Angel: 'Must be something wrong with him. "West Hollywood"?' Kate: 'Daddy, no. Angel's just not my type.' A word of explanation about Trevor Lockley's question: during the 1970s West Hollywood was known for its progressive social environment and the city attracted a large number of gays. It is still regarded as the gay capital of Los Angeles.

The Charisma Show: Cordy crouched over the demon's body waving a hacksaw shouting, 'Found it,' is a definite highlight, especially after Wesley has just commented on how sensitive women can be around the subject of demons.

L.A.-Speak: Cordelia: 'Maybe it was having a bad *skanky-rag* day.' And: 'No lurky minions from Hell will get in here.'
Delivery Man: 'Just your average *Joe-Stink* homeless-guy.'
Angel: 'It was an "evil thing" in terms of that word. It just wasn't an *evil* "evil thing".' Kate: 'There are not-evil "evil things"?' Angel: 'Well, yeah.'
Wesley: 'I think that it would be a fair intuitive leap to assume that the Kwaini was *jonesing* to get well.'

Cigarettes and Alcohol: 'Up again all night, is it? Drinking and whoring. I smell the stink of it on you.' Trevor Lockley drinks a glass of Scotch.

Sex and Drugs and Rock'n'Roll: Wesley says that the demon drug is very similar to PCP (phencyclidine). 'I did identify "eye of newt" as one of the ingredients, but one suspects added chiefly for taste rather than kick.'

'You May Remember Me from Such Films and TV Series as . . .': A former ice-skater (once ranked twelfth in the US), Julie Benz auditioned for the role of Buffy Summers in 1997. Although unsuccessful, her consolation was becoming Angel's sire, Darla. She later starred as the sinister Kate Topolsky in another of this author's favourite series' *Roswell* and in *As Good As It Gets* and *Satan's School for*

Girls. Henri Lubatti plays David Sherman in *Felicity*, Eliza Szonert was Danni Stark for two years on *Neighbours* while Glenda Morgan Brown appeared in the movie *Dreamers*.

Don't Give Up the Day Job: John Maynard is also a Hollywood producer, working on *Loaded*, *All Men Are Liars* and the classic SF movie *The Navigator*. He was also technical adviser on *Bloodmoon*. Mark Ginther played Lord Zedd in *Mighty Morphin Power Rangers: The Movie*, but is best known as a stuntman on such movies as *Hoffa*, *Joe Versus the Volcano* and *Hologram Man*. Michael Vendrell, the series stunt co-ordinator, is a martial-arts expert and served as a specialist on *Commando*. He was Sean Connery's stunt-double on *The Rock*.

Logic, Let Me Introduce You to This Window: When Angel trails the delivery man the frost on his breath can be seen. This also applies, even more obviously, to Angel and Darla in the scene where Angel rises from the grave. There is no dent on the driver's side fender of Angel's car, though one was apparent in **13**, 'She'. Did he get it fixed? Darla's wig in the newly filmed scenes is more elaborate and a different colour to the one used in the footage culled from *Buffy*: 'Becoming' Part 1.

I Just *Love* Your Accent: Wesley refers to Kate as 'skittish'. More extremely dodgy Irish accents are on display. This is probably Boreanaz's blackest hour, because he's required to carry it off for such a large number of scenes. There are times when the accent doesn't so much 'slip' as 'crash to the ground and shatter into a million pieces'.

Motors: The licence on the Blue Circle Delivery van is 5W99765.

Quote/Unquote: Barmaid, on Liam: '[He's] God's gift all right.' Darla: 'Really? I've never known God to be so generous.' Barmaid: 'His lies sound pretty when the stars are out. But he forgets every promise he's made when the sun comes up again.' Darla: 'That wouldn't really be a problem for me.'

Kate: 'Look, no offence. I think you're probably a pretty decent guy for what you are, but let's keep this strictly business . . . I'm not your girlfriend.'

Cordelia: 'Move your entrails.'

Angel, on Kate: 'Ever since she ran me through with a two-by-four things have been different.'

Angelus, about to kill the father he hated: 'Strange. Somehow you seemed taller when I was alive . . . To think I ever let such a tiny, trembling thing make me feel the way you did.'

Notes: 'You're a layabout and a scoundrel and you'll never amount to anything more.' A brilliant reformatting of the series, telling (in more detail than before) Angel's *Year One*-style origins. The clever juxtaposition of Kate's uncomfortable relationship with her father (previously glimpsed in **6**, 'Sense and Sensitivity') and Angel's troubled past is neatly handled and the acting from all concerned is excellent (despite the accents).

Angel's Christian name when he was alive was Liam. He was born in 1727 and had a younger sister called Kathy whom Angelus killed (along with his mother and father) after he became a vampire in 1753. The family had one servant, a chambermaid called Anna. The scenes of Darla siring Angelus are taken from *Buffy*: 'Becoming' Part 1. Several important points here: although the date of Liam's death confirms the on-screen information of *Buffy*: 'Becoming' Part 1, it contradicts several other bits of dating in *Buffy* (notably Willow's observation, taken from *The Watchers' Diaries*, in 'Halloween' that Angel was 18 years old in 1775 and still human). It seems that vampires take their 'age' from the time that they actually become a vampire (see, for instance, Spike's age as given in *Buffy*: 'The Initiative') though in Angel's case this is *still* a couple of years away from the dates given in *Buffy* episodes during 1997–98 (that Angel was either 240 or 241) and with the statement in the *Angel Demo Reel* that he is 244 in 1999.

He should be 246, at least. (It's also worth noting that the *Demo Reel* says that Angel was 27 when he became a vampire; here, the priest says he's 26.) There are approximately eleven people at Liam's funeral, including the priest, his mother, father and sister and several upset-looking ladies. The inscription on his gravestone reads 'beloved son'.

Darla tells the newly revived Angelus: 'Welcome to my world. It hurts, I know, but not for long. Birth is always painful,' echoing similar sentiments expressed by Angel in *Buffy*: 'School Hard'. Angelus's first victim was the grave-yard groundsman, followed by his sister, who believed he had returned as an angel (this is possibly where his nickname derives from).

Cordelia's birthday was a fortnight ago. Angel claims he didn't know. She suggests that they use her birthdate for the office's security code so that he'll have eleven and a half months of typing it in and no excuses not to remember next year. When she does input a code, she uses '0522' which many fans have taken as meaning that her birthday is 22 May; however, there is no confirmation of this. Angel Investigations appear to have purchased a digital camera that Cordelia uses when tailing the delivery man. Angel reminds Trevor that they met at his retirement party (see **6**, 'Sense and Sensitivity').

Trevor Lockley (1938–2000) was on the police force for 35 years. Angel tells the vampires attacking Trevor: 'The minute his soul leaves his body, I am through this door to kill you both,' which confirms that a vampire may not enter uninvited a live dwelling. Angel uses the dual stake contraption seen in **1**, 'City Of' and **3**, 'In the Dark'.

The scene with Trevor and Kate eating hot dogs was filmed in Marina Del Rey.

16
The Ring

US Transmission Date: 29 February 2000
UK Transmission Date: 21 April 2000 (Sky)

Writer: Howard Gordon
Director: Nick Marck
Cast: Marcus Redmond (Tom Cribb),
Douglas Roberts (Darin McNamara),
Scott William Winters (Jack McNamara),
Anthony Guidera (Ernie Nellins),
Chris Flander (Mr Winslow), Marc Rose (Mellish),
David Kallaway (Doorman),
Juan A. Riojas (Val Trepkos),
Michael Philip (Announcer), Mark Ginther (Lasovic)

Darin McNamara stumbles into the office asking for Angel. He tells them that his brother, Jack, was kidnapped the previous night. He has a gambling problem and was heavily in debt to one of his bookies, Ernie Nellins. Angel visits Nellins and buys information that leads him to Beechwood Canyon and some Howler Demons. Angel finds the demons in underground tunnels and beats them until they tell him where Jack is. Angel lurks outside a nightclub and then gets into the cellar. In the bar Angel briefly meets a woman called Lilah, then he discovers a crowd gathered around a pit where two demons are fighting to the death. The ringmaster introduces the next two fighters as Angel spots Jack in the crowd. He follows Jack into a darkened room where someone turns a spotlight on. Angel is blinded as he realises he's been set up.

Angel awakes in a cell. Around his wrist is a thick metal cuff that he can't remove. Jack warns Angel against stepping over the red line on the floor. Angel must wear the cuff until he has 21 kills in the ring; if he survives he will be released. Angel refuses to fight and Jack tells him, in that case, he'll die. Wesley and Cordy are worried about the missing Angel. Wesley retraces Angel's visit to Nellins and shows huge bravery in finding out where Angel is. He and Cordelia pose as detectives to gain entrance to the club. Angel and the demon Baker begin to fight, but it's obvious Angel is doing little more than defending himself against his opponent. Wesley and Cordelia watch, horrified as Angel eventually assumes his vampire face and kills his opponent. Angel, upset at what he has been forced to do, walks out of the ring.

Angel tries to get the other demons like Trepkos to rebel. Another demon taunts Angel, telling him his kill was a lucky one. Angel assures him it's not the first life he's taken. Wesley and Cordy try to devise a way to rescue Angel using one of the bracelets that Cordelia stole from the ring. Jack taunts Angel about his kill. Angel pulls Jack over the red line into their confinement area. Holding Jack by the throat he is eventually subdued after Darin shoots his brother dead to get at Angel. The guards shock Angel into unconsciousness again while the other demons merely sit and watch. Angel wakes up in the offices of Wolfram & Hart with Lilah. She says she has convinced Darin to sell Angel's contract to the firm. Angel is free, as long as he forgets all about the ring. Angel tells the guards to take him back. In tonight's match Angel must fight Trepkos who already has twenty kills.

Wesley manages to open the cuff. The ringmaster announces the fight between Angel and Trepkos. Angel tries to talk to Trepkos, telling him, even when they remove the cuff after the fight, he'll still be their slave. Trepkos tells Angel he'll kill him quickly and once they are in the ring, he attacks. Cordelia feigns being lost to allow Wesley entrance to the locker room. Wesley asks one of the demons, Cribb, where Angel is. Cribb tells him he's fighting Trepkos and will be dead in a matter of moments. Wesley shows him the key to the cuff and promises to free them all if he'll help. The demon sticks out his long tongue and snatches the key from Wesley's hand. The crowd is booing Angel because he's not fighting back. He is forced to defend himself and trips the demon and places the pointed end of a staff at Trepkos' throat but hesitates, as the crowd calls out for the killing blow. Angel refuses to kill Trepkos. Trepkos gets to his feet and attacks Angel, but hesitates, then drops his fist. Wesley attacks Darin with a gun as the demons, freed by Cribb, come crashing into the ring. Cordelia helps Wesley push Darin into the ring below. Cribb snaps a cuff on Darin's wrist and Trepkos picks Darin up and throws him out of the ring. He instantly disintegrates. Cordelia tells Angel that Wesley devised the key. Angel tells them they did great. They freed . . . demons.

It's a Designer Label!: Love Cordelia's black evening dress.

References: The bracelets used are similar to the restraint devices in *The Running Man*. The television shows *Jeopardy*, *Wheel of Fortune* and *Jerry Springer*, Tim Burton's *Beetlejuice*, the Marvel superhero Captain America, *Robin Hood*, Bob Marley's 'Exodus' ('Set the captives free'), Bernstein and Sondheim's *West Side Story*, Mahatma Gandhi (1869–1948), Moses and, obliquely, actor Keanu Reeves (*Bill and Ted's Excellent Adventure*, *Speed*, *The Matrix*) are mentioned or alluded to. Howard Gordon also wrote *The X-Files* episode 'Firewalker', which featured a character Daniel Trepkos. Tom Cribb (1781–1848) was an English bare-knuckle boxer. Dare I mention how much like *Spartacus* the whole thing is? Or *Fight Club*? (Not to mention a couple of *Star Trek* episodes, 'Bread and Circuses' and 'The Gamesters of Triskelion').

Bitch!: Cordelia: 'Every night it's *Jeopardy*, followed by *Wheel of Fortune* and a cup of hot cocoa. Look out, girls, this one can't be tamed.' Wesley: 'I'll admit, it may not be as intoxicating as a life erected on high-fashioned pumps and a push-up bra.'

The Charisma and Alexis Show: Cordelia and Wesley pretending to be *Dempsey and Makepeace* is one of the highlights of the season: Cordelia: 'I'm Detective Andrews and this is Detective Yelsew. Show them your badge and write down their licence plate number four three niner, Peter, Charley, Edward . . .' Winslow: 'You'll be hearing from my lawyer tonight.' Cordelia: 'Are you aware that you've purchased tickets to an unlicensed sporting event?' Wesley: 'Answer the detective.' Winslow: 'If it's illegal what are all these people doing here?' Cordelia: 'We're trying to do you a favour, Mr Winslow.' Wesley: 'Something's going down tonight. Something with *the man.*'

L.A.-Speak: Cordelia: 'The bookie who may get his *jollies* cutting off people's extremities?'

Cribb: 'Bloodsucker is crazier than I thought.'

Cigarettes and Alcohol: Lilah is something of a boozer, drinking red wine in the bar, a whisky when watching one of the bouts, and champagne in her office with Angel. Lots of crates of Carlsberg lager can be seen in the bookies' office.

Sex and Drugs and Rock'n'Roll: Cordelia: 'Someone ought to create an inter-demon dating base. You know, like Archfiend dot org, where the lonely and the slimy connect.' Wesley tells Cordelia he leads a rich and varied social life. Wesley: 'He wrote 'claw-like hands'.' Cordelia: 'Could be a mixed breed, smell?' Wesley: 'Sulphuric.' Cordelia: 'Add a Porsche and hair plugs and I've dated this guy. A lot.'

'You May Remember Me from Such Films and TV Series as . . .': Douglas Roberts was Richard Yzerman in *L.A. Law*. Scott William Winters played Clark in *Good Will Hunting* and also appeared in *The People Vs. Larry Flynt*. Stephanie Romanov began her career as a model at the age of fifteen, working for *Elle*, *French Vogue* and *Vanity Fair* before moving into acting with the role of Teri Spenser in *Melrose Place* and *Models Inc.* She has also appeared in *Due South* and in movies including *Spy Hard* and *Dark Spiral*. Anthony Guidera features in *Armageddon*, *The Rock*, *Species* and *The Godfather: Part III*. On TV Juan Riojas has appeared in *West Wing* and *Walker, Texas Ranger* while his movies include *Conspiracy Theory* and *In the Line of Fire*. For Marcus Redmond, see **5**, 'Rm W/a Vu'.

Don't Give Up the Day Job: James E. Mitchell, the assistant fights co-ordinator and David Boreanaz's martial-arts trainer, has a lucrative sideline as the movie stand-in for George Clooney in *Out of Sight*, *Batman and Robin* and *From Dusk Till Dawn* among others. He also doubled for Mel Gibson in *Payback*. Nice work if you can get it.

Logic, Let Me Introduce You to This Window: How does Angel know in which drain in Beechwood Canyon the Howler Demons are hiding? During the bout with Trepkos, Angel's mouth is bleeding as he lies in the dirt. When he rises, most of the blood is gone. The hole in Angel's shirt switches sides several times. Trepkos has the same problem as Angel: his metal cuff and leather cuff switch wrists during their fight. After Angel refuses to make the killing blow on Trepkos, he stands and moves away. Note that there is no wound in his side.

I Just *Love* Your Accent: Wesley: 'A name rife with *single-entendre*.'

Ernie: 'You're from another country, right? [Wesley pulls a crossbow from behind his back] What are you, Robin Hood?'

Quote/Unquote: Cordelia: 'You'd think people would get enough gratuitous violence watching *Jerry Springer*.'

Wesley: 'These Octavian matches date back to the Roman Empire. I'd heard rumours of a revival.' Cordelia: 'Couldn't they have just done *West Side Story*?'

Notes: 'How does it feel to be a slave?' A very brutal subject matter handled in an oddly dispassionate manner makes for an episode that it's difficult to feel strongly about. 'The Ring' features some nice stuff (Wesley's on good form, particularly his heroic use of a crossbow), but the main story just rambles and, after a while, bores.

Angel speaks Spanish, Russian and Italian. Wesley talks to Kate on the telephone after Angel goes missing. Cordelia once owned a palomino horse called Keanu, 'before the IRS took him away' (see **1**, 'City Of'). She still keeps a lock of his hair in her bracelet. Wesley mentions the Vigories of Oden Tal (see **13**, 'She').

There are a dozen species of demons indigenous to L.A. county. Jack and Darin run the illegal sporting venue XXI, which is located under the Parker Bros warehouse. The signs in Nellins' office read: 'Danger Hot Girls' and 'We Have Ice'.

Did You Know?: Many of the drawings on the *Demons, Demons, Demons* database are sketches by Joss Whedon used to create the monsters for *Buffy* and *Angel*. These include the demons from 'Gingerbread' and 'The Wish', a Kailiff demon from **5**, 'Rm W/a Vu', a Kawaini demon from **15**, 'The Prodigal' and a Brachen demon from **9**, 'Hero'.

Lost Angel?: David Boreanaz believes that Angel as a character has 'evolved and he's taken on a totally new lifestyle being in the environment that he's in'. He told *The Big Breakfast* that 'it's refreshing to see him mixing with people and trying to find himself in the human realm. He's [been] closed off from that society and he's finding his place now. We're opening his character up and it's good to see him smile and be part of the human race.'

17
Eternity

US Transmission Date: 4 April 2000
UK Transmission Date: 28 April 2000 (Sky)

Writer: Tracey Stern
Director: Regis B. Kimble
Cast: Tamara Gorski (Rebecca Lowell),
Robin Meyers (The Masseuse)

Angel and Wesley discuss their means of escape from a dire situation, but they realise there is no way out and resign themselves to another hour of torture, as they watch

Cordelia's ghastly performance in *A Doll's House*. After the play, they dodge her questions regarding quality. Cordelia spots Oliver Simon, the famous talent agent, coming out of a nightclub accompanied by Rebecca Lowell, a television actress. A car lurches out of the darkness and heads for Rebecca. Angel dives across the street, pushing her to safety. Once she has recovered, Rebecca asks Angel if he makes a habit of saving people and Cordelia tells her that it's his purpose in life and hands Rebecca their card. The following morning, Cordelia boasts that she made the front page. Her elbow is visible in a picture of Rebecca. Angel seems disappointed that his rescue wasn't mentioned in the paper. Rebecca arrives and invites Angel to her house, saying that she is being stalked.

Rebecca throws a house party. Once all the guests have left she goes to check the lock on her door. Angel crashes through it, just in time to save her from an intruder already inside the house who makes his escape. Rebecca rushes to Angel as he climbs to his feet. Unfortunately, they are standing in front of a mirror and she sees the lack of Angel's reflection. Angel says he's not what she thinks. Rebecca says she knows he's a vampire and asks if he drinks blood. He says that he does but assures her he's not a killer. Rebecca seems fascinated and unafraid.

Wesley tells Cordelia that Angel spent the night looking after Rebecca. Cordelia warns about Angel and the danger of him experiencing 'true happiness'. She says she is going to check on Rebecca, her one and only link to stardom. Angel answers the door to find Cordelia wearing a large wooden cross. Angel does his best to curtail Cordy's inquisitiveness explaining that Rebecca has gone out for lunch. He admits to revealing his secret to the actress. Rebecca meets Oliver, where he informs her that she must read for the part in a new series. Rebecca is indignant that a star of her calibre should have to read for a part. Back home, Rebecca works out while complaining to Angel about the indignity of this. The housekeeper brings a suit, which Rebecca hands over to Angel, explaining she has a premiere to attend and can't go without her bodyguard. At the premiere, a man in a tux and carrying a gun follows them. Angel and Rebecca exit through the back of the theatre. Angel hears something above them and sees the man about to shoot Rebecca. He shoves her aside then attacks the stranger. While the police take Angel's statement, Rebecca tells Oliver their attacker is a stuntman and she knows Oliver set it all up. Oliver confesses, assuring her that he'd never have allowed her to get hurt. As he tells her that no one stays young for ever, Rebecca looks at Angel. Cordelia and Rebecca spend a day shopping together and Rebecca pumps Cordy for information about Angel. Later that evening Rebecca shows up at Angel's apartment with a bottle of Dom Perignon and makes herself comfortable. Rebecca spills her drink on Angel's shirt, but when he goes to change, she puts a drug in his drink.

Cordelia tells Wesley that she made a mistake by giving Rebecca information about Angel, including the details on how one becomes a vampire. Angel tells Rebecca that he hurt a lot of people, hence his quest for atonement. Rebecca notes that he deserves some happiness. She offers herself, telling him to make her a vampire. Angel begins to get angry, telling her she has no idea what she's asking. Angel drags her to the kitchen where he opens the refrigerator and sprays blood into her mouth. Then he realises he's been drugged. Rebecca says she just wanted him to relax. Angel says that he is perfectly happy and bites her shoulder before becoming Angelus. He tells Rebecca that he's never killed a famous person before. Rebecca accuses him of trying to scare her and says it's not working. She tries to escape but he blocks her way, promising to torture her for hours so she can determine if she wants that type of lifestyle. Rebecca struggles to her feet and says she's through running. She hits Angelus with a candlestick and runs to the elevator. Wesley and Cordelia meet her in the office where Cordelia accuses her of sleeping with Angel. Rebecca admits she gave him Doximall, a tranquilliser that induces bliss. Wesley explains that it's not true happiness and suggests they vacate the premises until the effects wear off. The lights go out and Wesley tells Angel what he's experiencing is a chemical suggestion. Angel tells Wesley that his name is Angelus, knocking him out. He then taunts Cordelia, imitating her acting style. Cordelia grabs a bottle filled with water. She tells him it's holy water, blessed by the local priest. Angelus says she's bluffing. Cordy tells him she's prepared herself for this every single day. She throws the water on him and he recoils. Wesley takes advantage of the distraction, knocking Angelus into the elevator shaft.

Angel finds himself chained to his bed. Cordelia wonders if he's still evil. Angel asks about Rebecca who, Cordy informs him, won't be retaining him as a bodyguard. Wesley says it's best to put it all behind them. Angel tries to tell Cordelia that he didn't mean what he said about her acting, but she cuts him off saying it would be best if he didn't try to weasel out. At least Angelus was honest. Angel meekly calls after her and Wesley, but there is no response.

Dudes and Babes: Rebecca Lowell is a beautiful actress best known for the character of Raven whom she played on the TV series *On Your Own*, which ran for nine-and-a-half years. Rebecca has been famous since she was fourteen.

It's a Designer Label!: Rebecca's impressive wardrobe is seen in a series of stunning evening dresses. Those vampy sunglasses seen when she visits Angel are outstanding. She wears a baseball cap with a Japanese symbol on it at one point but we'll forgive her. Compared to such elegance, Cordelia's white sweater and shiny red pants and Wesley's cream tie stand no chance.

References: Cordelia appears in the play *A Doll's House* by Henrik Ibsen, in the role of Nora Helmer. There are references to *ET – The Extra-Terrestrial*, Emma Thompson, *Entertainment Tonight*, *Batman* (again), *The E! True Hollywood Story*, *The National Enquirer*, *Fright Night*, Ernest Borgnine, *The Wizard of Oz* ('What're you going to do? Melt me?'), the *Los Angeles Times*, plus the Emmys and the Oscars. Rebecca: 'Bela Lugosi, Gary Oldman, ❧

they're vampires.' Angel: 'Frank Langella was the only performance I believed' refers to actors who played the Count in *Dracula* (1931), *Bram Stoker's Dracula* (1992) and *Dracula* (1979) respectively. No Christopher Lee? *Philistines*. There's a great bit of TV industry mockery. Cordelia: 'It was a seminal show. Cancelled by the idiot network. I was going to picket them but I didn't have any comfortable shoes . . .'

Bitch!: You forget how cutting Angelus is when you haven't seen him for a while. On Cordelia's acting: 'You were really, let me tell you, *bad*.' Cordelia: 'Stop it.' Angelus: 'Why? *You* didn't. I mean, I've been to Hell, but that was *so much* worse.'

Cordelia: 'You *slut!*'

The Charisma Show: Her incompetent eavesdropping on Angel refusing to take Rebecca as a client ('*Are you insane?*') and her fake-vision are highlights. Some good comedy with Boreanaz too. Angel: 'You brought a cross?' Cordelia: 'Along with three double half-caf, non-fat, skinny lattes.' Angel: 'And a cross?' Cordelia: 'Judging by the outfit, I guess it's safe to come in. Evil Angel never would have worn those pants.'

As some fans have pointed out, Charisma plays three separate characters here. Her normal role, the bad-actress-Cordelia in the opening scenes and an Oscar-winning-Cordy towards the end. A truly fine bit of acting. Her comic timing remains impressive. That '*Pffft!*' at the end being the perfect final touch.

L.A.-Speak: Cordelia: 'Angel is the Dark Avenger. Only not too dark. Happy dark.'

Oliver: 'This will be all over the tabs come morning, Bec. We might as well just put our own spin on it first.'

Masseuse: 'You have to be proactive with deterioration.'

Cordelia: 'He could be helping us both. Think of the *Karma*.'

Cordelia calls Wesley: '*Dufus*.'

Angelus: 'There wasn't a dry eye in the house, everybody was just laughing so hard. Maybe you can get Raven here to coach you, then you'd actually *suck*.'

Cigarettes and Alcohol: Rebecca brings a bottle of Dom Perignon champagne to Angel's apartment.

Sex and Drugs and Rock'n'Roll: Doximall is the drug that Rebecca uses on Angel ('just a little happy pill'). As Wesley notes it's a 'powerful tranquilliser. It induces bliss.' 'Remind me to get the number of your dealer before I kill you,' Angelus tells Rebecca.

Wesley: 'What sorts of questions?' Cordelia: 'Where does Angel hail from, what's his favourite colour, what kind of aftershave he wears? The exact specific details on how someone could make themselves into a vampire?' Wesley: 'Surely, you don't think . . .?' Cordelia: 'What? That she'd try to manoeuvre Angel into an exchange of bodily fluids in order to make herself eternally young and beautiful, thus saving her failing career? Gee, now you mention it . . .'

'You May Remember Me from Such Films and TV Series as . . .': Tamara Gorski played Megan Torrance in *Poltergeist: The Legacy*, and Doctor Alexandra Corliss in *Psi Factors: Chronicles of the Paranormal*. She was also Morrigan in *Hercules: The Legendary Journeys* and has appeared in *Forever Knight*, *Highlander*, *The Kids in the Hall* and *Earth: Final Conflict* along with the movie *To Die For*.

Don't Give Up the Day Job: Director Regis B. Kimble began as an editor (working on series like *Matlock*) and it was in that capacity that he first worked on *Buffy the Vampire Slayer*, before graduating to directing on the classic 'Earshot'.

Logic, Let Me Introduce You to This Window: When Angel first looks at the car it has a huge cloud of exhaust fumes coming out of the tail pipe, the camera is away for less than a second, then returns to show none whatsoever. As

Angel opens the door into the alley, his reflection can be seen in the surface of the door. When the bookcase is knocked over in Rebecca's house, various vases go flying but none of them break, even though there is the sound of glass breaking. Watch closely during the scene when Angel goes to change his shirt, you'll notice no sign of his tattoo. Angelus has blood on his hand after force-feeding Rebecca some blood. But in the next shot his hand is clean. When Rebecca shows up in Angel's apartment with the champagne it is 8:25; at the scene's completion some moments later, the clock still says 8:25. When Rebecca puts the Doximall in Angel's glass it turns cloudy and doesn't seem to be dissipating very fast. But as soon as the camera cuts to Angel walking back into the room, the champagne is clear again.

Confronting Angelus, Wesley is wearing a pair of slacks, when he pushes Angelus down the elevator shaft he has a pair of jeans on; in the final scene the slacks are back. The length of Rebecca's hair changes quite dramatically between the opening scene and the next in which she appears. Concerning Angel's appreciation of Frank Langella's *Dracula*: when, exactly, did Angel *see* this since he's never been seen to have a TV (in this episode he confirms he doesn't possess one) and in *Buffy*: 'Enemies' he noted that it was 'a long time' since he'd been to the cinema. Did Rebecca invite Angel into her home off-screen? There's also discontinuity with *Buffy*: 'Surprise'/'Innocence'. In those stories it is established that one moment of perfect happiness will turn Angel into Angelus even if he doesn't feel much happiness after the transformation. Yet here it is implied (and subsequently confirmed) that he will only remain Angelus as long as he is experiencing the effects of the drug and that once he comes down he will revert. If that's the case, why did it take eight episodes and a spell to revert him in *Buffy*, Season Two?

I Just *Love* Your Accent: When Cordelia mentions *ET*, Wesley thinks she's talking about Emma Thompson. Tasteful. He also says, in response to Cordelia's comment about television seasons: 'And they say there are no seasons in Los Angeles.'

Motors: The car that drove at Rebecca was a 'green, freshly painted '76 Chevy Nova'.

Quote/Unquote: Cordelia: '[Angel] can fight off Donkey Demons who rip people's guts out, but he can't help one defenceless actress from a psycho? What is your *thing*?'

Rebecca: 'You're not a killer?' Angel: 'I gave that up.' Rebecca: 'Well, there is a support group for everything in this town, I guess.'

Wesley: 'Angel's moment of true happiness occurred because he was with Buffy. Do you realise how rare that is . . . ? What are the odds he'd find it with an actress?' Cordelia: 'And what's that supposed to mean?' Wesley: 'I meant TV actress.' Cordelia: 'Save it.'

Angel: 'You looked into that mirror and all you saw was yourself. That's all you ever see, Rebecca, and that's what really frightens you. This isn't about the way the studio, the network or the fans see you. It's about how you see yourself.'

Cordelia: 'You don't think I wasn't ready for this, do you? Why do you think I have a stake stashed in my desk? A cross in my bag? I think about this happening every single day.'

Notes: 'You walk a fine line, Angel, I don't envy you.' This one is *really* good. A very clever examination of the pitfalls in the quest for eternal youth that takes an oddly dispassionate view of all of the characters (Cordelia is at her most narcissistic and it's difficult even to feel sympathy with Angel when you see Angelus at his worst). Tamara Gorski is excellent and the direction is among the series' best. Amazingly, no one dies.

There are several references to Angel going to Hell in *Buffy*: 'Becoming' Part 2, while Cordelia's: 'You weren't around the last time Angel went mental. I, on the other hand, was on the first wave of the cleanup crew,' refers to the final episodes of *Buffy*, Season Two. Angel remembers

Oliver giving him his card at the party in **1**, 'City Of'. He wears a **44** long. Angelus suggests that Wesley has an inferiority complex.

When Cordelia notes, 'They close off stores for her. Oh, and lunch at Mirabelle's. I had the most to-die-for veal fillet with a light truffle marinade,' she's referring to the exclusive **Mirabelle Restaurant & Patio Bar** on Sunset Boulevard. Wesley has a pager. The tabloid in Rebecca's house is the *Global Snooper*. There are approximately fifteen people in the audience for Cordelia's play which doesn't, indeed, count as a 'crowded theatre'.

Critique: In an article in *TV Guide* as part of a series entitled *What Can I Watch With My Kids?*, Joe Queenan noted: 'Personally, I enjoy *Angel* because it is well written, it addresses the issue of sin and redemption, it does not trot out the same story every week and it is far less camp than *Buffy*. My wife says she enjoys the show because of the eerie lighting and the creepy cello music . . . I have no idea why my kids enjoy the show.'

Previously on *Buffy the Vampire Slayer*: 'This Year's Girl', 22 February 2000/'Who Are You?' 29 February 2000: Faith dreams that she and Buffy are friends; Buffy apologises for being unable to stay, she has to get ready for the arrival of 'little sis'. Faith notices that she is bleeding and finds the knife that Buffy stabbed her with is still in her. Faith looks pleadingly at Buffy and asks, 'Are you ever gonna take this thing out?' Buffy plunges the knife in further.

Xander attempts to fix the faulty blaster that Professor Walsh gave Buffy when she sent her off to die. Giles comments that Buffy has been patrolling for three days and could use some rest. Buffy is determined to find Adam. Willow brings up the subject of Riley. Buffy says that the Initiative tell her that he's fine, but she doesn't trust them. Back in Faith's mind, she and Mayor Wilkins are having a picnic. Buffy arrives and stabs the Mayor with Faith's knife, coldly telling Faith, 'I told you I had things to do.'

Buffy gets Willow to hack into the Initiative security system so that she can rescue Riley, just as Riley appears, asking, 'Am I really worth all that?' Faith dreams again. She's running from Buffy and the knife. Faith falls into a grave and Buffy jumps in after her. Back at the hospital, Faith's eyes suddenly open. In the basement a girl asks a confused Faith for directions. Faith tells her that she needs to get to Sunnydale High School. The girl tells Faith that the school isn't there any more. It was a tragedy: lots of students died, along with the Principal and the Mayor. Moments later Faith leaves the hospital, wearing the girl's clothes. A nurse explains to a doctor and a policeman that Faith is missing. Then she goes to the phone. 'It's happened,' she says. 'Send the team.' Faith looks at what's left of the school and then walks through downtown Sunnydale. She finds Giles's house, where she eavesdrops on the Scooby Gang talking about Adam. The phone rings and Giles passes it to Buffy. When she hangs up, Buffy tells them that Faith has escaped. Buffy knows that Faith won't be hard to find, but wonders what they're going to do when they find her. Riley asks, 'Who's Faith?' The next day at university, Buffy tells Willow that she told Riley the basic story of Faith, but without some of the Angel details. Buffy tells Willow that if she were Faith, she'd get out of town, just as Faith turns around saying, 'You're not me.' Buffy asks Faith if she's all right. Faith replies that she is ready for payback. She tells Buffy about a dream she had in which Buffy wasn't even dating the guy that she almost killed Faith for. As the two begin to fight, the police arrive and Faith runs.

Xander and Giles run into Spike. Xander says they're looking for a rogue-Slayer and describes her. Spike appears concerned, wondering, 'Is this bird after you?' Xander confirms that she is and Spike offers up his help. 'I'll head out, find this girl, tell her exactly where all of you are and then watch as she kills you.' Outside the hospital, the nurse greets the arrival of a helicopter and three men. Faith is approached by a demon, telling her that it has a remembrance from a friend. She kills it and takes an envelope containing a videotape. Breaking into an office, she puts the tape in the VCR and sees the Mayor on screen. He tells her that if she's watching this, he must be dead. Even though the doctors tell him that she won't wake up, he doesn't believe them. Unfortunately, her days will be numbered; there won't be a place for her in the world any more. He instructs her to open a box that he left for her and she finds in it a silver device. Giles comes home to find the men from the helicopter sitting in his house. 'Hello, Rupert,' one of them says.

Buffy tries to convince Riley of how dangerous Faith is. Riley is sure that Buffy is leaving something out. All she will tell him is that Faith comes after the people she loves. Faith attacks Buffy's mother. She takes Joyce to her bedroom and goes through her make-up drawer, putting on lipstick. She asks Joyce how she looks. Joyce says, 'Psychotic.' Faith says that she's found a stockpile of letters from Buffy, implying that Buffy hasn't been home in a while. Faith insists that Buffy is too into her own life to worry about her mom. Buffy bursts through the window. Joyce reaches for the phone as the girls fight. Faith hears sirens, she gets out the silver device and grabs Buffy's hand as a light pulses. Buffy throws a punch and knocks Faith out. Joyce asks if Buffy is OK and wonders what the device is. Buffy throws it down and stamps on it, saying it's a weapon that didn't work. 'Are you sure you're OK?' Joyce wonders. 'Five by five,' 'Buffy' reassures her.[9]

'Buffy' watches 'Faith' being moved to the ambulance on a stretcher. A detective confirms that 'this Faith chick' is dangerous and as he leaves, 'Buffy' says, 'She truly is.' The women go inside and Joyce wonders what drives Faith to such behaviour. 'Buffy' reasons that maybe Faith likes being that way, but Joyce insists that Faith must be unhappy. In the bath, 'Buffy' relaxes in her new body. She stands by the mirror and practises being Buffy, rehearsing

---

[9] The Buffy/Faith body-swop in 'Who Are You?': 'Buffy' refers to Faith inhabiting Buffy's body and 'Faith' refers to Buffy inhabiting Faith's body. Confused? You will be . . .

lines like 'You can't do that. It's wrong.' 'Faith', meanwhile, is fighting to get away, trying to explain what has
happened. 'Buffy' finds Buffy's passport and a credit card
and books a flight out of Sunnydale. Joyce tells 'Buffy' that
Giles called. 'Buffy' picks a lipstick on Joyce's dresser.
Joyce notes it's the one Faith used earlier. 'Buffy' tells
Joyce to burn it.

An armoured truck charges in front of the vehicle
carrying 'Faith'. Two men take 'Faith' into the truck 'by
order of the Watchers' Council'. 'Buffy' arrives at Giles's
to discover that 'Faith' has been captured by a special
operations unit of the Council. 'Buffy' finds this amusing.
Anya says that she and Xander have plans for sex and
'Buffy' jokes that she wouldn't want to cut into *that* seven
minutes. Xander and Anya are offended, but 'Buffy' tells
them to lighten up, reassuring the Scooby Gang that they
can have their fun and she'll be out doing her job. We next
see 'Buffy' dancing at the Bronze. She bumps into Spike,
whom she doesn't recognise. Spike tells her to 'sod off', she
begins to walk away, which only offends him more. He
asks if she knows why he hates her so much. 'Because
I'm a stuck-up tight-ass with no sense of fun?' she asks.
Spike says that pretty much covers it. 'Buffy' pushes Spike
against a wall, telling him 'I could ride you at a gallop until
your legs buckled ... I've got muscles you've never even
dreamed of. I could squeeze you until you popped like
warm champagne and you would beg me to hurt you just
a little bit more. And you know why I don't? Because it's
wrong.' She giggles and walks away. In the sewers, the
leader of a group of vampires is complaining that it's too
crowded for hunting. Adam finds them. He says he has
been thinking about vampires: on their fear of death and
how being immortal causes them to fear it more than those
to whom it comes naturally. He says that he relates to the
fact that they are between two worlds. 'Faith' finds her
wrists chained. She tells one of the Council men,
Weatherby, that she is really Buffy. The leader, Collins,
isn't convinced. She's just a package and he doesn't care
what's inside. Weatherby tells 'Faith' that the Watchers'

Council used to mean something, but she perverted it and spits in her face. At the Bronze, Willow and Tara spot 'Buffy' who says she got tired of patrolling. Willow goes to get a drink. 'Buffy' immediately realises that Willow and Tara are a couple. Tara begins to stutter and 'Buffy' mocks her. Willow points out a vampire. 'Buffy' hesitates before remembering that she's supposed to slay it. She finds it feeding from the girl and kills it. 'Buffy' tells the girl that she'll live but the girl grabs 'Buffy''s hand in gratitude. Willow tells 'Buffy' that Tara isn't feeling well and wonders if 'Buffy' is going to Riley's.

'Faith' tries to escape, capturing one of the Council men, Smith. 'Faith' orders the others to unchain her or she'll kill him, but Collins says that before every mission they put their affairs in order. He apologises to Smith and he and Weatherby walk away. Weatherby says that getting her across the border is going to be difficult and Collins isn't even sure if the Council can get them passage. Riley is surprised when 'Buffy' shows up at his door. 'Hi, baby,' she greets him. Tara tells Willow that Buffy wasn't herself; a person's energy is supposed to have a unity, but Buffy's was fragmented, like something forced where it doesn't belong. Willow worries that Buffy is possessed and Tara says they can access the Nether Realm. 'Buffy' climbs on to Riley's lap and kisses him. They go to bed, 'Buffy' asking what 'nasty little desire' Riley wants to try out ('Am I a bad girl? Do you wanna hurt me?'). Riley is confused and wonders what game she is playing. They make love. Riley tells 'Buffy' that he loves her. 'Buffy' pushes Riley away, asking, 'Who are you? What do you want from her?' Adam tells his minions that he has something they don't, the knowledge of his purpose. To extinguish life. He asks the vampires what they fear most.

'Buffy' puts on Riley's shirt and leaves. She runs into Forrest, who says that she's not letting Riley get much rest. 'Buffy' tells him that she's been fighting demons since before he could shave. 'Yeah,' he agrees, 'you're a killer.' 'I am not a killer,' says 'Buffy', 'I'm *the Slayer* and you don't know the first thing about me.' Collins has got word from the Council that they can't get passage; they order that 'Faith' be terminated. He points his gun at 'Faith' but she wrestles it away with her feet and escapes. 'Faith' arrives at Giles's. She tells him that she is really Buffy, but Giles doesn't believe her. 'Faith' tells him to look into her eyes and be intuitive and reminds him of the time that Ethan Rayne made Giles into a demon then rattles off some other facts that only Buffy would know. Willow and Tara arrive and confirm 'Faith''s story. She hands over a contraption that will allow 'Buffy' and 'Faith' to switch bodies again. Xander calls, telling Giles to turn on the TV. Three 'disfigured' men have taken church parishioners hostage. 'Buffy' is at the airport when she also sees the news. Inside the church, the vampire tells the congregation how his fear was stupid. Outside, a police sergeant confirms that he's been ordered to defer command to Riley who orders them to back off until the troops arrive. Riley heads towards the church and spots 'Buffy', who plans to charge in. 'I'm Buffy,' she says, 'I *have* to do this.' Giles, Willow and Tara create a diversion to allow 'Faith' entry. She sees Riley and throws her arms around him. 'It's OK, miss,' a surprised Riley says. 'Faith' begins to explain, but instead asks how many are in the church. Riley asks 'Who are you?' Inside, 'Buffy' tells the vampires that she won't allow them to kill these people, 'because it's wrong'. The leader realises that she's the Slayer. He tells her that they aren't afraid of her or anything any more, Adam has shown them the way. Suddenly, he turns to dust and 'Faith' appears behind him. 'Buffy' and 'Faith' furiously fight, with 'Buffy' beating 'Faith''s head against the floor, screaming at her that she's nothing but a disgusting, murderous bitch. 'Faith' grabs 'Buffy''s hand and light passes through them as they revert to their own bodies. Faith gets up and runs. Buffy confirms to Riley that Faith has disappeared and that the Watchers' Council are gone too. As Riley berates himself for not realising, Buffy discovers that he slept with 'Faith'. 'I slept with *you*,' Riley says. Buffy comments that she doesn't think Faith is coming back. Faith, meanwhile, is sitting alone on a train.

18
Five by Five

US Transmission Date: 25 April 2000
UK Transmission Date: 5 May 2000 (Sky)

Writer: Jim Kouf
Director: James A. Contner
Cast: Tyler Christopher (Wolfram & Hart Lawyer),
Rainbow Borden (Marquez/Gangbanger),
Francis Fallon (Dick), Adrienne Janic (Attractive Girl),
Rodrick Fox (Assistant DA),
Thor Edgell (Romanian Man),
Jennifer Slemko (Romanian Woman)

A young man, Marquez, is attacked by demons but is saved by Wesley and Angel. Meanwhile, at a bus station, a man waits to greet unsuspecting young girls arriving in L.A. He makes the mistake of finding Faith. She attacks him, taking his wallet and keys. Borsa, Romania, 1898: Darla leads a blindfolded Angelus telling him she has a surprise for him. She pulls off the blindfold, revealing a terrified gypsy girl, wishing him happy birthday.

Angel shoves Marquez into his office, warning him that if he doesn't do what's right, Angel won't be there to save him next time. Cordelia tells Wesley the boy isn't going to do his civic duty. Wesley says he has faith in Angel's ability to convince him otherwise. At a nightclub, Faith is dancing. She provokes an argument with a woman and punches her face, the fight escalating into a brawl. Faith continues to dance.

The next morning in court, the Wolfram & Hart lawyer Lindsey McDonald is denying that his firm tampers with witnesses and demands a dismissal of the charges against his client as Marquez and Angel enter the courtroom. Back at the firm, Lindsey is on the phone with his superior, admitting he is responsible for underestimating Angel. He agrees that Angel has been a costly liability to the firm. He hatches a plan along with colleagues Lee Mercer and Lilah Morgan to hire a rogue slayer. At Wolfram & Hart offices, Lindsey tells Faith that there's an outstanding arrest warrant for her in Sunnydale and that if she works for them, they can get her off the murder charge. When Faith asks who it is she's to kill, Lindsey tells her Angel. Faith instantly agrees.

1898: Darla finds Angelus cowering. She asks if he's playing a game. Angel laments that for 140 years they've been killing and their victims are all dead. Darla demands to know what's happened. Angel tells her the gypsy girl's people did something to him. He can remember every person he's killed and begs her to help him. Darla realises that they've given him a soul and in disgust attacks him, telling him to get out. Angrily she drives the tormented Angel into the street.

Wesley wonders what ramifications they can expect from Wolfram & Hart. Angel, Wesley and Cordelia are on their way to meet a new client when Faith arrives armed with a crossbow. Faith fires but Angel catches the bolt. Faith laughs and tells them this is going to be fun. Angel talks to Giles on the phone. Wesley is upset that Giles didn't inform him that Faith had come out of her coma. He was, after all, her Watcher. Cordelia asks what she can do and Angel tells them both to not make themselves a target. Wesley argues they need to band together and reminds Angel that Faith is not a demon, but a very sick girl. Later Angel finds Faith in the office. He says he's glad she stopped by. Faith pulls a gun, telling Angel she'll give him one chance to kill her, and tosses it to him. Angel fires, but the gun is loaded with blanks. Angel gives the gun back and asks Faith if she's considered that he might enjoy killing her. Faith wonders if that would be a moment of true happiness. She says if he doesn't kill her, she will kill him. She fires the gun but this time the bullet is real. Faith tells a wounded Angel that the games have begun and jumps through the window.

Angel walks into the Wolfram & Hart office building. Making his way to Lindsey's office, Angel goes through his desk. Lindsey walks in and Angel asks him where Faith is. Lindsey warns Angel that they have a highly sophisticated security system and that he'd like to stick around, but he has a dinner appointment. Amused, Angel tells Lindsey they'll meet again. Wesley and Cordelia try to enter her apartment, but Phantom Dennis slams the door shut. Once inside they discover that it wasn't Wesley that Dennis was worried about, but rather Faith.

1898: Angelus roams the streets. Seeing a group he tells them he's hungry and one of the men tosses him a coin. A woman screams that he's a monster and the men drag him into an alleyway. Angelus emerges and attacks the woman but he is unable to kill her.

Faith speculates on how different things may have been if Giles had been her Watcher as Angel comes crashing through the door. Faith holds a knife to Wesley's throat and asks Angel if he's ready to play. She admits she's been hired to kill Angel. Faith screams that no one can take her and she and Angel crash through the window, a dumpster breaking their fall. The battle continues in the street, Faith telling Angel he doesn't know what evil is and that she's bad. Angel ignores her demands that he fight back. Faith screams that she's evil, then begs Angel to kill her before falling into Angel's arms, sobbing.

Dudes and Babes: Faith's back; look out! Wesley: 'A fight in a bar, several arrests made and a woman fitting Faith's description was involved. However, not arrested.' Cordelia: 'She charm her way out?' Wesley: 'Apparently she managed to break a policeman's jaw with his own handcuffs before she disappeared into the night.' Cordelia: 'For Faith, that *is* charm.'

Denial, Thy Name is Faith: As previously hinted at in *Buffy*: 'Consequences', 'Enemies' and (especially) 'Who Are You?', Faith suffers from a severe self-loathing which is why actually *becoming* Buffy had such an attraction for her. Just as in the final sequence of 'Who Are You?', Faith, in Buffy's body, beating *herself* and screaming how 'evil' she is, so in this episode the poignancy of Faith's battle with Angel is highlighted by her desire that he should kill her. Not so much denial as horror at what she has become.

It's a Designer Label!: Cordelia's rich blue top and Faith's red top vie for attention though both are trumped by Faith's leather-gear in the club. Check out Marquez's hilarious *Boyz 'n' the Hood* threads.

References: The title, Faith's catchphrase, is a radio communications call-sign meaning 'loud and clear'. The Dalai Lama, Elvis, Spike Lee's *Do The Right Thing*, *The Game* and the American Bar Association are name-checked and there is a reference to Spider-Man ('your friendly neighbourhood vampire').

Bitch!: Concerning the events of *Buffy*: 'Consequences'. Wesley: 'She's not a demon, Angel, she's a sick, sick girl. If there's even a chance she can be reasoned with ...' Angel: 'There was. Last year I had a shot at saving her. I was pulling her back from the brink when some British guy kidnapped her and made damn sure she'd never trust another living soul.' Cordelia: 'It's not Wesley's fault that some British guy ruined your ... Oh wait, that was *you*. Go on.'

Faith is described by the guy she beats up as 'the bitch from Hell', while Lee also refers to Lilah as 'a bitch'.

The Charisma Show: Eclipsed by a Tasmanian-Devil performance by Eliza, Charisma nonetheless gets some marvellous moments: 'I knew it when you brought him in last night. Someone with that much body art is gonna have a different definition of civic duty.' And: 'OK, Elvis, when you're a big star, you can get away without carrying cash. And, while we're on the subject, I think one of us should apply for a small business loan, just to get us through the rough spots. I mean, what's a thirty-year-loan to you?'

L.A.-Speak: Marquez: 'Yo *ese*. What the hell you burning there, man? Smells like ... Yo, you're hanging in the wrong place, man. My boys ain't gonna be too happy when they get here and see what kind of a mess you made.'

Cordelia: 'You don't change a guy like that. In fact, generally speaking, you don't change a guy. What you see is what you get. Scratch the surface and what do you find? More surface.' And: 'You can always tell when he's happy. His scowl is slightly less scowly.'

Faith: 'Who is *we*? And why do they know me when I don't know *Jack* about you?' And: '*Dude*, I'm getting paid. They hate you almost as much as I do.'

Sex and Drugs and Rock'n'Roll: Faith dancing. Pure sex.

'You May Remember Me from Such Films and TV Series as . . .': Eliza Dushku made her film debut aged eleven in *That Night*. She went on to play Emma in *Bye Bye Love*, Missy in *Bring It On* and Dana Tasker in *True Lies*. Tyler Christopher was Nick Cassadine in *General Hospital*. Rainbow Borden has appeared in *Punks*, *Random Acts of Violence*, *The Limey* and, ironically, the 1998 movie *City of Angels*.

Don't Give Up the Day Job: Jim Kouf is the writer of several movies, including *Stakeout*, and was producer of *Con Air* and the 90s cult-favourite *Kalifornia*. His only acting role came in the 1981 film *Wacko* (which he also wrote), something he shares in common with fellow producer David Greenwalt (see **1**, 'City Of'). Francis Fallon is guitarist with L.A. rock band Ester.

There's a Ghost in My House: On reaching the apartment Dennis shuts the door in Cordelia and Wesley's face, trying to warn them that Faith is inside. Wesley: 'Dennis? Your ghost, I presume.' Cordelia: 'Yes, he's jealous. [Loudly] Don't worry, Hell will freeze over before I have sex with *him*.'

Logic, Let Me Introduce You to This Window: How did Angel enter Faith's borrowed apartment? At the bus depot when Faith is coming down the steps, there's a pair of sneakered feet with anklets behind her on the pavement. When the shot pans up, the same girl is just coming off the stairs. Cordelia's apartment was 212 in 'Rm W/a Vu'. Here it's number 6. She had no neighbours to the left nor across the hall from her door, but now she does. When Faith tells Wesley he has a stake up his 'English Channel', it looks like there was a different bit of dialogue that got overdubbed. In the initial shot of the kitchen counter in Faith's apartment, there are no knives in the canister. Next shot they magically appear. Presumably Angel and Darla's parting in Rumania in 1898 was the last time they met until 1997 in Sunnydale; however, this contradicts information given in *Buffy*: 'Angel'.

Why doesn't Phantom Dennis physically restrain Faith? It's been established that he can move objects about, so what's to stop him clobbering her with a chair?

I Just *Love* Your Accent: Wesley's finest hour: 'I was your Watcher, Faith. I know the real you. And even if you kill me there's just one thing I want you to remember.' Faith: 'What's that, love?' Wesley: 'You are a piece of sh . . .' *Nice one.* This after Faith has told him: 'Face it, Wesley, you really were a jerk. Always walking around like you had some great big stake rammed up your English Channel.' Plus a use of the word 'ruffian' in a non-ironic way. Faith's 'where's that stiff-upper-lip?', however, *is* dripping with irony.

Motors: Faith arrives in Los Angeles on a Greyhound bus.

Quote/Unquote: Angel: 'Your name Marquez? Good, I hate saving the wrong guy.'
   Angel: 'You'd think with all the people I've maimed and killed, I wouldn't be able to remember every single one.'
   Wesley: 'Seems you're taking this personally.' Angel: 'Well, she tried to shoot my own personal back, so yeah.'

Notes: 'Feel young, do ya, Faith? You're looking pretty worn out to me.' Probably the highlight of the season, as the astonishing Eliza Dushku brings her many talents on to *Angel* with devastating effect. Includes – definitively – the finest moment of *Angel* so far: Wesley dropping the knife that Faith used to torture him in slow motion and

Faith collapsing into Angel's arms begging him to kill her. Truly epic.

Faith says she likes black. She left Sunnydale, according to Giles 'about a week ago' (see *Buffy*: 'Who Are You?'). Faith dancing wildly at a club is reminiscent of her antics in *Buffy*: 'Bad Girls.' The alley where Angel and Faith fight is the same one used in 3, 'In the Dark' where Angel was captured by Marcus and Spike. Wesley seems to sleep on Angel's couch. Lindsey says he has the entire conversation with Angel recorded on hi-def tape. His assistant is called Jesse. The three lawyers that we see at Wolfram & Hart have the initials 'LM'. Coincidence? Lilah says that green is her favourite colour, that she looks good in diamonds and loves riding in limousines.

The Rumanian street scenes were filmed at Universal studio's 'Little Europe'. The bus depot set seems to be the same one used for Sunnydale bus station in *Buffy*: 'Inca Mummy Girl'.

Soundtrack: Rob Zombie's 'Living Dead Girl' and the APM Dance Indie Mix instrumental 'Pressure Cooker'. Robert Kral told Rob Francis, 'For **18**, "Five by Five", there was this scene where there was this strange seagull crying-type sound that was in the background for a second. I thought David Greenwalt would think it was in my music track and to ask me to remove it and I would have to tell him it that I couldn't because it was actually on the production track: recorded during filming. I got the comments back on the score and David said he loved that sound. "Can I hear more of that?" he asked. I explained to David [that] I had no idea what it was. However, I found a very similar bendy string orchestra-type sound, but spookier, as if the strings are crying one by one, so I added it to that scene.'

19
Sanctuary

US Transmission Date: 2 May 2000
UK Transmission: 12 May 2000 (Sky)

Writers: Tim Minear, Joss Whedon
Director: Michael Large
Cast: Alastair Duncan (Collins), Jeff Ricketts (Weatherby),
Kevin Owens (Smith), Adam Vernier (Detective Kendrick)

Angel puts Faith to bed and tells her to get some rest.
Faith calls him back and, for an instant, imagines staking
him. Cordelia, with a horribly swollen cheek, talks to an
even more bruised and battered Wesley. Angel asks if there
are doughnuts, which sparks an argument, Wesley telling
Angel that he doesn't understand why Faith is being
treated so kindly after what she did. Angel reminds Wesley
that they aren't in the business of giving up on people.
Angel says that they can't pick and choose who gets saved.
Cordelia tells him she's taking a paid vacation as she has
no desire to be around Faith. At the apartment where
Faith held Wesley captive, the police are gathering evidence. A detective tells Kate Lockley that Faith is the
prime suspect and says there are rumours she has 'super
powers'.

The Wolfman & Hart lawyers discuss the failure of their
plan. Lindsey admits the senior partners will not be
pleased. Lee suggests that they kill Faith. Faith asks if she
is a prisoner but Angel tells her she's free to go. He
reminds her she faced a similar choice once before and asks
if she liked the way things turned out. Faith asks Angel to
help her. Wesley meets the Watchers' Council group in a
bar. Collins tells Wesley that the Council have made a
mistake and offers to reinstate him if he'll turn over Faith,
reminding him how dangerous a rogue slayer can be. They
provide him with a sedative that will render Faith unconscious so that they can get her back to England for

rehabilitation. Wesley agrees, under one condition: they are not to harm Angel.

Angel tells Faith that the first thing she has to do is apologise to Wesley. Faith argues there are some things you can't take back. She says that Buffy was her only friend and she repaid her by sleeping with her boyfriend. Realising she's inadvertently told Angel that Buffy is with someone else, Faith apologises and Angel tells her that saying sorry isn't so hard. Wolfram & Hart send a demon after Angel and Faith. Faith kills it and then stares at her blood-soaked hands, horrified. Angel tries to comfort her just as Buffy arrives.

Buffy says that Giles told her Faith tried to kill Angel and was worried. Faith attempts to apologise to Buffy but Buffy threatens to beat her to death. Buffy and Angel begin to fight over Faith, so Angel sends Faith upstairs. Buffy sarcastically accuses Faith of playing Angel, but he explains it was a cry for help and that he can relate to Faith. Buffy says that she can't since, unlike them, she has never 'murdered anyone'. Wesley comes downstairs with Faith, telling Angel they must leave because the Collins' group are expecting him to hand her over. Faith heads for the roof with Buffy following her.

Lindsey decides it's time to change tactics. He goes to see Kate and tells her that they have an enemy in common and shows her a picture of Angel who, he says, is harbouring Faith. On the roof, Buffy tells Faith she's not running. Faith begs Buffy to tell her how to make things better as Collins shoots at them. Together they leap to the adjacent building as a helicopter hovers above. Downstairs Weatherby points a crossbow at Angel and asks Wesley if the sacred oath he took as Watcher was meaningless. Wesley says he swore to protect the innocent and shouts to Angel to get to the roof as he draws Weatherby's fire before stabbing him with the syringe. Buffy exchanges punches with Collins. As she takes out her combatant, Angel leaps through the skylight and grabs the helicopter's base, pulling Smith from his seat. Angel orders the pilot to land. Faith, meanwhile, has fled.

Kate asks Angel where Faith is, but he remains silent. Kate orders his arrest and Angel is handcuffed and whisked away. Wesley and Buffy arrive at the station as Kate tells Angel that his cell affords him an excellent view of the sunrise. Angel sees Faith sitting handcuffed across the room saying that she wants to confess. Buffy thinks Angel should have told her what was going on. Angel replies it wasn't any of her business. It was *her* idea that they stay away from each other. Buffy retaliates by claiming she came out of fear for him; Angel believes she came for vengeance. Buffy says she's in love with someone she trusts. Obviously hurt, Angel tells her it's nice she's found someone but that he's not allowed to. He says she should go. Buffy sadly reflects that Faith has won again. Wesley asks Angel if he wants to go after Buffy. Angel says that he does. Wesley tells him he's done the right thing with Faith. Angel disagrees: 'Faith did it.' Wesley expresses hope that Faith finds peace. Angel says he thinks she has a chance.

Dreaming (as *Buffy* Often Proves) is Free: Faith's dream of killing Angel. That girl really has got some nasty stuff floating around in her head. She also has a flashback to her murder of Alan Finch in *Buffy*: 'Bad Girls'.

Denial, Thy Name is Buffy: Buffy is horrified that her greatest enemy seems to have her claws into her former lover and this colours her actions for the rest of the episode.

It's a Designer Label!: Kate's chunky grey sweater puts in another appearance.

References: *The X-Files* (Kendrick: 'Everybody knows you've gone all-Scully. Anytime one of these weird cases crosses anyone's desk, you're always there.' Kate: 'Scully's the sceptic.' Kendrick: 'Huh?' Kate: 'Mulder's the believer, Scully's the sceptic.' Kendrick: 'Scully's the chick, right?'). When Faith channel-surfs she sees a fragment of a 1940s *Superman* cartoon.

Third & Long, the bar where Wesley meets the Council, is really in New York, located on 3rd Avenue close to the Empire State Building.

Bitch!: Wesley calls Faith this at one point.

The Charisma Show: She's only in it for a few moments, but she gets one great line, telling Wesley: 'If it's any consolation, it really does look like you were tortured by a much larger woman.'

L.A.-Speak: Angel: 'Paid vacation?' Cordelia: 'Like I'm gonna stick around here while psycho case is roaming around downstairs, with three tons of medieval weaponry. *Not.* Oh and I'm thinking, sugar high, maybe not a great idea.'

Lilah: 'It's strictly a handshake deal.' Lindsey: 'Not that it's necessary for you to have hands for us to do business with you.' Lilah: 'That was speciesist of me, I apologise.'

Buffy: 'You hit me.' Angel: 'Not to go all schoolyard on you, but you hit me first.'

Wesley: 'She cleaned your clocks, didn't she?'

Angel: 'For a taciturn shadowy guy, I got a big mouth.'

Cigarettes and Alcohol: Lilah drinks whisky in Lindsey's office (see **16**, 'The Ring'). In the pub, Wesley and the Council Elite drink, variously, Guinness, lager (or possibly cider) and brown ale. Collins smokes in the bar despite there being a 'No Smoking' sign (as there are in all bars in California).

Sex and Drugs and Rock'n'Roll: The sexual tension in the Angel/Faith/Buffy scenes are something to see: Angel: 'She's not going to run.' Buffy: 'Why would she? When she has her brave knight to protect her? Does she cry, pouty lips, heaving bosom?'

Later, Angel tells his former love: 'It's nice you moved on. I can't. You found someone new. I'm not allowed to, remember? I see you again, it cuts me up inside, and the person I share that with is me. You don't know me any more, so don't come down here with your great new life and expect me to do things your way.'

'You May Remember Me from Such TV Series as . . .': Alastair Duncan has appeared in many TV shows, including *Blossom*, *Sabrina the Teenage Witch*, *Babylon 5* and *Highlander*.

Don't Give Up the Day Job: Adam Vernier is possibly best known for a role he didn't get. As a six-year-old he narrowly lost out to Danny Lloyd for the part of Danny in Kubrick's *The Shining*.

Logic, Let Me Introduce You to This Window: At the end of the 'Previously on *Angel*' scenes, we see Faith and Angel in the alley, kneeling as we left them at the end of 'Five by Five'. Wesley was in the middle of the alley but in this sequence, he is standing to the side. Everyone's bruises go through startling changes throughout the episode. Faith's, for instance, vacillate between raw to nearly invisible and back again. Also, the cut on Buffy's lip from Angel's punch disappears entirely in one scene, only to reappear later. Faith killed the assassin demon. Where did it go? How 'Elite' is the Council team? They have automatic weapons and yet they miss everything. So, Angel *does* have a TV, despite what he told Rebecca in 'Eternity' (maybe he's just got it?).

I Just *Love* Your Accent: Wesley gets to display moments of dry laconic wit, asking Angel: 'Developed a sweet fang, have you?' His anger when he says, 'Don't you dare take the moral high ground with me after what she did,' is heartfelt.

We learn about the machinations of the Watchers' Council: Weatherby: 'Wouldn't cough up the dosh for the airfare home, would they?' Wesley: 'They wouldn't.' Smith: 'All those alchemists on the Board of Directors and they still make us fly coach. *Miserly bastards.*'

Wesley: 'I have some conditions of my own, one actually. No harm must come to the vampire.' Weatherby: 'Oh, don't be a *ponce*.' Presumably Joss Whedon watched a lot of darts on TV while he was in England? Weatherby has a wonderful Jack Regan moment: '*SHUT IT!*'

Quote/Unquote: Angel: 'It wasn't too long ago that you were the one making the case for her rehabilitation.' Wesley: 'It wasn't too long ago that I had full feeling in my right arm.'

Buffy: 'Giles heard that she tried to kill you.' Angel: 'That's true.' Buffy: 'So you decided to punish her with a severe cuddling?'

Lee: 'This is getting ridiculous. The first assassin kills the second assassin, sent to kill the first assassin, who didn't assassinate anyone until we hired the second assassin to assassinate her.' Lindsey: 'All right, this obviously isn't working.' Lilah: 'You *think*?'

Notes: 'What do you want to do? You gonna throw me off the roof, again?' Doesn't quite have the spirit and the dark, nefarious undertones of the previous episode, but this is a superb mini-action movie (including helicopters, machine-guns and rooftops) in which Buffy, for once, is the enemy and Faith's redemption is the crux.

The trio of Council soldiers comes to L.A. to recapture Faith and bring her to justice in England having failed to catch her in Sunnydale (see *Buffy*: 'Who Are You?'). They try to entice Wesley into helping them by promising his reinstatement. Sunnydale is said to be north of Los Angeles. Faith eats Wesley's popcorn. She says she can live off the stuff.

Joss Whedon's Comments: Asked for his favourite episodes of the first season, Joss noted: 'Seventeen, eighteen and nineteen ['Eternity', 'Five by Five', 'Sanctuary']. We get into some very interesting and creepy personal stuff with our characters and the people around them and they made me more excited about the show than I've been yet.'

Tim Minear's Comments: 'Eliza is a force of nature. Just amazing. Faith is a fantastic character who, in my opinion, flourishes in *Angel*. If I have anything to say about it, she'll be back. But then, I really don't. But the potential is certainly there.'

Previously on *Buffy the Vampire Slayer*: 'The Yoko Factor', 9 May 2000: The Initiative commander, Colonel McNamara, talks via video to someone at the Pentagon. Morale is low since Professor Walsh's death and the escape of the prototype, Adam. The politician says that the incident with Riley Finn was unfortunate. The colonel suggests that he won't be hard to find, he'll stay close to his girlfriend. The politician looks at a file and says that their data banks don't have much on Buffy Summers. 'She's just a girl,' McNamara tells him. 'She's a lot more than that,' Spike tells Adam, who thinks Buffy makes things interesting. Adam asks why Spike fears Buffy. Spike replies that he doesn't fear anything, he's just had bad luck. 'I will make you whole again,' says Adam. Spike notes that Buffy's friends are important too. Adam suggests taking them away from her. Spike likes the idea and tells Adam he'll take care of them. Adam asks what he intends to do. 'Not a blessed thing, they're gonna do it for me.'

Xander brings fugitive Riley clothes to wear. Riley wonders if Buffy has come back from Los Angeles yet. Riley senses that Xander doesn't like Angel either. 'It's not like I hate the guy,' Xander says. 'Just the guts part.' He asks Riley how much Buffy told him about Angel. 'Everything,' Riley says. How he went evil, she cured him and he left. 'One moment's happiness,' Xander comments and explains *exactly* how Angel lost his soul, realising that Buffy left that part out of the story. He tries to reassure Riley that it's all ancient history. Giles is playing guitar and singing 'Freebird' when he is startled by Spike's arrival. Spike tells Giles he knows a way to get files from the Initiative and he's willing to trade. Giles agrees, but Spike says that's not good enough – this deal is for the Slayer. Giles says that he's Buffy's Watcher. Spike points out that he's actually her *former* Watcher and that she hardly listened to him even when he was in charge. She treats Giles, Spike notes, 'like a retired librarian'. Depressed, Giles pours himself a drink. Tara and Willow play with their new kitten, Miss Kitty Fantastico. Willow says she hasn't dealt with the housing situation, but mentions there are some off-campus places for groups. Tara believed that Willow would be dorming with Buffy again, but Willow's not sure. 'It hardly feels like we're roomies now.' The next day, Riley goes to Buffy's room, telling her that he got tired of sitting around. Buffy says that Angel upset her in Los Angeles. When asked how, she doesn't want to talk about it. Xander and Anya get some military fatigues for Spike who comments that Xander won't make it very far in boot camp. Anya is furious to hear that Xander is joining the army. Xander says he's doing no such thing and asks Spike where he heard this. Spike says Willow and Buffy were talking. Xander is furious that the girls think of him as a useless lunk. 'They look down on you,' Anya confirms. Buffy patrols the woods and encounters Forrest. He asks if she's killing humans now and suggests they go their separate ways. Buffy heads towards a cave where, it turns out, Forrest is also going. Forrest says he blames her for getting Riley to commit treason and ruining his future. 'Future doing what?' she demands. In the cave they find Adam waiting for them. Buffy tries to shoot him but Adam knocks the blaster from her hand. Forrest is killed and Buffy barely escapes with her life. Spike arrives at Giles's where Willow and Tara are waiting. He hands Willow several computer disks and she loads one into her laptop. Unfortunately, the disks are encrypted; Spike asks Willow if she can crack it. She replies that it'll be difficult, prompting Spike to comment that she's not the computer whiz she once was. She insists that she is. He tells her that he heard Buffy and Xander saying how she was too busy with the new thing to work with computers as much, that it's a phase and she'll get over it. He comments that if a person wants to be a witch that's their business. 'I knew Buffy was freaked,' Willow responds angrily.

Colonel McNamara is informed that Initiative cell capacity 'maxed out' three days ago. They enter the communications centre and hear a mayday from one of their patrols being attacked. Riley listens to the same call and hurries to the location. There he finds a dark-clad figure-of-the-night-type-thing. 'Riley Finn,' it says. Riley asks if he should know it to which the creature replies they have a friend in common. 'Angel,' Riley states.

Angel wants to know if the welcoming committee was his idea. Riley says he heard that Angel was all peaceable now and wonders, 'What could've happened with Buffy that would make you lose your soul?' Angel says that's none of his business, he's here to see Buffy. They fight and Angel beats the crap out of him. Buffy returns to her room to find Angel. She asks him if he came to see her because he thought of something even more hurtful to say. Riley bursts into the room and points his gun at Angel. Buffy fumes, 'You've got to be kidding me.' 'You actually sleep with this guy?' Angel asks Buffy. Buffy steps between them and shoves them apart, threatening to send them both to the hospital if she sees one more display of testosterone poisoning. Buffy demands to know what Angel thought he was doing by pounding on her boyfriend. He says he was trying to make things better. Buffy can't help but laugh. He came to apologise for the way he spoke to her in L.A. Buffy admits that he wasn't completely wrong. They don't live in each other's worlds any more. Angel noticed how intense things are in Sunnydale and offers to help. Buffy thinks the best thing he can do is leave. He understands and starts to walk off, but he turns around to tell her something about Riley. 'I don't like him.' She smiles and thanks him again.

Spike tells Adam that tearing the Scooby gang apart was easier than he thought. It's the Yoko Factor, he says, asking Adam if he has ever heard of the Beatles. Adam says he liked 'Helter Skelter'. Spike explains how they were important and when they broke up everybody blamed Yoko, but she just happened to be there. It's the same with kids, going off to college and growing apart. Adam is pleased that the Slayer has been separated from her friends. Buffy asks Riley how badly he's hurt. He says he doesn't know; the night is still young. He admits that he doesn't know much about Angel or her relationship with him, he just asks that if she's going to break his heart to do it fast. 'What? You think Angel and I . . .?' She tells him of course 'that' didn't happen. Riley explains that when he found out what makes Angel lose his soul, he assumed the worst, especially when he saw him bad. She assures him that Angel isn't bad. 'Seriously?' he asks. *'That's* a good day?' Buffy asks if she has ever given him reason not to trust her. He admits that she hasn't. Buffy then has to tell him that Forrest is dead. Riley is devastated.

Buffy goes to Giles's apartment where Willow is unable to crack the encryption. Frustrated, Buffy says she can't wait around, that maybe she should go back to the cave and track Adam. Willow tells her that she might get lucky and Adam will rip her arms off. Giles, more inebriated than ever, says 'You never train with me any more. He's gonna kick your arse.' Buffy is shocked. He apologises for being honest. Xander offers to help but Buffy tells him he's not going. Xander remarks that she and Willow can do the superpower thing while he 'putts around the Batcave with crusty old Alfred'. Giles points out he's no Alfred, because Alfred had a job. Buffy says Willow isn't going either. 'Great,' Willow says, 'then when you have your new "no arms" we can all say, "Gee, it's a good thing we weren't there getting in the way."' Xander offers to get Buffy some new fighting pants. Buffy tells them this isn't helping. The argument continues, Buffy saying, 'I need both of you. Just not now.' Willow wants to know exactly how Buffy needs her. She adds that Xander would be great in the army, but wonders if the umbilical cord between him and Anya could stretch that far. Xander knew she didn't like Anya, but Willow counters by saying she'll leave being judgemental to him and Buffy. Buffy tells them if she was any more open-minded about some of the choices they made, her whole brain would fall out. Xander reminds Willow not to forget how superior Buffy is. 'You guys, stop it. What happened to you today?' Buffy asks. But Willow tells her it's not just today, that things have been wrong 'since Tara', because Buffy can't handle the fact that Tara is her girlfriend. Xander disagrees, saying it started when they went off to college and forgot about him. Then he turns on Willow in shock. 'Tara is your *girlfriend*?' Buffy tells them that's enough and asks them if they want to help. Buffy suggests they can all go into the cave with Willow and Xander attacking her and the funny drunk drooling on her shoe. 'I guess I'm starting to understand why there's no ancient prophecy about a Chosen One "and her friends".' She hurries out of the apartment, saying that if she needs help she'll go to someone she can count on.

Adam has a visitor. 'I've been waiting for you.' 'And now I'm here,' Riley replies.

20
War Zone

US Transmission Date: 9 May 2000
UK Transmission Date: 19 May 2000

Writer: Garry Campbell
Director: David Straiton
Cast: Michele Kelly (Alonna), Maurice Compte (Chain),
Mick Murray (Knox), Joe Basile (Lenny),
Sean Parhm (Bobby), Sven Holmberg (Ty),
Rebecca Klingler (Madame Dorion),
Kimberly James (Lena), Ricky Luna (James)

A young girl is followed by a gang of vampires, who think they have trapped her in an alley. In reality it's an ambush as Gunn steps forward, carrying a sword along with other young vigilantes armed with stakes and crossbows. They kill several vampires but one of the youngsters is badly injured and they retreat to their headquarters, beneath an abandoned building. Gunn's sister, Alonna, questions his tactics, claiming he has a deathwish.

Cordelia, Wesley and Angel meet billionaire David Nabbit at a party at his home. He tells Angel that he was photographed in a demon brothel and is being blackmailed. Angel visits Madame Dorion and Lena, from whom Angel discovers that the blackmailer is called Lenny. Angel is watched from the shadows by Gunn and his group who overhear Angel making arrangements to retrieve the photographs from Lenny the following night. Nabbit writes a huge cheque to Angel Investigations. Cordelia and Wesley thank him for his generosity though they remind him that the job is not yet finished.

Lenny meets Angel but as the pictures are delivered two demons attack Angel. Weak from the fight, Angel is unprepared for a further attack by Gunn and his gang. The young vampire hunters drive him into a warehouse. He escapes from a series of elaborate traps and grabs Alonna, using her as a shield. Gunn tells Angel they're going to kill him, but Angel releases Alonna as a show of faith and then saves her life when Alonna inadvertently falls on a trip wire. Gunn lets Angel go, but warns him not to come back.

Angel asks Wesley to find out where the kids live and surmises that there must be a vampire nest nearby. At the nest Knox, the leader, complains to his group that they've become lazy and kills Ty, his right-hand man, as an example to the others. Alonna argues with her brother and Chain, believing that Angel could be of use, but they are unwilling to trust him. Angel finds the nest and beats information from one of the vampires. Meanwhile, tear gas is thrown through the teenager's warehouse window, but it's a trap as the vampires snatch Alonna and whisk her away in a van.

Angel finds the group preparing to rescue Alonna. He warns that they are walking into a trap. Gunn floods the room with sunlight, forcing Angel into a meat locker. At the vampire lair Gunn goes in alone and finds Alonna, but he is too late; she has become a vampire. Alonna tells him not to be sad, she's stronger than ever and explains that there's no guilt or grief. She argues that they can stay together for ever. Angel fruitlessly tries to escape until Cordelia and Wesley free him. Alonna reminisces with Gunn about their childhood and how he always protected her. Gunn sadly says goodbye to his sister and kills her.

Angel arrives and tells Gunn that they need to get out. Gunn's friends rush into the building, just as the vampires come out of hiding. Knox taunts Gunn about Alonna. Angel tells Knox that L.A. is *his* territory. Knox asks Angel who he is. He replies, 'The name's Angelus,' and then kills the vampire. Wesley and Cordelia sit on a park bench discussing how hard a life the youngsters have led. Angel and Gunn are on a rooftop. Gunn says he doesn't need any help. 'No,' Angel tells him, 'but *I* might,' and vanishes into the night.

Dudes and Babes: There are lots of babes at Nabbit's party. Sadly, he doesn't know any of them, even if one or two appear to know him. More are in evidence at Madame Dorion's including the alluring Lena who tickles Angel's manhood with her tail. Knox's vampire gang includes punks, skins and rastas.

It's a Designer Label!: The series first 'anorak'. Since Gunn's wearing it, no sarcastic comments will be made. Gunn's sweatshirt has 'New York' printed on it and he wears various coloured bandanas in this and subsequent episodes. Cordelia's party dress is lovely, as is her maroon scarf.

References: The TV series *The Naked Truth* is mentioned. Gunn's gang of vampire hunters and their armoury is reminiscent of *Mad Max 2: The Road Warrior*. The sequence where Angel runs the gamut of traps may be a homage to *Raiders of the Lost Ark*. Nabbit mentions playing Dungeons and Dragons as a teenager and that 'some of us really got into it'. This could be an allusion to the memorable TV movie *Mazes and Monsters*. Alonna quotes from Beck's 'Loser' ('So why don't you kill me?'). Variations on the 'You expecting someone else?' opening have been used in *Doctor Who* ('The Caves of Androzani') and a *Phantom Menace*-spoof trailer for *Austin Powers: The Spy Who Shagged Me*.

The Charisma Show: The regulars continue to develop their witty badinage. Wesley, on what Cordelia is smelling:

'Camembert I believe.' Cordelia: 'No. Money. I like to smell a little money once in a while.' Angel: 'She's not just saying that. Hide some in the office some time and watch her. It's uncanny.'

Classic *Double Entendre*: Cordelia: 'I like David. It's such a strong, masculine name. It just feels good in your mouth.'

L.A.-Speak: Lena: 'Just don't do that face thing . . . Look, Ma, no hands.'
  Alonna: 'It shouldn't have gone down the way it did.'
  James: 'I suck, OK?'
Knox: 'Stupid human street trash. For seventy years we ruled this neighbourhood. Used to be decent people lived here. Working people. And now? You can't even finish one without wanting to puke.'

Yo, a Haven for the Bruthas, Homeboy: Even if it is in the gutter . . .

Cigarettes and Alcohol: Cordelia drinks what looks like champagne at Nabbit's party.

Sex and Drugs and Rock'n'Roll: Madame Dorion's is a demon brothel in Bel Air. Wesley notes, 'The Watchers' Council is *rife* with stories about it.' David Nabbit has been there twelve times: 'I always said that I would make a billion dollars in the Software market and learn to talk to girls. Still working on step two.' The conversation between Wesley and Angel over the incriminating black-mail photographs is hilarious. Wesley: 'Oh my.' Angel: 'It's upside down.' Wesley: 'Certainly not something you'd want to have framed.'
  Cordelia: 'Perspectively speaking, I might want to prostitute myself to billionaire David Nabbit.'

'You May Remember Me from Such Films and TV Series as . . .': J. August Richards played Richard Street in the TV mini-series *The Temptations*. David Herman provides voices on both *Futurama* and *King of the Hill* and played Michael Bolton in the movie *Office Space*. He also had a role in *Born on the Fourth of July*. Rebecca Klingler has appeared in *The Green Mile*, *Titanic*, *LA Confidential* and *Copycat*. Kimberly James was Furrier in *Mystery Men*.

Don't Give Up the Day Job: A former Mouseketeer on *The Mickey Mouse Club*, Ricky Luna spent much of his childhood in his family's trapeze circus act, 'The Flying Lunas'.

Logic, Let Me Introduce You to This Window: As Cordelia bandages Angel's ribs where the stake penetrated his chest, there appears to be no corresponding hole in his shoulder blade, though the stake went in through his back. He also has no wound in his hand where he caught the crossbolt. Even though vampires heal fast (as noted on several *Buffy* episodes) Angel still sports bruises.

I Just *Love* Your Accent: Wesley's exclamation 'Good Lord,' suggests that somebody has overdosed on *The Avengers*.

Motors: There's a wonderful attack on L.A.'s pollution record. Cordelia: 'There's nothing like riding in a convertible with the top down to make you see the sun and sand. Smell that salt air?' Wesley: 'That's not salt.' Cordelia: 'I don't think it's air either.'

Quote/Unquote: Nabbit: 'Are you familiar with *Dungeons and Dragons*?' Angel: 'I've seen a few.' Wesley: 'You mean the role-playing game?' Angel: 'Oh, game? Right.'

Cordelia: 'Did someone find out you were a big nerd?' Nabbit: 'No, that's actually public record.'

Gunn: 'I don't need advice from some middle-class white-dude, that's *dead*.'

Gunn: 'What are you doing here?' Angel: 'Skulking, professionally.'

Angel: 'I'll be around.' Gunn: 'I don't need no help.' Angel: '*I* might.'

Notes: 'You expecting somebody else?' Another fine episode, 'War Zone' is about the dichotomy of Los Angeles and includes a star-making performance by J. August Richards. The plot is thin in places, but the verve and energy of the (mainly young) cast more than make up for this, particularly in several fine fight sequences.

When asked what he wants, Angel replies: 'Love, family, a place on this planet I can call my own.' The bridge in the opening sequence has been the backdrop of other episodes, including **11**, 'Somnambulist'. As kids, Gunn and Alonna lived in a shelter on Summer Street.

Soundtrack: Gunn's character theme is a variation of Angel's.

Joss Whedon's Comments: Concerning the introduction of another pair of semi-regular characters – Gunn and David Nabbit – Joss Whedon told Rob Francis: 'It's becoming clear that *Angel* works in a similar way to *Buffy*. The main characters are the people we are most invested in. We thought of it more as an anthology when we first devised it but that clearly is not going to be the formula. It's going to be more *Buffy*-like and we need a reserve of characters who have all different opinions. Wesley and Angel have a lot of similarities and so we wanted some voices in there that are unique.'

21
Blind Date

US Transmission Date: 16 May 2000
UK Transmission Date: 26 May 2000

Writer: Jeannine Renshaw
Director: Thomas J Wright
Cast: Jennifer Badger Martin (Vanessa Brewer),
Keilana Smith (Mind Reader #1),
Dawn Suggs (Mind Reader #2),
Charles Constant (Security Centre Guard),
Scott Berman (Vendor),
Derek Anthony (Dying Black Man),
Rishi Kumar (Blind Child #1),
Karen Lu (Blind Child #2), Alex Buck (Blind Child #3)

Angel finds a dying man in a warehouse and is attacked by
a blind woman with incredible strength who leaves behind
only her sunglasses. Cordelia comes up with a suspect,
Vanessa Brewer, who is on trial for double homicide and
is represented by Wolfram & Hart. In court, as Lindsey
McDonald makes his closing arguments, Angel throws the
sunglasses to the woman who catches them without
turning round. Lindsey's boss, Holland, congratulates
Lindsey on his victory in court and confesses that Vanessa
gives him the creeps. Holland expresses concern for
Lindsey, who admits he's stressed. He tells Lindsey he'd
like to see him move up in the firm and says that he knows
Lindsey is questioning his future. He asks Lindsey to create
a past for Vanessa, as she will soon be involved in a case
that will require a strong defence, concerning children.

When Angel learns that Vanessa has been acquitted, he
is enraged. He laments that he can't fight Wolfram & Hart
and the judicial system and questions his place in the
world, confessing that he misses the simplicity and clarity
of things when he was evil. Just as Angel complains that
nothing ever changes, Lindsey tells Angel that Vanessa is
going to kill some children. There are files in a vault at
Wolfram & Hart that explain everything but the firm
employs mind-readers and if he tried to acquire them he'd
never get out alive. He has devised a plan: he'll leave his
pass so Angel can gain access to the vault, but only if a
diversion can be created to get past the Wolfram & Hart
shaman who can detect the presence of a vampire on the
premises. Angel tells him that won't be a problem. Angel
meets Gunn to ask for his help. Lindsey returns to
Wolfram & Hart while Angel gains access through the
tunnels. Lindsey creates a distraction to make sure Angel
isn't spotted on the security cameras; while Gunn is
making a scene in the lobby, and two of his posse drop a
bundle next to him, Angel climbs into the basement. In the
surveillance room, the vampire-detecting shaman begins to
squeal just as Gunn opens the bundle to reveal a startled
vampire. Angel retrieves the ID badge, as Lindsey watches
him on the monitor. Once inside the security room, Angel

is attacked by a demon that Lindsey warned him about. Thanks to Wesley, Angel has a powder, which he blows in the demon's face, nullifying it. Angel finds the files and loads them into his briefcase. He's about to leave when he is mysteriously drawn to an ornately carved cylinder. Picking it up, he sets off the alarm. He escapes just before the doors shut.

Upstairs, Lilah, Lee and Lindsey watch as Holland escorts two odd-looking women into one of the offices. Lindsey tells his cohorts they are mind-readers. All the lawyers gather to face them. Lee is discovered to have been meeting with another law firm and is shot. Holland then dismisses the lawyers, except Lindsey. Angel gives Cordy the encrypted disks while Wesley inspects the object which, he discovers, is an ancient Aramaic scroll. Angel admits he doesn't know why he took them and Wesley says he'll translate them.

Holland says he knows Lindsey betrayed the firm. He assures Lindsey that he is not going to have him killed, because he believes he just needs a few days to think things over, and allows him to leave. Cordelia telephones Willow, who talks her through decrypting the disks. Cordelia gets into the files and discovers that Brewer's powers come from studying the Nan Jin. They also discover that the three blind children, seers, are being brought together. Lindsey arrives and says that the children are a threat to Wolfram & Hart. Angel and Lindsey go to the safehouse in which the children are being kept to find Vanessa has beaten them to it. They fight. Angel using his ability to remain absolutely still to combat the blind woman's extrasensory powers. Finally he stabs Vanessa with her own cane.

Wesley tells Angel that the Scrolls of Aberjian mention a vampire with a soul. He says that there is a design to the world and he has a place in it. Holland is cleaning out his office when Lindsey returns to Wolfram & Hart. Lindsey tells his ex-boss that he's made copies of the files to ensure his safety. Holland admires Lindsey for standing up to the firm and offers him his own job because he's going upstairs. Lindsey sits at his new desk and gazes out over the lights of L.A.

Dudes and Babes: Vanessa Brewer's LAPD profile says: 'Date of Birth: July 18, 1967. Place of Birth: San Francisco. Citizenship: United States. Gender: Female. Hair: Brown. Eyes: Blind. Height: 5'6". Weight: 122. Misc: Blind eyes, no visible iris. Known Associates: None. Arrests: 1 misdemeanour (12 July 93 – Driving w/o a license); 2 felonies (23 Apr 95 – Aggravated assault; 6 Oct 99 – Double Homicide); convictions 0; on bail (trial in progress).' In her latest case, defended by Lindsey McDonald, she was acquitted. She wasn't born blind but lost her sight at the age of 21, the loss being self-inflicted. She spent five years studying in Pajaur with the Nan Jin (cave-dwelling monks). She reached enlightenment and can now 'see' with her heart and not her mind.

Denial, Thy Name is Lindsey: Suffering a 'crisis of conscience' over the activities of Wolfram & Hart, Angel tells Lindsey that he has the chance to change. However, his mentor, Holland, who hand-picked Lindsey when he was a sophomore because of his 'potential', offers the lawyer the one thing he cannot refuse: 'the world'.

It's a Designer Label!: Cordelia's red T-shirt is excellent; but for garish quality, check out Gunn's orange sweatshirt and, even worse, the vampire's leather trousers. *Very* 1980s.

References: Wesley: 'No blind demons. Perhaps Angel's discovered a new species.' Cordelia: 'What, Hellen Kellerus homicidalus?' refers to author and educator Helen Keller (1880–1968). Also referenced, *Superman*, Peggy Lee's 'Is That All There Is?', *Etch-A-Sketch*, the Rubik's cube and 'LAPD online' (the site Cordelia goes to for research. This page looks nothing like the real LAPD Online page). The removal of the disks from Wolfram & Hart is very *Mission: Impossible*. The eyes of the girl are reminiscent of the eyes of the children in *Village of the Damned*. 'The righteous shall walk a thorny path' may be an allusion to *Tantra Six of Tirumantiram*.

Bitch!: Lindsey: 'Sorry I'm late. Hope I didn't worry anyone.' Cordelia: 'We just figured you were dead.'

The Charisma Show: The charming scene of Cordelia talking to Willow on the telephone.

L.A.-Speak: Cordelia: 'That's not the real *whammy*.' And: 'I thought *born-again guy* was gonna do it.'

Angel: 'I'm smelling a whole lot of fear. Big, stinky, mortal terror.'

Not Exactly a Haven for the Bruthas: Gunn anti-Wolfram & Hart rant: '*Whoo-hoo*. My God. They told me it was true, but I didn't believe them. Damn, here it is. Evil white folks really do have a Mecca. Now, now, girls, don't get all riled up. Did you just step on my foot? Is that my foot you just stepped on? Are you *assaulting* me, in this haven of justice? Somebody get me a lawyer, because my civil rights have seriously been violated. Oh, I get it. You all can cater to the demon, cater to the dead man, but what about the *black man*?'

'You May Remember Me from Such Films and TV Series as . . .': Sam Anderson was Kevin Davis in *The Cape*, Dr Keyson in *ER* and has also appeared in *Forrest Gump*, *La Bamba* and *The X-Files* episode 'The Pine Bluff Variant'.

Don't Give Up the Day Job: Dawn Suggs directed the 1990 movie *Chasing The Moon*.

Logic, Let Me Introduce You to This Window: Lindsey tells Angel that the secret vault is on sub-level two, but when Lindsey exits the elevator it warns him that he is entering sub-level three. When researching Vanessa's history it is stated that she was born on 19 July 1967 and at the age of 21 joined a group of blind monks in another country for five years, but her police record says she was arrested for driving without a licence on 12 July 1993, which is only four years after she would have joined the monks. The credits say Jennifer Badger Martin plays 'Vanessa Weeks', but she is called Vanessa Brewer throughout the episode.

Quote/Unquote: Angel: 'It's their system and it's one that works . . . Because there's no guilt. There's no torment, no consequences. It's pure. I remember what that was like. Sometimes, I miss that.'

Wesley: 'There *is* a design, Angel. Hidden in the chaos it may be, but it's true. And you have your place in it.'

Notes: 'Are you telling me self-mutilating, psycho assassin chick reached enlightenment?' This one rambles a bit, though some of the set-pieces are terrific and there's an excellent performance by the dryly sinister Sam Anderson and another smashing little cameo moment from J. August Richards. The main let-down is the unconvincing rationale behind Lindsey's sudden change of character-motivation.

In a mini-crossover, Willow Rosenberg helps Cordelia, via the telephone, decrypt the Wolfram & Hart files. We learn that Willow has just finished decrypting disks stolen from the Initiative (and also saving the world again), placing these events in the middle of *Buffy*: 'Primeval'. Also note that Willow says 'hey' to Wesley. In real life Alyson Hannigan (who plays Willow) and Alexis Denisof were dating.

Angel's father (see **15**, 'The Prodigal') was a silk and linen merchant. Lee Mercer held talks with another law firm, Klein & Gabler. His employment with Wolfram & Hart was subsequently terminated. With extreme prejudice. Lindsey went to Hastings Law School. He was poor but ambitious, one of six children from a very deprived background. The Wolfram & Hart lawyers call their clerks 'the amoebas'.

22
To Shanshu in L.A.

US Transmission Date: 23 May 2000
UK Transmission Date: 2 June 2000

Writer: David Greenwalt
Director: David Greenwalt

Cast: Todd Stashwick (Vocah),
Louise Claps (Homeless Woman),
Daren Rice (Uniform #1), Jon Ecklund (Uniform #2),
Lia Johnson (Vendor), Robyn Cohen (Nurse),
Susan Savage (Doctor), John Eddins (Monk #1),
Gerard O'Donnell (Monk #2),
Brahman Turner (Young Tough Guy)

Wesley is still trying to translate the prophecies of Aber-jian. 'Shanshu' is a pivotal word in the text and he's having difficulty finding its meaning. Cordelia sees in the paper that Wolfram & Hart have promoted Lindsey. Wesley laments that Lindsey had the opportunity to change. After a brief visit from their nerdish acquaintance David Nabbit, Wesley announces that he knows the meaning of Shanshu: 'Death.'

Two monks perform a ritual, conjuring the demon Vocah. He is greeted by Holland, Lilah and Lindsey. Both Cordelia and Wesley are amazed that Angel shows no concern at the prophecy, then Cordelia has a vision about a homeless woman being attacked by a demon. Holland explains to Vocah that the Scroll of Aberjian was stolen by Angel. The demon reminds them the scroll is needed for the raising of the very thing that will tear Angel from The Powers That Be. Lilah says that Angel hasn't had time to study the text. Kate finds Angel in a dark alley consoling the woman he's just saved. Kate demands to know what attacked the woman and when Angel tells her, she becomes hostile, reminding him that she hasn't forgotten it was 'his kind' that killed her father. Wesley suggests that Angel consult the Oracles, but he says he doesn't need their help. The Oracles, meanwhile, already have a visitor, Vocah, who kills them.

Cordelia visits a market, looking for a gift for Angel. Vocah follows her, brushing her hand as he passes. Cordelia suffers terrifying vision after vision and falls screaming to the ground. Vocah then enters Angel Investigations, breaks into the cabinet, removes the scroll and places something in its place. Angel finds Cordelia in hospital. The doctor tells Angel they've given her drugs but nothing seems to work. She says that Cordelia may die if they are unable to sedate her. Wesley goes to the weapons cabinet to retrieve the scroll. Angel arrives just as the building explodes.

Angel finds Wesley and carries him to safety. After another angry confrontation with Kate, Angel goes to see the Oracles, but discovers that they've been murdered. The ghost of the woman Oracle appears to Angel, complaining that so far, she doesn't like being dead. She explains that Vocah is the assassin. He's trying to weaken Angel, stripping away all of those close to him. When Angel asks how he can stop Cordelia's torment, the Oracle reveals that he needs the scroll to cure her. Angel, with Gunn protecting Cordelia and Wesley, goes to Wolfram & Hart and follows Holland, Lilah and Lindsey to where Vocah is performing a revival ritual. Vocah stops the ritual, sensing something is wrong. Angel comes crashing in and kills Vocah with his own scythe. Lindsey grabs the scroll and continues with the ritual. Bright light blasts from the box, throwing Lindsey across the room. The group hurriedly leaves with whatever was revived. Lindsey grabs one of the ritual crosses and uses it to hold Angel at bay planning to burn the scroll. Angel throws the scythe, severing Lindsey's hand. Picking up the scroll, Angel returns to the hospital where Wesley translates a passage that takes away the multiple visions. Cordelia tells Angel she saw people needing help and Angel assures her they will help them.

While Cordelia makes lunch, Wesley apologises to Angel; he can't tell him what was raised in the mausoleum. Wesley also realises that he's made a mistake. 'Shanshu' doesn't mean death, it means 'live'. He tells Angel that his destiny is to become human. Of course all of this will take place after he has survived many battles, but he *will* live again. Lilah, Lindsey and Holland look at the box from the crypt. Holland tells Lindsey that the senior partners were pleased by his sacrifice. Lilah peers into the box and tries to pacify the creature within: Darla.

Dreaming (as *Buffy* Often Proves) is Free: Cordelia's terrifying vision-overload ('I saw them all. There is so much pain. We have to help them').

Denial, Thy Name is Kate: As hinted at by Kendricks in **19**, 'Sanctuary', Kate seems to have become an object of ridicule to her LAPD colleagues (note the conversation between the two officers: 'Told you she'd show. She listens to the nut-calls on our scanner.' 'Are you sure she doesn't pick up the radio waves on her brain chip?'). She tells Angel that she doesn't care about 'most people and what they think of me. What I do care about it ridding this city of your kind.' This leads to a major confrontation in the aftermath of the attacks on Cordelia and Wesley. 'I'm glad we are not playing friends any more,' says Kate. 'There is a thing called the law.' Angel: 'This isn't about the law, this is about a little thing called life. I'm sorry about your father. But I didn't kill your father. I'm sick and tired of you blaming me for everything you can't handle. You want to be enemies? Try me.'

It's a Designer Label!: Cordelia's fringy-yellow blouse and her lovely red patterned top are obvious highlights, especially when lined up alongside Wesley's chunky blue sweater. Watch out for a 'Mayhem' T-shirt on sale behind Cordelia when she goes shopping. Lilah's short black skirt is also worth keeping an eye open for.

References: 'Shanshu' is a late-imperial genre of didactic writing incorporating the teachings of Confucianism, Buddhism and Daoism. Given what 'Shanshu' is said to mean, *To Live and Die in L.A.* takes on a new meaning. References also to the 'Magic eight-ball' toy, Judas Iscariot's betrayal of Jesus to the Pharisees for 30 pieces of silver, ouija boards, *Pinnochio* and the discount store Pennysaver. Geographical locations mentioned include the San Fernando valley towns of Reseda and Tarzana.

Bitch!: A couple of 'Cordelia-Special' moments in the final scene: 'I just hope skin and bones here can figure out what those lawyers raised *sometime* before the prophecy kicks in and you croak.' And: 'Typical. I hook up with the only person in history who ever came to L.A. to get older.'

Lilah tells Lindsey: 'Remember when Robert Price let the senior partners down and they made him eat his liver?'

The Charisma Show: 'Nobody gets my humour,' bemoans Cordelia after an inappropriate joke has fallen on deaf ears. 'I thought it was funny,' says a straight-faced Angel.

Some of Charisma's best acting of the year, especially in the hospital. Plus, the wonderful scene where Cordelia and Wesley discuss Angel's lack of connection to humanity over doughnuts and Cordelia's subsequent suggestion that they get him a puppy.

Cordelia, on David Nabbit: 'A very wealthy man with just no life at all.' After Wesley has revealed that the prophecies say that Angel will die: 'He certainly took that well. Is this that opportune time to talk about my raise?' On the prophecy itself: 'Angel faces death all the time, just like a normal guy faces waffles and French fries. It's something he faces every day like lunch. Are you hungry?'

L.A.-Speak: Wesley: 'After all you did for him he sells his soul for thirty pieces of silver.' Cordelia: 'Actually he sold it for a six-figure salary and a full benefits package.'

Nabbit: 'That was *awesome*. Can we do it again? . . . I just popped by to hang. I blew off my board of directors because tonight it's my turn to be dungeon master. What do you think of my cape?' Cordy: 'Shiny.'

Cordelia: 'Well, that *sucks*.'

Gunn: 'Lot of hungry people're gonna appreciate this. You're doing God's work here. If God was a busboy he'd look just like you. Toss it up, brother.' And: 'Yo, heads up.'

Gunn: 'I know this *fool*. That was entertaining. What y'got under that hood?' Angel: 'I need your help.' Gunn: 'I figured you didn't roar in here to ask me after my health. Pretty good, by the way. You getting enough iron? You look a little pale. OK, it's traditional in the human world to humour people who've done favours for you in the past.'

Cigarettes and Alcohol: On discovering that he will eventually become human, but not for a while, Angel tells his friends not to open the champagne yet. Cordelia prepares some blood for Angel and says he shouldn't be embarrassed drinking it in front of her and Wesley because 'we're family'.

Sex and Drugs and Lexicography: Wesley believes 'Shanshu' isn't an Aegean word but instead 'descends from the ancient Magyars. Its root is proto-Hungaric.' He later discovers that 'Shanshu has roots in so many different languages. The most ancient source is the Proto-Bantu and they consider life and death the same thing, part of a cycle. Only a thing that's not alive never dies. It's saying that you get to live until you die.'

After Cordelia has her 'scratch'n'sniff' vision, she asks for a painkiller. In hospital, the doctor suggests Ativan to sedate her ('We're trying a number of different drug therapies. Do you know if she has any allergies?' Angel: 'I don't think so. Drugs won't help her.')

'You May Remember Me from Such TV Series as . . .': Todd Stashwick appeared in *Spin City* and *Law and Order*.

Logic, Let Me Introduce You to This Window: Darla was dusted by Angel in *Buffy*: 'Angel', wasn't she? Let's hope the production team have a really good explanation up their sleeve next season. Considering he's just had his hand cut off, there's a surprising lack of blood all over Lindsey as Angel grabs the scroll from him. When Cordelia leaves the art stall she is carrying two shopping bags, which mysteriously disappear after Vocah touches her. During her visions at the outdoor market, her bracelets switch from Cordelia's left wrist to her right and back again. When Angel first opens the weapons locker, the left-hand door has three sais hanging on it. Vocah opens it a short time later and there is only one sai, and a slim dagger. Watch the doughnut that Wes and Cordy share. It's never the same half-eaten condition two shots running. When Angel knocks off Vocah's mask, it is mysteriously back in place when Angel kills him. Cordelia opens a bottle but in the next shot she's clapping her hands together and the bottle is on the table in a different spot, with the cap on.

Motors: Unsurprisingly, Wolfram & Hart own the biggest black limo you've probably ever seen, along with a green Isuzu truck used to transport crates containing the Hell-raised.

Quote/Unquote: Wesley: 'Apocalyptic prophecies aren't exactly a science.'

Cordelia: 'If I ever meet these Powers That Be I'm gonna punch them on the nose. Do you think they *have* a nose?'

Vocah: 'I am summoned for the raising, the very thing that was to bring this creature down to us, tear him from The Powers That Be. And *he* has the scroll?' Lilah: 'We're not unaware of the irony.'

Vocah: 'The old order passes away and the new order is come. He that was first shall now be last and he that was dead shall now arise.' Female Oracle: 'And he that is trespassing shall now depart.'

Lilah: 'Aren't we going to be late?' Holland: 'You never want to be on time for a ritual, the chanting, the blood rights, they go one for ever.' And, on arriving at the ceremony: 'They haven't even gotten to the Latin yet!'

Notes: 'Don't believe everything you're foretold.' A turbo-charged end to the season with one of the most spectacular bits of pyrotechnics ever seen on US TV, some great Hell-like imagery and a shocking final revelation.

Angel Investigations is room 103 of its building. Room 101 is Casas Manufacturing, 104 is John Folger, DDS (see **11**, 'Somnambulist') and 105 is Herbert Stein. According to the prophecy the beast of Amalfie (a 'razor toothed six-eyed harbinger of death') is due to arise in 2003 in Reseda. Cordelia buys paints for Angel at a stall called 'Art Attack'.

Lindsey is now a Junior Partner in Wolfram & Hart. The Oracles bleed like humans.

Soundtrack: Grant Langdon performs 'Time of Day' in the sequence where Cordelia goes shopping in the open market.

Did You Know?: While it is every fan's dream to contribute to their favourite show, few actually get the chance. Not so for Tam Cox of North Carolina, who seized an opportunity to showcase her design skills on the Angel Investigations office set. Responding to frequent references regarding the lack of suitable coffee-making facilities (particularly the need for a grinder in **13**, 'She'), Tam designed the *Angel Automatic 2000* – a coffee grinder packaged in a stylish box depicting images from the show and a version of Angel's tattoo. The production team (in particular David Greenwalt) were so delighted to receive the *AA2000* that the grinder was given a spot on top of Angel's fridge during filming of **22**, 'To Shanshu in L.A.'.

Critique: *Science Fiction World*'s Michael Wright wrote enthusiastically about the season believing the series 'opted for the traditional route of playing off the season's slow build in fine style, giving us a final confrontation with the forces behind Wolfram & Hart and a slam-bang head-to-head with the agents of evil. This is a series which really established itself, putting down strong roots for future seasons and using the occasional crossovers with *Buffy* to excellent effect. The characters of Angel and Cordelia have developed strongly and in some unexpected directions now they've moved to centre stage instead of being part of an ensemble cast, and Boreanaz and Carpenter were ably supported by Glenn Quinn as Doyle and Alexis Denisoff [sic] as Wesley, who both brought depth and subtlety to what could so easily have been one-note 'side-kick' roles.'

John Mosby, in *DreamWatch*, found the season 'hugely enjoyable [with] oodles of dark potential, some lessons learned about the strengths of an ensemble cast and then a great cliff-hanging ending. What more can we ask?'

The Angel Novels

Eager to match the worldwide success of their *Buffy* series, Pocket Pulse quickly began to publish *Angel* novels. As with *Buffy*, these actually arrived in the UK some months ahead of the show via specialist shops like Forbidden Planet.

not forgotten

Writer: Nancy Holder
Published: April 2000
Tagline: The price for immortality is steep . . .

When Angel rescues workers from a sweatshop factory, he is bitten by a snakelike demon who warns him that 'this world does not want you'. He, Cordelia and Doyle become involved with a group of Indonesians who are trying to raise Latura, a God of the Dead. This is linked to an ancient demon, Golgothla, whom Angel encountered before he was sired.

It's a Designer Label!: The reverse: Cordelia is shopping in an unfashionable market when she encounters Jusef Rais and becomes caught up in the plot.

References: Angel tells Kate he is living 'la vida loca' like Ricky Martin. *Batman*, *The Bone Collector*, *Charmed*, *Jeopardy*, *Big Trouble in Little China*, *How to Marry a Millionaire*, *The Wizard of Oz*, *Indiana Jones*, *Star Wars*, *Rolling Stone* magazine, *Die Hard V*, Monopoly.

The Charisma Show: A classic Cordelia line: 'No! My dates only die in Sunnydale, okay? Not here too!'

L.A.-Speak: The book is, irritatingly, riddled with it.

A Haven for the Bruthas: Focuses on the Indonesian population and makes the point that over half the children in L.A. are non-Caucasian.

Cigarettes and Alcohol: Angel and Doyle end up in an Irish bar. It's noted that Cordelia is too young to drink.

Sex and Drugs and Rock'n'Roll: An emergency driver overtly comes on to Angel.

Logic, Let Me Introduce You to This Window: Even the author realises that cellphones shouldn't work underground, but never explains how they do; the flashback to Galway is set in 1752, but only a fortnight before Angel was sired. Alice's journal is misdated to 1920, rather than 1930.

I Just *Love* Your Accent: Cordelia asks Doyle if he has a green card.

Notes: Angel has visited Thailand/Siam at some point in the past. This is set two months or so after *Buffy*: 'Graduation Day' (although this contradicts the impression from **1**, 'City Of' that it has been some time since Angel and Cordelia last saw each other). Doyle can't drive a manual (stick-shift) car.

redemption

Writer: Mel Odom
Published: June 2000
Tagline: History can repeat itself . . .

Whitney Tyler plays Honor Blaze in *Dark Midnight* – a TV show about a vampire DJ – but people are trying to kill her because they think she really is a vampire. When Angel meets her, she is the double of Moira, someone who Angel believes died in Galway in 1758 who was trying to kill him and Darla. In fact Whitney *is* Moira, who was possessed by a banshee when Angel killed her and is being hunted by her own former co-hunters, the Jesuit Blood

Cadre. Angel eventually realises that she is possessed and helps the Jesuits persuade the girl to exorcise herself.

Dudes and Babes: A couple of rich leather-clad L.A. kids slum it in an alley and are set upon by vampires.

Denial, Thy Name is Kate: Kate is recommending Angel and helping him, although she tells him that she wants to know a lot more about why he's doing what he does.

References: *Charlie's Angels*, *Salem's Lot*, *Forever Knight* (see **Notes**), *A Current Affair*, *Winnie the Pooh*, *Pollyanna*, *Little House on the Prairie*, *Snow White*.

The Charisma Show: Cordelia deduces that Whitney hasn't had a childhood – a vital clue to her real nature.

Not Exactly a Haven for the Bruthas: A cabbie is given dialogue that even Ian Fleming would have found racist.

Cigarettes and Alcohol: We open in a bar where Angel and Doyle are drinking beer.

Logic, Let Me Introduce You to This Window: There was supposed to be a 'Scottish rebellion' in 1758, apparently. Angel is still making references in mortal terms in 1758, five years after he was sired. Whistler is alleged to have taught Angel how to hide after he regained his soul, yet according to *Buffy*: 'Becoming' Angel didn't meet Whistler until 1996.

Notes: Whitney's show *Dark Midnight* allows a lot of riffs on a vampire TV series, although its central conceit – a vampire DJ – echoes LaCroix in *Forever Knight*. Wolfram & Hart are mentioned in passing. Filming takes place outside a bar called 'Hannigan's'. Doyle calls on Mama Ntombi, a wise seer woman and Angel seeks help from occult investigator Bascomb, whom he knew about before coming to L.A.

Two further *Angel* novels are planned for 2000: **close to the ground** is, says author Jeff Mariotte, 'about what happens when Angel gets too close to the case he's supposed to be working on – trying to protect a spoiled Hollywood brat. [He] ends up in trouble himself. It's got a lot of Celtic mythology scattered throughout it, with a healthy dose of black magic and some inside movie studio stuff that comes from my own experience.' November sees the release of **shakedown** by acclaimed SF author Don DeBrandt. In this, 'Doyle has a vision involving a seismic shift, which leads Angel to a group of Serpentine demons.'

The Angel Comics

As with their TV and novel counterparts, it was inevitable that Dark Horse's monthly *Buffy* comic would be followed by a similar *Angel* series. The *Buffy* stories had accurately captured the quirkiness and aesthetics of the TV show and its mixture of horror and humour. In many ways Joss Whedon (a self-confessed comics' fanboy since childhood) had created, in another media, characters and situations more suited to the world of superhero comics than anywhere else. As Scott Allie of Dark Horse notes: 'Joss did an interview [with *Comic Buyers Guide*]. He talked about how in the comic we don't have the same budget restraints as the TV show.'

Highlights of the *Buffy* series include a three-part retelling of Buffy's origins (a *very* DC/Marvel-style concept), the superbly drawn 'The Latest Craze' in the 1999 'Buffy Annual', the 'Bad Blood' arc (with some nice Cordelia characterisation) and 'Double Cross', a Doug Petrie story set in the aftermath of *Buffy*: 'Graduation Day' and featuring Angel.

The *Angel* comic story begins with the three-part 'The Hollower' (1999, later collected into a 64-page trade paperback). Written by Christopher Golden and drawn by Hector Gomez and Sandu Florea, this is the story of a malevolent evil that has followed Angel through his many lives, and features appearances by Darla, Spike and Drusilla. The continuity was pretty much later contradicted by **15**, 'The Prodigal', but it's fun nonetheless. (Angel's closest friend when alive was Liam McHugh, for instance.)

The monthly series began in November 1999 with the three-issue 'Surrogates', written by Golden, pencilled by Christian Zanier and inked by Andy Owens. This accurately captured the series vision of Los Angeles-*noir* and gave Doyle and Cordelia plenty to do as Angel is kidnapped in a story about a fertility clinic creating demon babies (it's not conceptually unlike **12**, 'Expecting'). 'The Changeling Wife' (issue 4), by Golden and artist Eric Powell, concerned domestic violence and featured Kate Lockley, while the three-part 'Earthly Possessions' (written by Golden and Tom Sniegoski, and with artwork by Zanier and Owens) introduced two semi-regular characters, attorney Rachel Hammerlin and Gaetano Noe, a defrocked priest and exorcist. In issues 8 and 9 ('Beneath the Surface'), corpses are cropping up in all sorts of places and Angel and Detective Lockley have different ideas about who's behind it, while issue 10 saw the beginning of a new multi-part storyline, 'Love For Sale', in which Cordelia has a vision about a Congressman just before he dies at the hands of a demon prostitute. It's impossible not to love a comic with a letters page called 'To Hell and Back'.

Further *Angel* adventures occur in *Dark Horse Presents* issues 153–155 (April–June 2000) containing the Golden/Sniegoski story, 'Lovely, Dark and Deep', with beautiful black and white artwork by Brian Horton and Paul Lee. Amusingly, Cordelia wins a part in a *Blair-Witch Project* type movie, but here, the horrors are for real.

Angel and the Internet

To series like *Angel*, the Internet is the only form of comment that is genuinely applicable. The only one that *matters*. *Buffy* has been called 'the first *true* child of the Internet age'. If this is accurate (and it pretty much is), then *Angel* is the first true *grandchild* – a series born on, and possibly (due to the instantaneous nature of fan reaction) *by*, the Net. Within weeks of *Angel* beginning a flourishing Net-fan community, it had spawned newsgroups and websites, often as annexes to already existing *Buffy* domains. As with most fandoms much of what has emerged is good but there's also a little downright scary element. This is a rough guide to get you started.

Newsgroups: The main *Buffy* usenet group, alt.tv.buffy-v-slayer, also includes lots of post concerning *Angel*, debating the merits of new and old episodes, likely developments and other topics of interest. In the past it's been an open forum with debate encouraged; however, the group has begun to attract, of late, a distinctly aggressive and overly vocal contingent who are unhappy with the current direction on both shows and want the world to know it. Hell hath no fury, it seems, like a bunch of overgrown kids with access to a computer. The group also features that curse of usenet, 'trolling' (people who deliberately send abusive and offensive messages to see what reaction they get). The *Angel* newsgroup, alt.tv.angel, actually began before the series, as a consequence of the popularity of David Boreanaz. This had somewhat humble beginnings (many initial posts were from fans of *Touched By An Angel* wondering why everyone was talking about vampires), but it's growing and has yet to acquire much of the cynicism and self-aggrandisement of the *Buffy* group. There's also some official input as writer/producer Tim Minear occasionally drops by. alt.fan.buffy-v-slayer.creative is a fan-fiction forum and carries a vast range of 'missing adventures', character vignettes, 'shipper' (relationship-based erotica) and 'slash' (same-sex erotica) stories, some of them of a very high standard. A UK newsgroup, uk.media.tv.buffy-v-slayer features gossip and spoilers from the States, but it also *stars* a number of extremely obnoxious and loud individuals, so is worth avoiding if you want a quiet life. There are also lively usenet groups in Europe (alt.buffy.europe) and Australia (aus.tv.buffy) where *Buffy* and *Angel* have big followings.

Posting Boards: *http://board.buffy.com/bronze/posting-board.shtml* is the official *BtVS* posting board, which includes regular contributions from Joss Whedon and other members of the production team and cast (writers like Jane Espenson and David Fury show up regularly along with some of the actors and former *Buffy* stunt co-ordinator Jeff Pruitt). This is an excellent forum (particularly as it features a direct line to the production office). The only problem is the sheer size of the thing. (When asked about his Internet usage, Joss Whedon told *DreamWatch*: 'I came to it late. I'm still: "What's download?"')

Websites: There are literally hundreds of sites on the Web relating to both *Buffy* and *Angel*. What follows is a (by no means definitive) list of some of the author's favourites which should give readers an idea of where to start. Many of these are also part of webrings that link to related sites. An hour's surfing can get you to some interesting places.

Disclaimer: Websites are transitory things at the best of times and this information, though accurate when it was written, may be woefully out of date after publication.

UK Sites: www.watchers.web.com (*The Watcher's Web*) is an award-winning and invaluable source of information and analysis on both *Angel* and *Buffy* from a largely British perspective. It includes numerous exclusive interviews, probably the most up-to-date news service on the Net, ratings figures and fan fiction (including some by this author). You can, literally, get lost in it for days.

http://buffy.acmecity.com/hellmouth/464/index.html (*Angel Investigations*) features well-written character profiles, a plethora of fan fiction and is designed for easy navigation.

US Sites: http://buffy.acmecity.com/watcher/403/ (*Two Demons, A Girl and A Bat-Cave*). An interesting domain which shares many qualities with the equally impressive *The Complete Buffy the Vampire Slayer Episode Guide* (www.buffyguide.com). Episode synopsis, reviews and character studies are the hallmark of this intelligently assembled site.

http://members.tripod.com/~Little__Willow/index.html (*Little Willow's Slayground*) is a delightful treasure-trove of photos, articles and reviews, plus all the latest news. Includes 'Who Says?', the VIP archive of the *BtVS* Posting Board, fun sections like 'The Xander Dance Club', cast filmographies and official web-pages for *Buffy* regulars Danny Strong (Jonathan Levinson) and Amber Benson (Tara). It's also a useful link to the charming *Keeper Sites* webring (www.geocities.com/stakeaclaim). Again it's possible to find something new on each visit.

http://www.geocities.com/Hollywood/Lot/8864/angel/angel-ws 2.htm (*Angel Music Pages*), a spin-off of the seminal *Buffy: The Music* domain, Leslie Remencus's beautiful and frequently updated site is devoted to the music on *Angel* (as indexed by artist, episode and song) plus interviews, tour dates, musical allusions, etc. An absolute gem.

http://rhiannon.dreamhost.com/angel/ (*The Angel Annex Presented by The Sunnydale Slayers*) is part of the 'Suns' group (www.enteract.com/~perridox/SunS/) and was, according to the authors, set up by 'a gang of people . . . who wanted to talk about, lust after and discuss in depth *Buffy the Vampire Slayer*.' It's great fun including fiction, well-written reviews, cast biographies and a link to the delightfully daft *World Wide Wesley*. Love the *FAQ* where they answer the question, 'So, it's not just a bunch of women who want to drool at Anthony Stewart Head,

David Boreanaz, Seth Green and Nicholas Brendon then?' with 'Oh no, we've got a few male members too!'

http://home.flash.net/~zax/angel1.htm (*Zax's Angel Page*) an excellent and well-designed site which features a lot of less obvious aspects of the *Angel* universe, with space given to the comics, novels and other merchandise, a large spoilers section and lengthy cast biogs.

http://www.geocities.com/~angelsecrets (*Angel's Secrets*). Chrystal's long-running website is devoted to all things Boreanaz and is always worth a visit. Includes a regularly updated news section with numerous links to obscure interviews.

http://sanctuary.digitalspace.net/ (*The Sanctuary Devoted to David Boreanaz and Angel*) prides itself on being 'the most comprehensive site on *Angel* on the Net'. It's certainly very good, with extensive fan-fiction, a very interesting rumours page ('The Runes') and a section containing impressive episode summaries.

http://www.geocities.com/thecityofangel/index2.html (*The City of Angel*) is another highly entertaining and enthusiastic fan-site with lots of detail on the episodes, a big section on 'creative fandom' (both fiction and artwork) and a chilling photo of the site-owner's cat!

http://slayer.simplenet.com/angelsoul/main.htm (*An Angel's Soul*) has an impressive media section (an invaluable research tool) containing interview transcripts and lots of good links.

http://slayerfanfic.com (*The Slayer Fanfic Archive*) is, as the name suggests, a site dedicated to *Buffy* and *Angel* fanfiction with links to related pages that offer all sorts of fan writing. For those yet to discover the joys of 'shipper' and 'slash' fanfic, this is the place for you.

www.webring.org/cgi-bin/webring?ring=angelshippers; id=22;list (*The Angel Romantics Web Ring*) is a series of sites dedicated to the romance inherent in the Buffy/Angel relationship.

Both Charisma and David have numerous unofficial web-sites: www.charisma-carpenter.com (*Charisma-Carpenter. Com*) and www.gate.net~woof/ (*Acute Angle – The Un-official David Boreanaz Site*) are among the best. There are also a couple of nice Wesley pages like www.angelfire.com/tv/wwp/index.htm (*Who Watches This Watcher?*). Curious-ly, one of the best *Angel* sites around is dedicated to a former cast member: www.ljc.simplenet.com/doyle/ (*Doyle – Glenn Quinn*) is a beautiful celebration of the series and of Glenn Quinn. Widespread coverage of all aspects of the show and a huge archive section make this a must-see for all *Angel* fans.

http://cityofangel.com (*City of Angel*) The design of this fine fansite is first rate and they have a lot of unique content, along the lines of *The Watcher's Web*, with production staff and comics interviews, a 'behind the scenes' section and excellent news coverage.

Redeeming Qualities

Marcus: 'You did terrible things when you were bad,
didn't you? And now you are trying so hard to do
good . . . What do you want, Angel?'
Angel: 'I want forgiveness.'

– 'In the Dark'

Redemption is one of the key elements in epic storytelling.
In hundreds of literary styles from the Greek and Roman
myths and the Bible onwards the quest for atonement to
transcend past unworthy deeds remains a beguiling and
fascinating one for most of an audience. Because, as the
man said, 'we've *all* got *something* to atone for.'

In *Angel*, the central character has more to purge than
most. A killer without compassion or feeling ('the meanest
vampire in all the land,' according to Doyle's fairytale
version of Angelus's origins), he spent over a century
engaged in deranged acts of torture, mayhem and ultravio-
lence. Angelus killed not through fear, or madness, or a
need to survive. He killed because he *enjoyed* it, and it's the
realisation of this (via a gypsy curse, admittedly) that
allows him to understand what he has to atone for. When
Doyle tells him that the Ring of Amara is 'your redemption. It's what you've been waiting for,' in 3, 'In the Dark',
Angel replies: 'I did a lot of damage in my day, more than
you can imagine.' Doyle asks: 'So what? You don't get the
ring because your period of self-flagellation isn't over.
Think of all the daytime people you could help between
nine and five.' Angel isn't satisfied: 'The whole world is
designed for them, so much that they have no idea what
goes on around them after dark. They don't see the weak
ones lost in the night, or the things that prey on them. If I
join them, maybe *I'd* stop seeing too . . . I was brought

back for a reason and as much as I'd like to kid myself, I don't think it was for eighteen holes at Rancho.'

It's a theme that is repeated over and over through the first season of *Angel*. All of the regular characters besides Angel have their own dark places and a need to shine some light on them. Like alcoholics giving up the drink (a metaphor the series intended to take very literally at one time) they have to realise themselves that they *need* to change before the process of redemption can begin. For Cordelia, in **5**, 'Rm W/a Vu', a new home offers her a fresh beginning. 'Working for redemption', as Angel puts it. 'I'm still getting punished,' she laments, 'for what I was, for everything I said in high school just because I could get away with it. Then it all ended and I had to pay. But [with] this apartment, I could be me again. Like I couldn't be *that* awful if I get to have a place like that?' 'Dammit, you're Cordelia Chase,' Angel scolds her. 'Are you just going to lie there like a weakling? Get off your ass and be *tough*.' It's when she comes to terms with her past – and, more importantly, makes someone else come to terms – that she receives her reward.

In **12**, 'Expecting', that process is continuing. She admits to Wilson that: 'In high school I knew my place and, OK, it was a haughty place and maybe I was a *tad* shallow.' As the season progresses, Cordy also accepts the 'gift of vision' from Doyle and The Powers That Be and, by **22**, 'To Shanshu in L.A.', has come to realise, through being exposed to *everyone*'s pain and suffering, that she and her friends have the chance to do real good: 'I know what's out there. We have a lot of evil to fight, a lot of people to help.'

Doyle discovers in **9**, 'Hero' that 'you never know your strength until you're tested' is not an empty slogan, but a necessary step to wiping out the past. Doyle thinks that Angel's actions in **8**, 'I Will Remember You' qualify him for special treatment: 'I would have chosen the pleasures of the flesh over duty and honour any day of the week. I just don't have that strength.' But Doyle, despite concluding, '*You* lived and loved and lost and fought and vanquished inside a day, I'm still trying to work up the courage to ask Cordy out for dinner,' and who in **7**, 'The Bachelor Party', tells Angel that his marriage failed because *he*, rather than Harriet his former wife, could not accepted his demon heritage, finally confronts his darkest secret – his betrayal of his own kind – in **9**, 'Hero'. This, it transpires, is why he was cursed. 'I'd only just found out about my demon side. I didn't know what it meant. The idea of having family obligations with guys that looked like big blue pin cushions was . . . too much to take.'

Even when Doyle has made the ultimate sacrifice, the theme of redemption (his and others) is weightily present in the immediate aftermath with both Cordelia and Angel (in **10**, 'Parting Gift' and **14**, 'I've Got You Under My Skin' respectively) struggling to cope with their personal grief and also facing their guilt. In the midst of this, Angel is further disturbed by 'killing dreams' and the discovery that one of the unfortunate souls he murdered during his Angelus days is still active (**11**, 'Somnambulist'): 'I'm sorry for what I did to you,' he tells Penn. 'For what I turned you into.' He genuinely means it.

The gap in Cordelia and Angel's lives is partly filled by the welcome return of Wesley, whose stereotypical stiff-upper-lip hides a decent and emotional man who cares deeply about his friends. But Wesley, too, has secrets. An unhappy childhood (**14**, 'I've Got You Under My Skin', something he shares in common with Angel in **15**, 'The Prodigal') and an inferiority complex (**17**, 'Eternity'). 'I'm a fool,' he says in **10**, 'Parting Gift'. 'The Council was right to sack me. I had two Slayers in my care . . . Fire me? I'm surprised they didn't cut my head off.' If Angel's salvation is the knowledge that he has the ability to make amends and if Cordelia's is by the (lengthy) process that opens up her world-view to the pain in others, then Wesley, ultimately, is redeemed as a character and a person by the loyalty he shows to Cordy and Angel (particularly in **19**, 'Sanctuary' – where he refuses to sell out his friend to the Watchers' Council even with the promise of reinstatement and forgiveness). For all three, the season is an emotional learning curve.

Redemption is key, also, to the ongoing story of Faith. In **18**, 'Five by Five', we see an anguished and world-weary figure; a girl sick of all the horror in her life and of the taint of evil within her. More even than her recent two-part appearance in *Buffy*, here we see Faith reaching, literally, the end of the line. Sadistically torturing her former Watcher, Wesley, for the simple reason that it will make Angel interested enough to kill her. That she chooses the path of redemption in **19**, 'Sanctuary' is almost entirely down to Angel's refusal to play the vengeance game, however much Buffy may want him to. By refusing to fight her, Angel forces Faith to face herself, and come to terms with who and what she is. In his argument with Buffy at the end of **19**, 'Sanctuary', Angel realises that *he* has changed, and that while Buffy has her own life to lead in Sunnydale, his priorities have been altered.

Redemption is there for other characters too. Gunn (in **20**, 'War Zone') survives the loss of the sister he has protected since they were children and emerges as a willing convert to Angel's crusade. It occurs also, though sadly briefly, for Lindsey McDonald (**21**, 'Blind Date') and equally temporarily Trevor Lockley (**15**, 'The Prodigal'). The former is seduced back to the dark side after a crisis of conscience, much to Angel's regret, while the latter dies with a halo, protecting the daughter he loved but never shared his feelings with. That such tragedy can be found amid the life-affirming qualities of *Angel* gives the series a poetic, almost Shakespearean touch – especially in its ruminations of the nature of how being redeemed actually works: 'There's no simple answer to that,' Angel tells Faith in **19**, 'Sanctuary'. 'I won't lie to you and tell you that it'll be easy because it won't. Just because you've decided to change doesn't mean that the world is ready for you to. The truth is no matter how much you suffer, no matter how many good deeds you do to try to make up for the past you may never balance out the cosmic scale. The only thing I can promise you is that you'll probably be haunted. Maybe for the rest of your life.'

For some, the price isn't worth paying. Kate Lockley won't be redeemed until she has learned to accept greater truths than those found in monochrome. The only things in life that are wholly black and white are Laurel and Hardy films and police officers' attitudes. Kate's disbelief in **15**, 'The Prodigal' that 'there are *not-evil* 'evil things'?' is a step away from a reality that she is fully aware of. Angel has saved her life on three occasions (**2**, 'Lonely Hearts', **6**, 'Sense and Sensitivity', **11**, 'Somnambulist'), yet Kate is unable to accept him as anything other than a monster of the kind that killed her father. Once Angel tires of trying to charm the hatred from her, his tirade in **22**, 'To Shanshu in L.A.' suggests that he views Kate as a lost cause.

When Wesley tells Angel in **19**, 'Sanctuary', 'I hope [Faith] is strong enough to make it. Peace is not an easy thing to find,' Angel's reply isn't a glib or unrealistic one. He, and the audience, are intelligent enough to know that 'working for redemption' doesn't come without a price – philosophical *and* metaphorical. 'She has a chance,' says Angel which is, ultimately, what the series is all about. It's the, literal, *Hope In Hell* – the dreams of someone in the gutter looking up at the stars. It's Cordelia's sudden realisation that the world doesn't end at her garden gate ('that was the *old* me,' she notes in **22**, 'To Shanshu in L.A.' aware that being taken to the edge of insanity has cleansed her of some worthless baggage). There's the maturing of Wesley from a hollow caricature into a man of great promise ('I've confronted more evil, slayed more demons, in short done more good while working with Angel than I *ever* did while in the Council's employ,' he tells Collins in **19**, 'Sanctuary'). The selflessness with which Doyle gave his own life to save a city but also two friends is mirrored in Angel's rejection of a life-altering gift and, later, the chance of true happiness with Buffy because it wasn't how the story was meant to end. And yet, ironically in Angel's case, the price of redemption may be worth paying in the end.

> Wesley: *'The vampire with a soul, once he fulfils his destiny, will "Shanshu". Become human. It's his reward.'*
> Angel: *'That'll be nice.'*
>
> – 'To Shanshu in L.A.'

The first season of *Angel* has seen each of the lead characters come to terms with who they are. They have all looked back at the demons in their own pasts – in some cases literally – and made the effort to overcome the weaknesses that those demons exploited. In the second season, it will be interesting to see how Whedon and Greenwalt use these purified characters against the backdrop of ever-present evil.

> Angel: *'Where are you gonna go? Back out in that darkness? I once told you that you didn't have to go out in that darkness. Remember? That it was your choice. Well, you chose. You thought that you could just touch it. That you'd be OK. But it swallowed you whole. So tell me how did you like it?'*
> Faith: *'Help me?'*
> Angel: *'Yeah.'*
>
> – 'Sanctuary'

Selected Bibliography

The following books, articles, interviews and reviews were consulted in the preparation of this text:

Abery, James, 'Where Angel Fears to Tread', *Shivers*, issue 71, November 1999.

'Angel Restores Faith', *DreamWatch*, issue 68, April 2000.

'Angel Season One', reviews of 'Rm W/a Vu', 'Sense and Sensitivity', 'The Bachelor Party' and 'I Will Remember You', Brian Barratt, *Xposé*, issue 42, January 2000.

Anthony, Ted, '12 Weeks After Columbine, Delayed "Buffy" airs', *Associated Press*, 12 July 1999.

Appelo, Tim and Williams, Stephanie, 'Get Buffed Up – A Definitive Episode Guide', *TV Guide*, July 1999.

Atkins, Ian, 'Fallen Angel', *Cult Times*, issue 47, August 1999.

Atkins, Ian, 'I Will Remember You' review, *Shivers*, issue 77, May 2000.

Baldwin, Kristen, Fretts, Bruce, Schilling, Mary Kaye, and Tucker, Ken, 'Slay Ride', *Entertainment Weekly*, issue 505, 1 October 1999.

Boreanaz, David, Landau, Juliet, and Marsters, James, 'Interview with the Vampires', interview by Tim Appelo, *TV Guide*, September 1998.

Boreanaz, David, 'Leaders of the Pack', interview (with Kerri Russell) by Janet Weeks, *TV Guide*, November 1998.

Boreanaz, David, 'City of Angel', interview by David Richardson, *Xposé*, issue 35, June 1999.

Boreanaz, David, 'Aurora Boreanaz', interview by Sue Schneider, *DreamWatch*, issue 69, May 2000.

Boreanaz, David, 'Good or Bad Angel?', interview by David Richardson, *Shivers*, issue 77, May 2000.

Bunson, Matthew, *Vampire: The Encyclopaedia*, Thames and Hudson, 1993.

Carpenter, Charisma, 'Charismatic', interview by Jim Boulter, *SFX*, issue 40, July 1998.

Carpenter, Charisma, 'Femme Fatale', interview by Mike Peake, *FHM*, issue 117, October 1999.

Carpenter, Charisma, 'Charisma Personified', interview by Jennifer Graham, *TV Guide*, 1 January 2000.

Carpenter, Charisma, 'In Step With . . .' interview by James Brady, *Parade*, 5 March 2000.

Cornell, Paul, '20th Century Fox-Hunting', *SFX*, issue 63, April 2000.

Cornell, Paul, Day, Martin, and Topping, Keith, *The Guinness Book of Classic British TV*, 2nd edition, Guinness Publishing, 1996.

Cornell, Paul, Day, Martin, and Topping, Keith, *X-Treme Possibilities: A Comprehensively Expanded Rummage Through the X-Files*, Virgin Publishing, 1998.

Fretts, Bruce, 'City of Angel', *Entertainment Weekly*, April 1999.

Gabriel, Jan, *Meet the Stars of Buffy the Vampire Slayer: An Unauthorized Biography*, Scholastic Inc., 1998.

Gellar, Sarah Michelle, 'Staking the Future', interview by John Mosby, *DreamWatch*, issue 61, September 1999.

Head, Anthony Stewart, 'Heads or Tails', interview by Paul Simpson and Ruth Thomas, *DreamWatch*, issue 69, May 2000.

'Hell is for Heroes', *Entertainment Weekly*, issue 505, 1 October 1999.

Holder, Nancy, *Angel: city of – A novelisation of the series premiere*, Pocket Pulse, December 1999.

Littlefield, Kinney, 'Avenging Angel', *The Orange County Register*, October 1999.

Middendorf, Tracy, *Insider: The Next Guest Thing*, interview by Shawn Malcom, *TV Guide*, 15 January 2000.

Mosby, John, 'UK-TV' in *DreamWatch*, issue 71, September 2000.

Nelson, Resa, 'Angel Makes Us Ask: Why Do Bad Boys Make Us Feel So Good?', *Realms of Fantasy*, February 2000.

Nelson, Resa, 'To Live and Die in L.A.', *Science Fiction World*, issue 1, June 2000.

Noxon, Marti, 'Soul Survivor', *DreamWatch*, issue 63, November 1999.

Queenan, Joe, 'Cross-Checked By An Angel', *TV Guide*, 15 April 2000.

Roush, Matt, 'The Roush Review', *TV Guide*, 11 December 1999.

Spelling, Ian, 'Biting Talent – An Interview With Charisma Carpenter', *Starlog*, May 2000.

Topping, Keith, *Slayer – The Totally Cool Unofficial Guide to Buffy*, Virgin Publishing, 2000.

Topping, Keith, 'Angel Delight', *DreamWatch*, issue 65, January 2000.

Tucker, Ken, 'Angel Baby', *Entertainment Weekly*, 3 December 1999.

Whedon, Joss, 'How I Got To Do What I Do', interview by Wolf Schneider, *teen movieline*, issue 1, March 2000.

Whedon, Joss, 'Whedon, Writing and Arithmatic', interview by Joe Mauceri, *Shivers*, issue 77, May 2000.

Whedon, Joss, 'Blood Lust', interview by Rob Francis, *DreamWatch*, issues 71–72, August/September, 2000.

Wright, Matthew, 'Endings and New Beginnings', *Science Fiction World*, issue 2, July 2000.

Wyman, Mark, 'Buffy Joins The Banned – A Fable for the Internet Age', *Shivers*, issue 68, August 1999.

Grr! Arrrgh!

Angel, like *Buffy* will return in the autumn. These are exciting times for fans of Joss Whedon's shows as the continuing and developing *Buffy* universe drags in more and more converts across the globe. *Angel*, by quickly establishing its quality and style, has now a fixed and important place within that universe, though it remains to be seen if the two shows will continue to crossover with such regularity. Joss Whedon has indicated in recent interviews that he would like to have Nick Brendon appear in an episode of *Angel* so that Cordelia and Xander's story can be concluded satisfactorily, while both Alyson Hannigan and Anthony Stewart Head have also expressed the wish to appear in future episodes of *Angel*. 'We know what arcs we want to see and who's going to be fighting who,' noted Whedon about *Angel*'s second year. 'What we don't have is a specific emotional mission.'

From the production team, it appears that Howard Gordon, Jeannine Renshaw and Tracey Stern are all moving on to other projects. Remaining with Joss, David Greenwalt, Tim Minear and Jim Kouf will be new additions Meredyth Smith and Shawn Ryan. Ryan was a producer on *Nash Bridges*. In addition, he co-wrote the film, *Welcome to Hollywood* and penned episodes of *Life with Louie*, one of which earned him a 'Humanitas Award' nomination. Smith worked as script co-ordinator on the first season of *Angel*. She was a fan and aspiring script-writer who caught the attention of the production staff.

Details on the second season are, as we go to press, very sketchy. Fan rumours surround an episode called 'Judgement', concerning a woman and her baby being targeted by evil forces trying to bring forth Armageddon. The baby is said to become the future's Joan Of Arc in a war between good and evil, but Angel initially picks the wrong side in the war. As with all fan rumours, this may turn out to be the product of someone's overactive imagination. What we *do* know is that Tim Minear will be writing the season's second episode and episode five (allegedly called 'Untouched') is by newcomer Meredyth Smith.

We may be seeing more flashbacks to Angel's past this year, as David Greenwalt recently confirmed: 'We'll be going back, but it may be [to] 30s or 40s L.A. We sold *Angel* as this gritty, urban thing, and we were going to show everything about Los Angeles. Then is was like, "Los Angeles is kind of boring; kind of spread out with a lot of freeway." When our shows are L.A.-specific they're great, but as we ground on through the year, I felt, "Too many goddamn warehouses".' 'Some of my favourites are Cordelia refusing to give up her haunted apartment; Angel saving Faith basically from herself when she doesn't even know she needs saving; Angel's own long journey back to sobriety from drinking blood for all that time; Wesley appearing as a "rogue demon hunter" and realising he's an utter failure, and then finding a little bit of success; Cordelia waing up eight months pregnant the next day after one not-so-casual date. These are all issues and shows that reverberate for me.' But for Greenwalt the main difference between *Buffy* and *Angel* is: 'There seems to be slightly less lesbianism, at the moment [on *Angel*]. I'm hoping to correct that in future.'

He, Joss Whedon and their writers and stars certainly *have* succeeded in producing a classic quest tale. With its emphasis on personal demons and the loneliness of the Big City, *Angel* has found its niche. What happens next could be *very* interesting.